A Bettor Way

A Bettor Way

A Winner's Guide To Wagering On Thoroughbreds

Dean C. Arnold

Library of Congress Number: 2005902425
ISBN : Hardcover 1-4134-9049-2
Softcover 1-4134-9048-4

This book was printed in the United States of America.

To order additional copies of this book, contact:
Xlibris Corporation
1-888-795-4274
www.Xlibris.com
Orders@Xlibris.com
28053

CONTENTS

SECTION 2: TIME MANAGEMENT

SECTION 3: DATA MANAGEMENT

SECTION 4: SPECIAL SITUATIONS

SECTION 5: PUTTING IT ALL TOGETHER

Introduction

For a number of years I have provided friends and horseplayers advice on how to bet on racing. Some just want the saddlecloth numbers of the winner. Others want me to give some inside scoop that makes my insight sound exclusive and foolproof. But others want to understand why I like the horses I do so that they can understand a methodology that produces results. This audience inspired *A Bettor Way*.

A lot of people I know are quite capable of finding winners on their own. But with simulcasts from a multitude of tracks, some 300 to 500 horses run in a single afternoon across North America. There is a massive amount of information to be digested, not all of which is on paper. Some of it only becomes available minutes before the race begins. The number of possible decisions you can make as a bettor on any given day, approaches infinity. Even at a "live" track offering just nine live races, the task of managing all the information and making appropriate decisions can seem impossible.

This book will help people build a methodology to tackle this overwhelming task better than ever before. My aim is to offer thoughtful, sensible advice to people ranging from part-time players to handicapping fanatics. This book will provide some insights regarding how to pick winners. But the focus is to show readers that selecting winners is important, and even critical. But that alone will not win you money.

There are two basic ways to deal with the betting aspect of racing. The first is casino style. You can approach the game as if it were another casino game of chance. Go to a casino and you can jump right in, and begin betting blackjack, craps, roulette or even the slots. Each hand, roll of the dice, or pull of the handle produces wins and losses. You stay and play hand after hand, round after round of your game of choice, until a) you run out of money, b) you run out of time and leave with whatever you have left, or c) you decide to stop and cash out with whatever you have remaining in your bankroll. You can wager on one round, or risk a small amount over and over dozens, hundreds, perhaps thousands of times. Unless you are a card counter or have decided a certain machine "is due," no one round seems to be a better or worse a proposition than another.

The second approach is more of an investment style. If you play the market, there are thousands of stocks, bonds, and funds you can invest in. You can buy and sell when you want. You can put all your money on one promising prospect, or spread it out amongst a variety of opportunities. Some opportunities will be riskier than others. Some are short term, some are long term. But when playing the market, you certainly do ***not*** buy and sell investments from all of the offerings every day. Thousands of stocks, funds, commodities, and currencies mean an infinite number of decisions—and you can't do it all.

So do you treat betting on horses like a casino game or an investment? My vote is clearly the latter. The wealth of information, trends, volatile prices, and opportunities lends itself to the investment strategy paradigm.

People treat it like a casino game, betting dozens of races each day, cycling that sum over and over as races go off every five minutes somewhere in North America. Yes, those people win money some days. Yes, some look at the *Daily Racing Form*, track program, tip sheets or newspapers. But can these people really make an informed decision about the many events in that little time? Not likely. I cannot, and I don't know anyone that does.

The more your bets tilt toward casino action instead of informed investing, the more likely you will lose money to the tune of the track take. Even worse, the take on horse racing is far higher than most popular casino games. These people would probably do better at craps tables.

Gambling, investing, whatever you call it—the keys to success are:

1. Being aware of overall percentages,
2. Finding accurate, pertinent information, and
3. Using the information to decide where the most value can be found.

Betting horse races is as complicated as playing the stock market, and none of the investment companies have a racing mutual fund (yet). The better your understanding of the vital information out there, the more likely your bets will be winning ones.

All handicapping aside, only you can manage or mis-manage your bankroll. Ultimately those who manage their bankroll best will win. Leave a winner. That means know the math, know when to go to the windows, and know when to go to the car and go home.

This book will:

— Show how management of your wallet on a daily basis and overall management over the course of the year are critical to success as a handicapper.

— Emphasize the importance of time management to a handicapper. This includes both preparation for the day's events and decision making right up to the start of each race.

— Provide big picture statistics in racing that will lead to new and fresh perspectives.

— Present handicapping tools, tactics and concepts that will alter how you look at races.

— Show how all of these concepts are combined into a sensible strategy that can be tailored to satisfy any bettor's individual approach to handicapping.

The Death Spiral

You're at Saratoga on a warm August day. You went over all the races the night before. You have opinions on all of the races, but you like the first, fourth, and eighth in particular. The national anthem has been played, and the changes that have been announced do not eliminate any of the horses you see as contenders.

With the $200 you brought, you bet $30 to win on the contender you admire in the first, and you throw in another $20 in daily doubles with several runners that look live in the second race. Your pick runs well, but is a near miss.

Before the second race you spend $36 in the Pick 3 trying to key your preferred horse in the fourth race. As long as you are using three horses in the second, you bet a $2 exacta box of the three of them for $12. When one of the horses you used wins but the other two run out of the money, you turn your attention to race three.

Live after the first leg of the Pick 3, you need any one of four horses to win. One of the four stands out more than the others. You key the standout over the other three in exactas, and bet $10 to win on him. If you are right, your Pick 3 will be live, and you'll also be entering the fourth race ahead for the day.

A longshot beats your horse to the wire (ouch) so you enter the fourth with no live Pick 3 tickets. You bet $40 to win on your second key horse of the day. Feeling a bit less confident, you spend $12, keying him in the place and show spots in $1 trifecta part-wheels. You go to the paddock and see your animal looking radiant. The horse is prancing as he heads out on the track for the post parade.

With 3 minutes to post you are sure your horse will win. You feel silly about the fact that if he wins, your win bet will pay less than if he runs second or third and your trifectas come in. So you head back to the windows, bet him on top in trifecta part-wheels, and double it ($2) because, after all, you should have more on him to come in first than to run second or third.

Midway through the stretch you wonder how your horse is going to get past six other horses, then close the 5-length gap that the favorite has opened on the rest of the field passing the 1/8th pole. You feel a glimmer of satisfaction when he grinds his way to second, but the trifectas don't include the number of the third place horse and the hefty win bet on a late-kicking stretch runner suddenly seems to have been a little overzealous, considering the way this track plays kindly to frontrunners. It is now 2:30 in the afternoon and it is beginning to turn into a long afternoon.

It's race five and you know the rest of the story because you've been here before . . . three races between you and that other good one you like in the eighth. You have $10 left, so you bet $5 on an advance wager—$5 win on your race eight pick—and hope you can turn the other $5 into something to really bet on the one you love.

You bet two $1 trifectas using one of the favorites over two pricey runners, no dice. It's a subtle reminder that the fifth race in New York is usually carded as the most wide-open affair of the day. The chance of hitting a trifecta with just two combinations was folly.

Nearing post time at race six, you feel silly holding a $3 voucher, but you stick it in the machine and press "$1," "Pick 3," "6," "with," "1, 2, 5," "with," "4," your horse in the eighth. Damn, why didn't you save more for the eighth? Your finger hovers over the "finish" button. Your eyes dart back and forth from "finish" to "start over." You pause, then press "start over", then "$3", "win", "6", "finish."

The 6 romps. The tote board shows final odds of 4/5.

With the seventh race approaching, you try to decide what to do with your $5.40 voucher. The three contenders you were going to use in the Pick 3 are at low odds, so you instead take notice of a 12-1 shot you overlooked before. He drifts all the way to 17-1 when you bet $2 Win/Place on him. Great, what to do with the $1.40 voucher, a buck more to win? A buck more to place? You pick option C, $1 exacta of your (now 19-1) shot over the favorite.

Your mid-afternoon love affair ends abruptly when your wonder-pick is sent charging eight-wide into the clubhouse turn by an apprentice that hasn't been on a horse this full of run in weeks. He hangs tough with the leaders into the far turn, but is still very wide and is getting hit with the whip on every other stride. The lagging TV ticker update shows him being in fourth at 21-1, just as he completely folds and is overrun by closers making their charge. The young rider buries his head in the horse's mane like he's ducking for cover as horses blow by to his left and right. By the 1/16th pole, he's faded to at least eighth and well beaten.

Five minutes later you are standing under a television monitor watching the race replay. You are so frustrated reliving this that you can't help but point out the calamity to strangers standing by you—*"He was full of run, the trainer must be ready to strangle the jock—LOOK HOW WIDE HE IS!"*

Ironically, watching the will-pays for the Pick 3 following the replay, you realize had you bet those three measly Pick 3s, you would now have a will-pay of $242 (divided by 2, for your $1 ticket of course) because the longest priced runner of your three choices in the seventh race hit. That amazes you, considering a 4/5 shot won the first leg.

With a $0.40 voucher in hand, and a $5 win bet, you feel dismayed about the doubles you can't bet with the ones you like in the finale. Your horse wins like a good thing, and pays $9.20. Your voucher and win ticket combine to a $23.40 voucher.

You want to bet something into the ninth, but not lose it all. Damn, you should be up for the day, you curse to yourself. $3 is an odd amount to bet but you'd like to have a $20 bill to go home with. $8 puts you at $15 and change, a nice and round number you can live with. You hate the favorite, who's getting overbet anyway.

You bet $2 to win on a horse that has some pluses going for it, then debate a trifecta box or $1 trifecta key, either one will cost $6. A box is safer, but a key gives you three horses under your pick instead of two others in a box with your horse. The $1 tri box wins if any one of three wins the race, but the other two must also finish in the money. The $1 tri key wins if your top choice runs first, and two out of your three hit the board. Your horse *should* win anyway, so $1 trifecta key is the way to go.

Your top pick runs second, and of course the two horses from your key that you would have put in the box run first and third. $290 trifecta—gone. The favorite was fourth. How hard was *that* $1500 superfecta!? *You don't even play the superfecta, but still . . .*

You not only should have finished up for the day. You should be filling out tax forms! You were so close all day. Half of these races you had figured out almost perfectly! You shudder to imagine what would have happened if you were watching Saratoga at a simulcast site along with five other tracks. Nine races and you are left mentally exhausted.

There must be a better way!

Transform Your Day To Profit

The before-and-after wallet check is the sincerest form of self-criticism.

This is a game where keeping score is quite easy. You leave the house with X amount of money at the start of the day. You place bets all day, and return home with X, plus winnings or minus losses.

Winning is possible if you know the math behind the game, how to manage a day's opportunities and challenges, the winning profile for any given race in question, and how to judge value in a given betting situation.

To make money at the races, just reading the *Daily Racing Form* is not enough. Just knowing trainer, breeding, track bias, and jockey stats is not enough. Having the most accurate speed and/or pace figures is not enough. Even being good at money management is not enough.

To make money at the races, you need to understand the mathematics behind the game. You need to know how to manage the entire day's opportunities and challenges. Handicapping each race with skill and objectivity is only a piece of the puzzle. In a variety of situations you need to know what factors are critical, and which are secondary. You need to know when your judgments are offering a chance to bet at odds more generous than the actual chances of winning. You also need to recognize when your best estimates do not present any real advantage over the rest of the betting public.

Like it or not, when you are at the track, every person you see is playing against you. There's a winner in every race, and somebody is going to cash a ticket. If it's not you, it's the schmuck next to you. The track takes your money, their money, simulcast money, OTB money, pools it together, keeps 15% to 25%, and then gives everything else back to the people holding winning tickets.

It's not the track that's keeping a small percentage you have to outsmart, it's the crowd betting alongside you. The track gets the same 15 to 25% regardless of who wins (unless there's a 'minus-pool' but let's not get into semantic arguments). The crowd gets 75 to 85 cents of every dollar you lose. You get to keep 75 to 85 cents of their dollar when you win and they lose.

Regardless of how you assess the runners and try to select the likely winners, you need to know how to optimally bet on your selections. You need "situational knowledge" of what to do and how to bet in a variety of circumstances. When do you concede that the favorite can't be played against? When do you bet $2 on a longshot and cheer? (When do you bet $40 on a longshot and cheer?) Should you start looking for sire information on the first time starters to see who can get the distance, or start comparing pace figures to see who can control the pace? What to do and when—that's the real challenge.

SECTION 1

Money Management

Racetrack Money Management: It's Tough To Be a Coach

It is harder to take advice from experts in activities you can already do, than in activities you are unfamiliar with.

I play golf, I make solid contact with the golf ball, and do fairly well. If I see my local golf pro for a lesson, he gives me advice that will change what I am doing. He has to do so in a way that I will accept even if it is awkward at first. The goal is to help me to go from doing something that works some of the time, to doing something that works more often. That is a tall order for my golf pro.

If I began a new sport instead, like kayaking, I would trust an expert's advice more because I have no base of skill and knowledge to reference. I have to trust him—it's all I have to go on.

The more you already know, the more experience you have to compare to the advice you receive. Yet in most sports, all of the professional athletes have coaches. The professionals have coaches, but amateurs often think they don't need coaching, advice, or help—handicapping is hard that way.

Every race run will have a winner.

Anyone that can put $2 through the mutuel window and call out a number will eventually stumble across winners now and then, so everyone thinks they know what they are doing.

There are no such illusions in golf, tennis, etc. Just because you can tee up the ball doesn't mean you might win a tournament. People that play amateur golf know they aren't in the same league as the pros.

Not so with handicappers.

You already know how to place bets, you know how to pick out information that helps you make your selections, and you cash tickets more often than "now and then." You may be ahead in the game for the month, for the year, for life. Your goal may be simply to pay for the cost of the hobby, or it may be something more ambitious, like paying the rent.

I will try to present this information as a coach and finesse it a little. I am trying to blend my advice with whatever is already going on in your head and hopefully working. Consider the information I present and incorporate it into your handicapping and betting. I think you'll find yourself better off in the long run.

There are no absolutes or sure things in racing. Learn what makes a handicapper a winner over time, not just on a given day. Learn how to optimize your bets—from reading this, being aware of the factors, and above all watching the races and being perceptive to what happened. Your results will improve.

An Introduction To Money Management: Managing Risk

Money management should be easy, right? You bring money, place bets, collect winnings, and go home with the winnings you collect. Well, at least you go home with whatever is left in your pocket. In reality, it is not that simple. There are many complex decisions to make. If you plan to bet 10 races, should you set aside 10% for each one to make sure you bet on each? Or should you bet a much higher percentage of your stake on the early events, hoping to make a score and parlay that into some bigger bets later on?

Such decisions need to be made based on your goals and your estimation of what opportunities the day's card offers. You need to try to ascertain where your best opportunities lie and come up with a plan that will make the best of the situation. This will vary every day and no mechanical system will suffice for all situations.

The best thing is to map out a general plan for yourself before the day begins. Having some idea of where your bankroll will be invested provides a framework for how your day—and your bets—will unfold.

Bankroll management is often treated as if you can only go through the day betting a portion of your original bankroll on one race at a time. This is not the case at all. With every passing race you can keep putting whatever money you have in your possession back through the mutuel windows, be it from home or from cashed tickets. On a good day you may have several times the sum you brought with you in your wallet after only a few races. Therefore you can go to the track with $200 in hand and put several times that amount through the windows.

If you start Race 1 with $100, bet $20, and cash a ticket, the bankroll is the leftover $80 plus whatever you cashed for, say $80. Now Race 2 is coming up and you have almost twice what you started the day with. *Do you adjust the size of your bets to risk more of your money?*

That all depends on your goals and personality. If your goal is to make profit without risking your original investment if at all possible, you may decide to stash your original bankroll and use the profits to try to make your score. It takes self control to stick with this plan and keep from going back into your original bankroll, and at least you won't lose for the day.

You may be the type that risks all the money at your disposal, with the philosophy, "You have to risk money to make money." After all, you brought the bankroll to bet with. However, recognize that if you plan to steadily increase your bets as the day goes on, you will risk more on later races than the early ones.

Racing is not blackjack, craps, or roulette—*all races are not equal propositions.*

If your early key races go well, you might decide to risk some of your profit on a later key race. That's one thing.

But if your "best bets" were in races 1, 3, and 6 and you make good money in them, the last thing you should do is risk winnings in races 7, 8, and 9. If "best bet" races called for $20 bets, non-key races should not get too much money, period.

There is nothing wrong with betting $5 in each and taking swings at longshots, value exactas, a late double, etc. But resist attempts to rationalize new key bets in the later races as an excuse to bet your bankroll. Fall into this trap and steam will be coming out your ears if you squander your profits on races you flagged earlier as poor betting races.

My final advice on the subject: One way or another, force yourself to quit while ahead.

Whether human nature or gambling psychology, this is the hardest thing to do in betting. It's like selling a stock that you've watched go through the roof. Although it is hard to do, you will thank yourself over the long term if you leave while you are ahead. When up for the day, many bettors tend to use the expression, "I'm playing with the track's money." They lose sight of the fact that the moment they cash a ticket, it becomes *their* money.

Whether they bring it home, use it to buy a hot dog, or use it to place more bets, they are risking their own capital.

As always, *your wallet keeps score very well. What remains in it when you leave the track is the final say in whether or not you won.*

How many races you were right about—doesn't matter.

How much you hit the daily double for—doesn't matter.

It's all about what's in the wallet.

Training Wheels: Learning Day-By-Day Money Management

If you are new to the sport or have been beaten up by it so many times that you want to start over by getting back to basics, here are several frameworks that I strongly recommend for several reasons. First, they are fairly simple. They will let you focus more on selecting good prospects. That alone will help you a great deal. Second, each forces you to put the bulk of your stake on the best insights you have. This puts you in a position where your day will probably be "boom or bust" based on your top picks, not by what you did with your money all afternoon.

Finally, the simplicity of these models will allow you to study what works and what doesn't. If you cash all your key bets, it will be a good day—but still pay attention to what works and what doesn't to improve your betting decisions over time.

Training Wheels On

Here is a betting framework for simple money management:

1. Take your day's bankroll.
2. Take 1/2 to 2/3 and split it equally among your "best bet" contenders (two or three horses).
3. Wager on each "best bet" to win only.
4. Put the win tickets in your wallet.
5. The remaining portion of the bankroll can be used throughout the day in any fashion. At least half your betting money is already in the wagers most likely to cash—a straight win bet on your "best bets."

For instance, if you have identified three "best bet" contenders in an afternoon's races, for every $100 you bring with you to bet, plan on betting $20 win on each of these three. Use the remaining $40 of each $100 for other activities.

With only two such contenders, two $30 win bets are in order. With four contenders, four $15 win bets.

With only one contender, you may not feel comfortable betting more than half your bankroll on a single race—all eggs in one basket. If a day appears to only offer one potential contender, it is much wiser to scale down your bankroll for that day and save it for better prospects. One $40 bet and $20 for exotics should satisfy the need for action.

As an almost golden rule, if you are interested in a horse because you really like *that* horse, you need to confine your betting to win or win/place only. The horse can be off your "watch list," from trip notes, or a lifelong overachiever. More exotic bets can waste an opportunity to capitalize on a runner you know about by relying on other runners you are not as familiar with.

If you can make yourself do this, you are taking the biggest step towards being aggressive while exerting some self control. You are putting enough of your money behind the horses that you like the most, and maximizing your chance to make a profit if you are right. Many overly aggressive bettors find themselves in a position of lacking capital when a really good, solid wager comes along.

Following this logic, you may have reserved only 1/3 of your bankroll for exotics. There are challenges in limiting yourself to this amount while still staying in a position to make money. How to optimally bet the 1/2 to 1/3 on exotics will be discussed later on in this section. The strategies can range from "supplement your win bet profits" to "try to make a 5- to 6-digit score."

This may seem overly simple, and even silly, to some reading this. Come home from the track a winner a few times when nothing else went right and you won't think it's silly at all. Winning is winning, no matter what method you use to do it—***and in this game your wallet keeps score.***

Strengths of this approach:

— This approach keeps "impulse shopping" from eating up all of your money.
— It puts muscle behind your top selections.
— It forces you to have a game plan early on and not make it up as you go along.

Weaknesses of this approach:

— Value must be anticipated for actual odds on all but the first race you bet.
— Last minute information is useless since your win bet is in your pocket.
— Even if some early bets win, if the bettor cashes while there are still races left to run, the "Tasmanian Devil" bettors will unload it on the remaining races.

Training Wheels Off

If you are accustomed to channeling 1/2 to 2/3 of your daily bankroll to your best bets, a more flexible routine can be developed, like the following:

— Write out a "big picture" game plan before the races start.
— Identify races that have opportunity to yield big payoffs.
— Develop a rough idea of what you will do for these races.
— Focus on win bets for most of your capital during the day.

If your handicapping is sound, you capitalize on races through exotics where you are really, really right. The win bets consistently yield profit even on races where you are only mostly right.

Strengths of this approach:

- This approach keeps attempts at big money within the realm of well thought out ideas.
- It meshes the "swings for the fence" with the rest of the game plan.
- If you are mostly right, it avoids, or at least cushions, the losses with successful win bets.

Weaknesses of this approach:

- It still only works if you are at least mostly right.
- It's difficult to stick to the plan in the actual execution of the day's bets.
- Even when you are ahead for the day, it is hard to resist betting on the remaining races of the day in an effort to make more money.

Big Stakes Day Bankroll Management

There are certain days when a track will host a marquee event, or several of them, when a number of high-profile races offer betting opportunities with well-known entries from around the country, or even the world. Examples include Kentucky Derby Day, the Breeders' Cup World Thoroughbred Championships, Florida Derby Day, and Travers Day at Saratoga. Any marquee event for a national level track where the highest quality card possible is assembled qualifies.

This poses unique challenges for the handicapper—many familiar names, contentious races, shippers, top jockeys from around the country. Possible added confusion comes from other tracks adding stakes, moving post times, etc. to get extra attention from the main event.

Top Outfits and Big Days

One point to remember as a handicapper: *Top outfits like to win on the big days.* Even if a top outfit can't win the big event, at least they can get their picture taken for a race on the undercard. Especially those stables shipping in for the big events. Their Grade I horse may lose, but the other horse in the trailer may do just fine.

Keep an eye out for "the other horse in the trailer," horses entered on the undercard with the same connections as a stakes entry shipping in from another racing circuit. It will come as no surprise to you that most horse trailers are built for two or more horses.

As long as a trainer is shipping his star in for the afternoon, the trainer is likely to bring another horse along for the ride. These horses may not be stakes material, but may be perfectly suited for a conditioned allowance or high priced claiming race, especially if shipping to a lesser circuit. This undercard race may even be an overnight handicap or minor stakes, but a well-intended allowance runner from a major track will often handle the locals just fine.

If an allowance for non-winners of three "other than" race (ALWN3X) is carded before the feature, a horse for a top conditioner that has struggled to clear this condition at a premier circuit may tower above the competition this afternoon. Bob Baffert and owner Mike Pegram (of Real Quiet and Silverbulletday fame) have referred to such wins as "beer money." The key to this angle is the assumption that the conditioner can choose any horse in the barn to best suit the conditions of the undercard races. The trainer will seize the best opportunity as long as he is already making the trip with his "A" horse.

If the horse trailer is arriving from a higher class circuit, consider that another added plus. Examples of a shipping-induced class drop would include from Belmont to Suffolk Downs (such as on MassCap Day), from Hollywood to Lone Star Park or Turf Paradise, from Churchill Downs to Thistledown, from Gulfstream to Tampa Bay Downs.

Naturally, high-profile connections may drive the odds down on such tag-a-long shippers. But on the assumption that the connections "mean business," you may want to adjust your acceptable odds accordingly.

Bettors in tune with this angle enjoyed numerous winning bets as Bill Mott shipped the great Cigar around the country back in 1995 and 1996. Cigar may have offered little value, but the Bill Mott trainees that accompanied him picked up more than a few wins on the "world tour."

Big Day Betting

Overall, on big days, focus on best betting opportunities and put your money there. Betting $5 on 10 different races makes less sense than betting $25 on the two best races and little or nothing on the rest. *Contentious stakes races make for tough exactas and trifectas.* Use live longshots in combination with your best bets, but try to make a score with a modest investment. Spreading too thin, or relying exclusively on exotics, can spoil a best bet that wins without you cashing.

Maintaining such self-control is more frustrating on these big days because with an exceptional undercard, so many races look tempting. Lots of horses will be deemed contenders. You may find yourself with strong opinions in twice as many races as you normally would. If this is the case, either decide to increase your daily stake for this special day, or make the decision to only bet the very best opportunities, even if that means passing on races that you would bet on any other day. Attempting to seize every opportunity can deplete your bankroll long before your main event occurs.

A word of caution: Distinguish rooting from handicapping. Because you know many names of competitors, you may find yourself "supporting" a dozen or more horses. Be sure that you don't confuse sentimental support with handicapping logic.

The Breeders' Cup World Thoroughbred Championships

And now for the "Big Event" strategy for surviving the ultimate Big Day: the Breeders' Cup World Thoroughbred Championships. Big Day equals lots of opportunity. It also means a tough day to survive with your bankroll intact.

As a fan you'll recognize many or most of the runners on the day's card. The only ones you won't recognize will be European shippers and obscure 2-year-olds. This is good and bad. You know more about them than the typical field. But having previous opinions of the runners can make it impossible to conduct an objective analysis.

At least half of the competitors in each Championship race can be considered a contender, even when there is an overwhelming favorite. These are like All Star games for horses, with regional heroes clashing to see who is best overall.

Typical stakes often have one or two stakes winners from the local circuit, several allowance winners taking a big step up, and maybe a stakes winning shipper or two from outside the region. The Championship races bring a full field of well-established stakes runners together.

How often does an afternoon of races occur where race after race, the 10 to 14 best jockeys in the world are pitted against one another? Put good riders on talented horses and you'll see some real match-ups.

Focus on the best ***betting*** opportunities and carefully make the distinction between rooting and wagering. In races where three or four contenders cannot be separated, consider using Pick 3s to include these horses in a minor investment when the other races have a single standout. Again, to belabor the point, don't get caught up in the moment and bet dozens of combinations in a frenzied attempt to cover the many talented competitors. It will be hazardous to your bankroll.

How To Play Six Tracks At Once On $300 a Day

Stay home.

Okay, you didn't take my advice and you are going anyway. Back to the original question, then. How do you play six tracks at once on a $300 a day budget?

First of all, you can't expect to win long term at the track if you are only bringing $300 but have $1,000 in bets in mind. Inevitably you will try to score early to build up a bigger bankroll that will cover your bets for the remainder of the day. Some days it will work, but more often, your early efforts won't build your bankroll to where you want. By mid afternoon, you will be looking at a list of upcoming opportunities and either trying to spread your small stake around to cover all of them, or you will be forced to perform triage to decide what gets bet and what gets passed over.

The Time Factor

So $300, 60 races, what to do? Over a 5-hour period, these races will go off every 5 minutes on average. Actually clusters of races will be run simultaneously at times, so decision making time is limited to such an extent that time management is one of the most critical aspects of modern horseplaying.

The 60-race card offers far too much information for any single bettor to analyze. Mutual fund managers don't study 500 companies per day. They may have researchers to do that, but even then they focus their research on specialties, sectors, certain markets, etc. You don't have a team of researchers, but you do have specialties you can focus on.

With $300/day, you are going to need to plan ahead of time which races will potentially yield good betting opportunities. Ask yourself, what contenders have I identified that may warrant a win bet? What races may offer a good exacta or trifecta wager? Are there daily doubles or Pick 3s worth investing in? Is there a Pick 6 with a big carryover worth an $8 to $12 flier? You have many options. On different days you will need to divide your bankroll in various ways, based on which options translate to the best opportunities. If you've read other works on handicapping, you've no doubt seen guidelines ranging from 50% win, 50% exotic or $200 win or win/place, $100 exotics or $150 win, $100 doubles and exactas, $50 super-exotics.

Generally, unless every time you head to the track you want to risk everything you brought to make a huge score, put enough of your bankroll into higher probability wagers to make a profit on days that your win bets are correct but exotics fail to pan out. Exotics have much lower probability of hitting, therefore they will cause short-term losing streaks much more frequently than win or place betting.

Start the day by assessing the potential opportunities, then use this as a roadmap to plan how to invest your capital.

Part of the planning process *must* include asking the question, "How much money am I trying to make by risking $300?" This answer is different for everyone. Some people will be happy to make $100 as long as there is limited risk of losing the entire $300 bankroll. Others will want to make $1,000 or more, and are willing to part with all $300 trying, as long as in the long run the winning days outrun the losing ones.

Here are some rough sketches of what you may think the day has to offer.

Planning Forecast—It's a Win Bet Day

Some days your planning may forecast four to six contenders as solid win bets, but with little chance to use these contenders in any form of exotics. At this point, a decision needs to made—to go home a winner today, divide your bankroll between those win bet contenders that offer good value once you see the odds.

You may want to hold back some amount ($50 maybe) for exotics that may pop up as an opportunity. After all, what if you get to one of your contenders and find the 7/2 odds you were hoping for, but a borderline contender you expected to see at 6-1 is at 20-1? You still want to proceed with your win bet on the 7/2 shot as a solid value bet, but suddenly there might be a great exacta value with this unexpected live longshot. This would be no time to be bound to a mechanical system, but you don't want to de-rail your plan to place a decent bet on the 7/2 shot either.

The important thing is this: recognize when a day looks like a "win bet" day with few exotics opportunities and adapt accordingly. Don't try to make this the day you sign IRS forms for a Pick 3 and two trifectas. If the opportunity isn't there, wishful thinking can't create it. But there may be solid win bets that you can plan and watch for. Going home with more money than you started with is the ultimate goal.

Planning Forecast—It's an Exotics Bonanza

Other days may be exactly opposite of win bet days. There may be no win bet contenders that look like standouts offering value, but there may be races where two to four horses could set up an exotics bonanza. Maybe you hate the favorite in the daily double, but give three other generously priced runners a good chance to win. Without favoring one of these contenders and trying to guess which one will actually win, you may be able to crush a daily double.

Suppose a maiden race has two contenders, two gray-area runners, and six throwouts. It's possible that the two equal contenders could go off at 4/5 and 4/1 which would lead you to a win bet on the 4/1 shot. But you won't know that until post time draws near.

In the meantime, a race with over half the field easily eliminated looks like an exacta/trifecta opportunity. Here the opportunity is not created by selecting either contender, but by identifying the six throwouts. Your plan should include the way you can take advantage of this situation. A win bet on one of the two contenders doesn't really make sense.

The Tug-Of-War

On days where exotic bets seem to be the wager d'jour, the chances of cashing a ticket are going to be much less than on days of win/place betting. In the back of your mind you know this. It is still hard to accept that sticking to your plan may lead to an entire day without cashing a ticket. Well into the day, you may not have hit anything but you have some lucrative races coming up soon. You may have the urge to abandon your plan and play it safe to make sure you cash a ticket—even if playing it safe removes any hope of getting value.

The challenge is to remain objective. If the exotics still make sense as post time approaches, stick to them. If a key contender is at much better win odds than you expected, you may want to change your strategy. Last minute information is critical, but as post time nears there is less decision making time. If you are going to change your strategy based on late odds, make it a rational, intelligent decision.

The Bankroll Situation

If your day has 10 bettable races, you ***do not*** want the amounts you bet in each of them to look like this:

$60, $50, $50, $40, $30, $25, $20, $15, $8, $2
Total: $300

Everyone who has been to the track even just a few times recognizes this pattern: ***a rough day.***

Starting off with sizable bets, the size decreases steadily as the day goes on. The majority of the $300 bankroll disappears early. Soon, only enough is left for token bets. Assuming the $2 final bet was not cashed for a $300+ trifecta, it was an ugly day doomed by poor bankroll management.

Instead, you would want the size of the bets to be based on value and chance of profit, not on what's left on the voucher. You may have five $40 bets, and five $20 bets, like this:

$40, $20, $20, $40, $20, $40, $40, $20, $20, $40
Total: $300

Admittedly, this is too simplistic. For one thing, it makes the dubious assumption that numerous propositions during the afternoon were equally inviting, but the points are these:

— Bets should be in amounts that are more or less predetermined based on your bankroll, comfort level, and goals. You can't expect to make a five-figure exotics score if you're not comfortable losing your $300 bankroll the majority of times you go to the track. The losses will hinder your judgment and soon you will deviate from your game plan trying to recover lost capital. Likewise if you bet large sums to place and show, you may cash several tickets and have little chance of tapping out in a given day, but your expectation for profit must be modest or you will feel like a failure even when you are successful.

— Bets toward the end of the day do **not** offer more or less value based on the time remaining or number of races left to wager on. The "best bet" of the day could just as easily be the last race as the first race.

— The size of bets later in the day should not depend on earlier success. If you hit some early races and want to try and use those profits to your advantage, no one is stopping you. Just remember the potential value of the later races on a day where you are blanked for the first five. Bet the later races based on ***their*** value and potential, ***not*** on how much you have remaining in your wallet.

It Begins With a Roar, and Ends With a Whimper

Before the first race everybody thinks that they have the day's card figured out. They expect to win, and expect to have plenty of money for the later races, but it rarely works out that way.

Quick Quiz: All other things being equal, the typical racegoer's biggest bet of the day comes on:

a) The first race,
b) The feature race, or
c) The final race.

The answer is "a." I know, you know, and everyone else that goes to the track knows people who bet big on the feature stakes. We also know people that bet a whole bunch on the finale in an all-or-nothing attempt to break the bank, especially if they've cashed a few tickets already on the card.

But the reality is, those people—just like nearly all other racegoers—usually bet the most on the first offering of the day.

Like the guy at the all-you-can-eat buffet that loads his plate with salad and dinner rolls and runs out of room before even getting

to the prime rib and seafood, the typical joe steps up to the first race ready to hit a big one. If he loses, there's plenty of money and races left to recoup. So he bets big, real big, often not realizing it. How many friends do you have that return to the window two or three times before the first race goes off? Waves of doubles, exactas, win bets, more doubles, more exactas . . .

By the time the feature race rolls around they may bet big—but only in proportion to the remaining bankroll! What's left is seldom anywhere close to what they began the day with.

When the finale is all that is left, that's when they "bet it all" although "all" is rarely all that much. A lot of tickets and a lot of action, perhaps, but little chance for long-term profit.

The Day Wears On, the Track Take Grinds Away

Added to the overzealous betting early on, the track take is a major factor in how much money is available for betting. To demonstrate this overlooked phenomenon, here is an over-simplified example: Assume that a finite amount of money, $1,000,000, is held by the public prior to the first race and there are no late arrivals or ATM machines to withdraw from. Now assume that 50% of the available money is wagered by the public in each race. Finally, assume the average track take across all betting pools is 20%.

In a 9-race day, here is what would happen with the public's funds:

Beginning Sum: **$1,000,000**
Race 1: $500,000 reserved, $500,000 bet, track take (20%): $200,000
New Balance: **$800,000**
Race 2: $400,000 reserved, $400,000 bet, track take (20%): $80,000
New Balance: **$720,000**
Race 3: $360,000 reserved, $360,000 bet, track take (20%): $72,000
New Balance: **$648,000**
Race 4: $324,000 reserved, $324,000 bet, track take (20%): $64,800
New Balance: **$583,200**

Race 5: $291,600 reserved, $291,600 bet, track take (20%): $58,320
New Balance: **$524,880**
Race 6: $262,440 reserved, $262,440 bet, track take (20%): $52,488
New Balance: **$472,392**
Race 7: $236,196 reserved, $236,196 bet, track take (20%): $47,239
New Balance: **$425,153**
Race 8: $212,576 reserved, $212,576 bet, track take (20%): $42,515
New Balance: **$382,638**
Race 9: $191,319 reserved, $191,319 bet, track take (20%): $38,264
Day's End Final Balance: **$344,374**

That track take grinds $1,000,000 down to $344,374! Almost 2/3 of the money ends up somewhere other than the hands of the public. Of course, the public doesn't bet 1/2 of all available funds each race, and simulcast money blurs the lines when trying to study what occurs on track. Also, different races offer differing menus of wagers, so that the sums bet are not consistent.

The grind is unstoppable, plays favorite to no individual, and is always a factor in what the public goes home with at the end of the day.

A look through the results of any track shows the combined effects of the public's lack of self control and the track take. Aside from big graded stakes that pull in big simulcast money, the daily handle (all pools considered) shows that the 1st race draws the biggest pool, the feature event second biggest, and the finale will have the smallest pools. Don't be like everyone else!

Find Your Game:

What Kind of Bettor Are You?

Here's one insight that applies to every bettor: Your personality has as much to do with how you will bet as any other factor you encounter at the track. Why? If you can't stomach losing and hate risk even if it leads to long-term rewards, you can't realistically expect measurable profit. You need to assess your temperament before adopting a wagering strategy.

Your betting might be characterized as much ado about nothing, or just for the fun of it. This book groups this kind of player into the "*risk-averse*" category. Betting is inherently a risky business, so a big challenge will be learning to accept or even welcome that risk. Within the handicapping arena, risk-averse bettors may be comforted when their pick is at unusually low odds, instead of seeing this a negative in the quest to make profit. This is all relative. A risk-averse handicapper is still much more comfortable with risk than the typical risk-averse citizen, who may stuff money into a mattress or only invest in the very safest choices.

The other extreme is someone that can't visit a wagering facility without succumbing to the desire to "Let It Ride" and take one big chance before leaving. This player would go home broke repeatedly without applying some strong self control. This group is referred to as the *high-risk* category, very comfortable with the most aggressive of risks.

Tactics For the Risk-Averse Player

For the risk-averse player, underlays and favorites are *not* the answer. Players that feel uncomfortable with a lot of risk are vulnerable to playing underlays. Vulnerable, due to a self-imposed mental barrier when the logic used to pick bets is:

"X is the favorite, and of all the horses is the most likely to win. How can I bet against the most likely winner? It must be the best choice to make a winning bet. You have to pick winners to cash tickets, and you have to cash tickets to make money."

This seems like flawless logic. Nevertheless, the favorite may be more likely to win than any other horse, but is still more likely to lose than win. Using this kind of logic, the risk-averse player—more than anyone else—finds it hard to pass a likely winner at unacceptably low odds—if the player in this category pauses to consider whether or not the odds are acceptable. Rather than pass the 6-5 horse that should be 2-1, the 6-5 odds are taken as a reassurance that "You are more on track than you even thought you were."

A Better Way For the Risk-Averse

The risk-averse player who really intends to make money needs to do one thing: migrate away from underlaid contenders towards high probability, fair value situations. Learn to pick and choose situations that have a high probability of winning but still offer fair value relative to the chances of winning. It is feasible to accept wagers at low odds as long as the chance of collecting on the bet remains solid. For example, getting 3/2 odds on something with a 50% chance of occurring is a huge value ($2 bet for $5 returned 50% of the time = $5 for every $4 bet, 25% profit) and cashing tickets will be a common occurrence.

Rather than accept underlays and console yourself with the knowledge that you have the majority opinion, look for anything with reliable value such as:

- — Class dropping claimers with recent speed figures as high as or higher than the cheaper competition.
- — Maidens that have already run faster than par (average winning time for maidens at that distance at that track).
- — ALWNX3 races, any horse that last ran in stakes, regardless of its finish position in that stakes race (unless it left the track in a horse ambulance, i.e. *vanned off* comment in the *Daily Racing Form*).

— Older maiden races, any horse that last finished second.
— Any debuting horse at odds of more than 3-1, with a sire or trainer that has a 25% or greater win percentage with first time starters.

These are just a sample of long-term high win percentage situations. Through your regular research, you can uncover many others. They may not lead to big win prices very often, but the betting public does have its occasional mis-read leading to a big payoff. Knowing that you are playing scenarios that frequently yield winners will help you resist the "underlaid but still likeliest winner" plays that are the undoing of many risk-averse players over the long haul.

Summary For Risk-Averse Players

Risk averse players will be helped in the long run if the following concepts are kept in mind to key on value and profitability:

— Even if playing longshots is not your style, there are plenty of opportunities to find overlays even at modest odds. A horse that should be 4/5 that pays 2-1 is a more than 100% overlay.
— Build a list of highly successful scenarios to look for. One to two dozen such angles can be enough of a portfolio to find several spot plays each day.
— Set aside a small percentage of your daily bankroll for exotics. These can be used to supplement a "best bet" win bet. If you handicap the race right and win, it is always nice to turn a base hit into a home run.

Control Measures For the High-Risk Player: Controlling the Fever

High risk does not imply educated risk. High risk does not imply calculated risk. "Wild stabbing" is a better description if this is your strategy for betting success, recklessly endangering your bankroll.

This section is geared for the person who is time and again lured by potential payoffs, who watches the TV screen looking for *huge* sums, and fabricates hypothetical situations that could produce those outcomes. Fabricating, because the person practically has to invent the scenario to make it sound logical.

For the typical high-risk player, the handicapping factors that matter most are whichever ones help the case of the selections he has in mind to produce a real payday.

These are people that fall in love with horses that they would not have considered contenders the night before. Stinging from a loss, they may look to the next race to redeem themselves. They may go after a longshot with little chance or plunge too heavily on undervalued exotics. These handicappers love cold exactas and doubles. Putting two "good ones" together and offering twice what a win bet will pay seems like a gift to them—even if the chances of success are far less than the odds would seem to indicate.

The sad part for many of these players is that once they are down, their focus never seems to shift to more reasonable propositions. Someone in this category who starts his day with $100 and already lost $75 of it, is not likely to see the 3-1 shot in the next race that should be 6-5 as an opportunity for a win bet of $15. If the horse wins at these value odds, he would cash for $60 and be a long ways back to even. It is more likely that the $15 will be invested in exactas and tris with longshots that will probably lose and cost the bettor a perfect chance to back a solid prospect.

Eavesdrop at the track before the last race of the afternoon and you will hear some of the most incredible fantasy suppositions imaginable.

"If the 5 horse steps up and runs with the favorite early, they may both weaken, and then the 2 should close better, and go outside both of them, which will hang him wide when the favorite tires and drifts out. That will set up my 7 horse to drop to the rail and come up on the inside, which the 7's jockey usually never does, but the 7 is wearing blinkers and that will keep him running straight as a string up the rail. So the jock's *got* to try to go through there. And with the favorite tiring and the 5 all done, the 2 and the favorite will complete the tri."

Now there's overthinking a race, and there's **overthinking a race**.

If you find yourself constructing complex if-this-then-that scenarios to justify how your exotic bets will work out, you are overthinking it.

The example above could instead be viewed this way:

"The favorite is a frontrunner that figures to face more pressure for the lead than he is accustomed to. This could really help a pace-presser I like (the 7). The 7 needs the favorite to tire in order to have a good chance."

If the 7 is at fair odds, a win bet on him should come first. If I had $20 left in my pocket and liked the 7, I would bet at least $15 if not $20 on him to win. If he wins, I cash a nice bet. Maybe I don't go home a winner for the day, but at least I made back a chunk of what I was down for the day. If I think the favorite is the only other contender, an exacta box might be good if the value is there. If it takes a highly complex scenario for a tri to hit, it is not a good bet.

Most high-risk bettors would use that $20 weighted heavily toward the exotics, with maybe $5 to win and $15 in exotics. The horse may win and the exotics still lose (after all, it's harder to hit the exotic). It is that fantasy of the "Mission Impossible" scenario all falling into place—"The 3 does this and the 5 does this and the favorite does that . . ."—that lures people away from reasonable or sensible or logical alternatives. A value horse to win may stare you right in the face, and you may not see it because you are focusing on who will run 2nd and 3rd and 4th and 5th.

A Better Way For the High-Risk Player

If a high-risk player intends to make money over time, it is important to capitalize on value opportunities with higher chances of hitting, usually through win bets. If planning to bet $20 on exotics using a key longshot, regularly bet $5 to win on that longshot. Being close on a handful of exotics tickets is not as rewarding as money in your wallet at the end of the day, and a small win bet will often cover the money bet on exotics.

Summary For High-Risk Players

High-risk players will be better served in the long run if the following steps are kept in mind to avoid chasing rainbows:

— If trying to make a "big score," identify the opportunities before the day begins, not with 3 minutes to post.
— Make sure that long-term win betting is profitable before you test your skills on exotics. If your win bet selections are not profitable over time, your exotic plays are even less likely to win.
— Always prefer a win pool overlay to a chance for an exotics score. If a horse you strongly feel has a 33% chance of winning is at 12-1, bet it to WIN! So what if the exacta and tri will-pays are huge? Your opportunity to cash on this overlay shouldn't be foiled by other runners not fulfilling their part of your exacta or tri tickets.

Handicapping Humor: Math Made Easy

Five handicappers embark on their annual pilgrimage to spend a long weekend at Saratoga. Each is there to win money and have fun. Here is a look inside the minds of these five bettors to see how they attack the betting windows.

Joe Math

Joe wants to survive without going broke. Joe's goal is to have enough money for a doublecheeseburger and a soda Monday night at the rest stop diner ($7.25). Joe realizes he loses 2/3 of his bankroll with each racing day, so here's how Joe plans his weekend: Friday morning, $600. Friday night, $200. Saturday morning, $195. Saturday night, $65.25. Sunday morning, $60. Sunday night, $21.75. Monday morning, $20. Monday night, $7.25.

Just to be on the safe side, Joe puts two quarters and a nickel under the floormat of the car before heading to Saratoga. For tolls, of course.

Al Math

Al has a system. A trifecta system. A complicated, high-risk trifecta system. A ten-horse field has 720 trifecta combinations. With Al's system, he will play 121 $1 trifectas, giving himself a 1 in 6 chance to hit the tri. Doing this 4 days in a row will cost $480 but gives him four tries at a 1 in 6 dice roll. The trouble is, the $2 trifecta will-pay would have to be $960 for a $1 tri to break him even.

Knowing perfectly well that the same $480 could afford him four $100 "best bets" to win, and $80 to play the exotics, Al is haunted by the realization that getting just 1 of 4 best bets home first at odds of 4-1 will pay better than even a $960 trifecta. For the system player like Al, life is a whirlwind of numbers and a nightmare of monster payoffs for the 600 unused combinations.

Jake Math

Jake is a class handicapper. It's not the class of the horses that concerns him—it's the class of the connections. Jake has a good set of binoculars and uses them in the paddock to see who's here. If the owner's a no-show, no bet. If the owner is here alone, the connections are interested in the outcome of the race. If the owner is here with friends and family, they are here to get their picture taken in the winner's circle. The bigger the entourage, the bigger the bet.

Spotting Dinny Phipps in the paddock surrounded by well-dressed admirers, Jake feels it is obvious that the Phipps Stable has their latest 2-year-old phenom cranked up early. Confirming this by seeing the trainer also wearing coat and tie, Jake senses it's photo time, and heads for the $50 min window while wondering how handicapping can be so simple.

Mike Math

Mike is an obscure angle player. The more obscure the angle, the more of his bankroll he is willing to risk. Today, he sees that the Voss horse is a fourth time off a layoff trying Lasix for the eighth time, whose odds are between 6 and 9 to 1, who is turning back after stretching out on the turf and changing to an apprentice rider.

Assuming everyone is on to this angle, the win pool is avoided in favor of a modified approach of Al Math. Unfortunately, the mutuel clerk will only give Mike a $20 one-way superfecta because he's using his watch for collateral and a promise of 10% of the winnings. Then again, angles like these don't come along every day. Mike feels lucky.

Jim Math

Alas, not everyone wants to be a professional handicapper. Jim's handicapping is completed in 2 minutes. He verifies the program number of every horse Jerry Bailey is riding and heads to the windows 20 minutes before the first race.

Surmising that the hot dogs are high fat but soft serve ice cream is a dairy product, Jim decides that even though the juice doesn't appear to be freshly squeezed, the vendor is a cute brunette. A $3.50 lemonade is not a bad deal.

Besides, if he eats now, he'll have plenty of time to call his girlfriend Kristen later. But then again, the blonde selling souvenirs would probably like to go to dinner so there's no reason to eat right away, besides Kristen has no idea when he'll call, and the only thing waiting for Jim back at the hotel is Joe. A wink decides it for him (and it wasn't Joe).

Probabilities and Their Impact On Bankroll Management

Bankroll management is very different if you're betting primarily "win-place-show" versus focusing your betting on the exotic pools. The higher the probability of a bet's success, the more often you'll be cashing tickets at the window. The risk-averse bettor will favor the types of wagers that are likely to hit frequently. This results in a steady cashflow from bankroll to wagering pools and back again. The high-risk player will favor wagers that succeed much less often. Thus the high-risk player can expect numerous outlays of money between rewards. In the long run, each style may show a profit or loss depending on the player's handicapping success. Yet the two approaches result in very different cycles of ups and downs on the balance sheet. Just like investors in stocks and bonds, increased risk leads to increased bankroll volatility. Each player must be prepared to manage the cashflow in and out of their bankrolls accordingly.

Even if you manage your money in an optimal manner, you may go home empty handed after a day in which you thought you did everything right. Is that luck? Partly. But you can predict how often you will cash tickets based on the chance of success of each wager you make.

A bettor may bet the favorite to show in every race, cash six tickets, and go home with a net loss. Over the course of the day, that person might be ecstatic about cashing so many tickets, then shocked at the day's end upon realizing that nothing was gained by doing so. On the other end of the spectrum, a bettor may bet Pick 3s for five straight days. On the first four days, not one ticket is cashed. On the fifth day, a Pick 3 finally hits and pays far more than all the money invested in the entire five-day span. Certain bets are more likely to hit, and those percentages can be factored into your strategy.

The various bets available at the track have widely different chances of winning. The chances of a bet hitting will vary based on many factors that can be grouped into three broader topics:

— The number of contestants (number of possible outcomes) in a race or series of races. Mathematically, a horse is more likely to win against four other competitors than against ten others.
— The probabilities behind the type of bet you place.
— The actual chances of your selection winning the race.

All the handicapping factors come into play in that last factor—the actual chances of the selection winning. For now, the other two factors will be discussed: the number of possible outcomes and bet-specific probabilities. First, let's focus our attention on some quick ways to calculate fair value.

Math That Insults Your Intelligence

Exact calculations of payoffs, chances of winning, etc. take time when the clock is ticking. Like a quarterback in the huddle, assess the general situation and go with the sensible play. The perfect plan of attack is useless if it takes 10 minutes to come up with and you have 2 MTP. The clock is running, and where the quarterback will get a delay of game penalty, you will get shut out and miss the opportunity entirely. It is important to have quick, reliable methods to assess value.

In order to make effective betting decisions, you need to convert your assessment of a race into an estimate of what odds your contenders should offer. If you frequently bet horses that offer odds lower than their chances of winning deserve, your long-term bankroll will suffer. In order to judge if the odds offered on your runners are "fair," you need to have your own notion of what a fair value is for your contenders.

Mechanical systems have attempted to do this, such as probability formulas, slide rules, and computer programs. The intent here is not to knock or question the accuracy of any of them—some are wonderful time savers. The goal here is to give a reliable no-cost rule of thumb.

Assess your runner's chances using the following brackets. If your choice offers better than these "fair odds," this will give you a healthy margin for value. You won't impress a math professor, but you will be in the right frame of mind at the track.

Rough Estimate Chances of Winning:	**Percentage**	**Rough Odds**	**Fair Odds**
Better Than Fifty-Fifty	50%+	< 1/1	7/5
Fifty-Fifty	50%	1/1	3/2
One-in-Three	33%	2/1	3/1
One-in-Four	25%	3/1	9/2
One-in-Five	20%	4/1	6/1
One-in-Six	18%	5/1	8/1
One-in-Seven	15%	6/1	9/1
One-in-Eight	12.5%	7/1	10/1
One-in-Ten	10%	9/1	12/1
Less Than One-in-Ten	<9%	10/1	15/1

Figure 1: Rough Estimate Chances of Winning

You don't need a degree in math to think in terms of percentages and "one in _____" chances. Rough calculations can be your ruler of value. Estimates are close enough considering:

— You don't have all the information so you can't make a precise prediction.

— The odds will change to some extent once you bet, so forget being right on target. Make safe general assessments. They are as accurate as you can (or need to) be, whether it seems that way or not.

— Because you do not have all of the information and the odds will fluctuate after you bet, you always need to give yourself a safety cushion to be reasonably assured that you will receive the value that you're expecting.

An easily-computed guideline for guaranteeing yourself "value" is approximately a 50% premium. A 50% margin of error may seem like a lot but is actually a safe guideline that is easy to calculate in the heat of the moment. Better to have a quick and dirty guideline than to get bogged down in math and either make a mistake or get shut out at the windows.

Size Does Matter!—Field Size Concepts

In any given race, field size influences the chances of winning more than you might think, and I'm not just talking about working through traffic on the racetrack. The number of contenders mathematically corresponds to the number of possible outcomes in a race.

In a 5-horse field, if a horse wins only 4 others can run second. In a 12-horse field, if the same horse wins, 11 others can run second. Even if the odds on the first 2 finishers are the same in both races, the 12-horse field exacta should pay much more than the 5-horse field exacta.

In a **5-horse** field, there are only 20 possible exacta combinations.
In a **12-horse** field, there are 132 possible exacta combinations!

In a **5-horse** field, there are only 60 possible trifecta combinations.
In a **12-horse** field, there are 1,320 possible trifecta combinations!

That's all you need to know. In larger fields, exacta and trifecta combinations *should* pay more! You can demand more value in big fields and can afford to be less demanding in smaller ones.

A quick math example to drive home the point: If I like an even-money favorite in a 5-horse field, I do some quick math to see if there's any value in the exacta with the horse I prefer in second:

— Chance of 1-1 favorite winning: 50% (0.50).
— Assuming the favorite does win, chance of any of the other four runners running second, regardless of respective ability, 1 in 4 or 25% (0.25).
— Chance of this exacta coming in: 0.50 x 0.25=0.125, or 12.5%, or 1 in 8.

With a 1 in 8 chance in the exacta, a $16 exacta payoff would be fair.

Since I prefer one of these runners, I am assuming its *actual* chances of getting second are better than that. This "all other things being equal" estimate lets me know what will earn me value.

Will I get $16 in the exacta pool? Probably not. With the favorite on top, the four exacta combinations are probably at $10, $14, $16, and $22, or something close to that. However, if the one I prefer in second is one of the higher paying combinations, I will get that kind of value. That's when an exacta makes sense.

Now, what about the fair value in a 12-horse field?

— Chance of 1-1 favorite winning: 50%, or 0.50.
— 11 other runners for second = 1 in 11 = 0.091.
— 0.50 x 0.091 = 0.04543, or 4 1/2%, or about 1 in 22.

In this case, a $44 exacta payoff is the blind fair value estimate.

In a 12-horse field, will there be exacta combinations paying $44 or more with the favorite winning? Absolutely. Will it be the combination with your second choice? Maybe, maybe not, but at least you have a good guideline for when your scheme is worth betting money on.

What can be learned from this? If the exacta will-pay with an even-money favorite over another horse you like is paying $20, the payoff is probably pretty fair if it's a 5-horse field. If it is a 12-horse field, it's not fair.

Remember, field size also matters because:

— Traffic becomes more of an issue in bigger fields.
— Post positions become more important where the field is large. It's easier to find position breaking on the outside of a 5-horse field. In a 12-horse field, it's a real challenge.
— Value should be considered relative to the number of entries.

Field size is just one variable that affects the chances of winning. Now we will look at how different types of wagers have significantly different chances of success depending on how these wagers are structured.

Exotic Bet Probabilities: Understanding Series Bets Vs. Parallel Bets

At every venue in North America, exotic wagering draws more money than the win, place and show pools. Attracted to the lure of huge payouts, most bettors eagerly add to the exotics pool but few realize the true chances of cashing the exotics ticket.

To help understand exotic wagering, there are two key kinds of propositions: Series Bets and Parallel Bets. Expecting things to happen one after another (first this, next that) are series events. Examples are the daily double or the Pick 3. Expecting several things to occur simultaneously (this and that must both happen) are parallel events. Examples are the Exacta, Quinella, Trifecta, and Superfecta.

Without getting into graduate level risk management theory, a shallow dive into the mathematic implications is in order.

Series Bets

Series bets are wagers where a sequence of events must happen one after another in order to win. True, to win *any* race a series of events must happen. The horse has to make it into the gate and leave in good order. The horse must get a clean trip and cross the wire first without interfering with anyone else. In that sense, every race is made up of a sequence of events.

For the purposes of wagering, however, the focus is on each horse's finish position in a race as a specific event. The payout is affected only by its placing, not the time, the path it took, or how the horse gets to the finish.

Racing applications: Daily Doubles, Pick 3s, Pick 4s, Pick 6s.

Series Bets: How This Translates To Betting

To cash a daily double ticket, you have to win the first race. If you don't have the winner in the first race, it doesn't matter what happens in the second. If racing is even canceled after the first race, the track pays off all tickets with the winner of the first race regardless of what selection was made in the second leg. (Severe weather will cause this from time to time so it's a good thing to tuck away in your memory.)

After winning the first race, you then have to win the second race. Only then do you cash the ticket. You have to be right on two races instead of one—have two fields accurately analyzed, two scenarios pegged.

To cash a Pick 3 ticket, first you win the first leg then the second, then the third. Miss any of the three and you get nothing. Close isn't worth anything. So what are your actual chances of winning series bets?

If you have a daily double ticket and the first racehorse is 2-1, there is only an estimated 33% chance you will be alive in the second leg. If the second leg horse is 2-1 as well, its odds of winning are also 33%. But there is only a 33% chance that you will be alive when you get to your second horse.

To find the odds of both winning, you multiply the percentages:

$$0.33 \times 0.33 = 0.1089, \text{ or roughly } 11\%$$

Did you know that two 2-1 favorites sweeping the daily double is a 9-1 or so proposition? That means a fair payoff on such a double is at least $20.

The only thing painful about that math lesson should be the realization that two 2-1 favorites don't pay over $20 very often!

For the Pick 3 probability, let's add a third 2-1 favorite in a third race. Its chance of winning is 33%, but after the first two legs there is only an 11% chance you'll be live when the gate springs for race 3. The chances of winning?

$$0.11 \times 0.33 = 0.0363 \text{ or about } 3.6\%$$

Now we're up to a 27-1 proposition, so the fair payoff is $56 or so. Will you get that in a 3-favorite Pick 3?

The more races in the bet, the more this effect is compounded. With three 2-1 favorites, the fair chance of winning was 3.6%. Add just one more favorite and turn the equation into a Pick 4:

$$(2/1) \times (2/1) \times (2/1) \times (2/1) = (0.33)4 = 1.2\%$$

As you would expect, using more horses in a given leg of a series bet gives you much better chances of surviving until the next leg.

If in the first half of a daily double you use the 1-1 favorite (50%), the 3-1 second choice (25%), and a 9-1 contender (11%), you now have a (50+25+11)% = 86% chance of surviving until the next leg. Now if you stick with the same 2-1 shot in the second leg (still 33%), your chances of cashing a ticket are:

$$0.86 \times 0.33 = 0.284 = 28\%$$

By covering the majority of contenders in the first leg, your 28% chance of winning the daily double is only slightly less than the 33% chance of winning the second leg outright (33%).

Now, you bought three daily double tickets, but only one can be a winner. The total bet is an important factor in determining overall profitability. To maximize profit, we want to bet as little as possible to make as much as possible. When evaluating these series-bet exotics, a valid comparison is against the return from straight win bets.

Will that one winning ticket pay more than betting three times as much on the horse in the second leg? If it will pay more, the double is a better bet than just win betting. If not, then the win bet was more of a value all along.

Covering 80% of the chances in each leg of a Pick 3 gives you a 0.80 x 0.80 x 0.80 = 0.488 or 49% chance of hitting it! More on how to make that work to your advantage later.

Series bets are won or lost based on the success of a bettor picking winners in race after race. Miss even one hurdle and all bets are lost. What happens to the remaining runners in each race is irrelevant.

Now for bets that are determined by the remaining runners in the selected race.

Parallel Bets

Parallel bets are wagers where multiple outcomes within the same race must be correctly predicted in order to win. To win the wager, all of the contingencies must be satisfied. Like series bets, the payout is affected by properly identifying placings of runners, not the time or how the horses get to the finish. Unlike series bets, the combinations all happen in the same race event.

Racing applications: Quinellas, exactas, trifectas, superfectas.

In the quinella, the two top finishers must both be determined:

A & B must both outfinish all other competitors.

In the exacta, the top two finishers must both be determined, and in the correct order.

A must outfinish all other competitors, B must run second.

In the trifecta, the top three finishers must be correctly predicted in the proper order.

A must finish in front of all other runners,
B must run second, and C must run third.

Finally in the superfecta, the first four finishers must be predicted in the precise order of finish.

A must win, B must run second, C must finish third, and
D must finish in front of everyone except A, B, and C.

Parallel Bets: How This Translates To Betting

To cash a parallel bet ticket, you have to correctly divine how multiple runners competing against each other in the same race will finish. If you don't have all necessary placings right, you get nothing for being close. Picking the winning horse on top in a trifecta ticket is worthless unless the second and third place finishers also run in the predicted order. Furthermore, final "win" pool odds do not effect the exotic payouts. The wagering pools are completely separate.

Payouts are determined simply by the share of the pool that the track will return to bettors, divided by the number of tickets correctly identifying the runner combination. The favorite in the win pool is not necessarily the horse most frequently used on top in exacta, or trifecta tickets. So how do you determine fair payouts for parallel bets?

True to their name, parallel bet payouts are based on the combined chances of all contingencies simultaneously being met. For example, the fair payout for an exacta would be the odds on the horse picked to finish first winning, **times** the odds of the horse selected to finish second beating all remaining horses but the winner.

This is not the same as multiplying the chance of each of the two horses winning. If horse A has a 50% chance of winning, and horse B has a 25% of beating all remaining runners, then the chances of that exacta combination winning is 0.50 x 0.25 = 0.125. In other words, if horse A has a 50% chance of winning, and B has a 25% of running second ***if A wins***, the probability of this exacta being successful is 0.125, or 12.5%.

Bettors often expect unrealistically large payouts when an odds-on favorite wins and a horse with high win odds runs second. If a favorite wins at 1/2, someone has to run second, and most of the field would be at longshot win odds.

The fact that a 20-1 shot gets second does not mean it was 20-1 to finish second behind the favorite, it was 20-1 ***to win*** the race, beating the favorite and all other runners! It may have had a 33% chance of running second given the favorite winning. In such an example the fair payout would be:

$$0.66 \times 0.33 = 0.2178 \text{ or about } 22\%$$

So a 9/2 payout or $11 would be more or less the fair exacta price.

In trifectas the math gets more complicated, and the chance of success drops off dramatically. If a 2-1 shot wins (33%), a horse with a 25% chance of getting the place spot finishes second, and a horse with a 20% of running third gets the show, the estimated chances of success is 0.33 x 0.25 x 0.20 = 0.0165, about 1.6%. The fair payout is in the neighborhood of $150 for a $2 bet.

Note there are no longshots in the above example. If the third place finisher had only a 10% chance of running third instead of 20%, the likelihood of success is halved, and the fair payout would have to double to make up for the added risk.

Superfectas include a fourth probability to be multiplied in the equation. Take the above trifecta example. Suppose it's an eight-horse field and the remaining five unplaced runners are all equally likely to get fourth place. That gives each a 20% percent chance of running fourth. So, multiply the trifecta success probability, 0.0165 times the chances of a selected runner finishing fourth, 0.20, and you get 0.0165 x 0.20 = 0.0033. The odds on this superfecta should be 303-1, for a payout exceeding $600; again with no longshots.

To get the same probability of success as the trifecta, you would have to cover all five of the horses in fourth place, getting a combined probability of 100% (20% for each). The cost of going this deep into any exotic ticket generally outweighs the potential return, so unless you were extremely confident in your analysis of the first three finishers, you would choose other betting opportunities.

There are two ways to look at these small probabilities (1.6% for our trifecta, and 0.33% for our superfecta picking one horse in fourth): either "Wow, the payouts are generous!" or "Wow, even with low-priced contenders the chance of hitting exotics gets pretty slim as the bets become more and more complicated!" The second assessment is the crucial point in this discussion.

Wagering and Cashflow Management: Accepting Cold Realities About Exotic Wagers

Exotic wagers attract more money from bettors than traditional win, place, and show wagering due to the chance for larger payoffs. Virtually every track takes a higher percentage of money out of exotic pools than other wagers. Yet the seemingly large payoffs mask the higher taxes. Bettors in general will gravitate toward exotic wagers using the favorite because the chance of winning a $100 trifecta seems more appealing than cashing a $4 win bet. Unfortunately, the exotic payoffs using the favorite are seldom a better value with respect to the true chances of winning, compared to W/P/S betting.

If the public is overbetting a favorite to win, it is almost certainly overusing it in exotics as well. Despite this, when a handicapper can isolate just a few contenders for the W/P/S spots, then exotics can be an opportunity to exploit the information known about all the competitors. The key is to focus on exotics when you conclude these pools offer value and not simply when win betting fails to offer the value you hoped for.

Exactas Vs. Win Bets

The more combinations you use, the more likely you'll win, but remember that keying a horse over five others in exactas ($10) may not pay as much as betting the same $10 to win. On the other hand, hitting a single $10 exacta may turn a good betting race into a real score.

Example: Horse A is a prime contender, and you bet $25 to win on it. You also want to bet some exotics. You think B is most likely to run second, with C, D, E and F also having chances. Investing $10 in the exacta pool, you can do one of the following:

Bet a $10 A w/B exacta or

Bet $2 exactas of A w/B, C, D, E, F.

If the A w/B combination is paying $40, and A w/C, D, E, F are paying between $40 and $70, you could either bet the one $10 exacta and try to cash in for $200 (plus your win bet)—a big hit from what you think is the most likely scenario. You could instead spread with the five $2 bets, and try to get $40 to $70 for $10 in bets.

If betting the $10 to win on A pays close to the $40 to $75 range, either go for the $10 straight exacta or just stick with the win bet.

Trifectas

Most people playing trifectas will go for a minimum of 6 combinations. Twelve, 18, or 24 is more likely. Although the payoffs can be great, many tris will fail to win. Betting $18 each on four trifectas a day would total $72 in one day for this type of bet—not a small investment. The few trifectas that are hit must pay for all trifectas bet *plus* profit to be worthwhile over time.

Daily Doubles

The same rules apply as for exactas. Too many combinations will lead to payoffs no better than betting it all to win. Betting fewer contenders decreases your chances of winning, but multiplies your payoffs relative to investment.

Pick 3s

To properly play the Pick 3, between $48 and $64 is required to make $1 Pick 3 part wheels. For every Pick 3 that you might play, you need that kind of capital set aside. Throughout the day, Pick 3s give the bettor more opportunity but also call for a separate stake to play.

Exotic Bankroll Complications

Suppose you bring $100 to the track, make three $20 win bets on your three prime contenders. You leave yourself $40 for everything else. You might be amazed how fast $40 can vanish on those other six or seven races plus exotics with your prime horses.

If you proceed this way, just one of your three prime bets winning at 4-1 or more will put you ahead for the day. If anything else hits, you do even better. But again, leaving yourself just $40 for exotic wagers leaves you with fewer options. Yes, you have a chance to make a big score. But you have nowhere near enough to bet exotics in every race. That $40 may be allocated for one or two exotic wagers in an effort to hit a home run. However, it should not be spread out in $1 or $2 bets in every race.

Longshots In Perspective

What if you like two longshots in an early daily double? The first horse you think has a 25% chance, and the second horse has a 15% chance. Statistically, the chance of both winning is 0.25 x 0.15 = 0.0375, or 3.75% (about a 1 in 28 chance).

This type of calculation applies any time you are counting on two longshots to perform. You can certainly bet on logical longshots. But counting on two or more longshots to step up in two consecutive races for a double or in the same race for an exacta or tri? Statistically, the chances of success are small. Not impossible—just smaller than you might think. **You will cash tickets more consistently if your betting strategy relies on only one miracle per bet.** You need to balance your search for value with sanity and reason.

If you are betting combinations that have a very small probability of success, be prepared for long losing streaks even if you are doing everything right. If you bet series of longshots strung together hoping for a 5-figure score, be prepared to wait all year. This does not mean you will come out a loser. It does mean that you must have enough capital to weather the long dry spells, otherwise that's exactly what will happen.

What does this teach the bettor to do? Consider the size of your bankroll when you decide how you want to wager. Unless your bankroll is big enough to survive the predictable dry spell, you may need to adjust your betting to a style that promises more consistent cashflow. You can't take advantage of exotic bets if you can't weather the ups and downs.

Exacta Myths and Methods

Despite the large variety of wagers offered on a typical race, the exacta remains one of the best wagering options at the races. When looking for value, handicappers usually start with the win pool, then the next place they look will be the exotics. With new wagers being invented with each passing year, the exacta is often forgotten in the menu of exotics presented to the bettor.

Yet the exacta is not boring. In fact, it provides opportunities to any bettor who takes the time to understand it. This section will discuss proven methods for success and when exactas are the way to go, while exposing common misconceptions.

The exacta is worth attention and study for many reasons. First, takeout on the exacta is usually the same or comparable to Win/Place/Show betting, much lower than Trifectas, Pick 3s, and Superfectas at most tracks. Second, the exacta has a higher probability of success than the "super-exotics." Tracks also show will-pay information—one of the few exotics bets that provide this information. The exacta consistently offers real value, especially in situations where the favorite is vulnerable to finish third or worse.

Finally, the exacta may be your "first, last, and only option" when no value can be found in the W/P/S pools. If you have assessed a race and have strong inclination about which runners will dominate the race, you want to capitalize on the situation by betting just about everything, up to and including the superfecta and Pick 3. But you may not be able to! Unfortunately, tracks limit the types of bets available in a given race. In contrast, the exacta is *almost always* an option.

Getting good value in exacta pools is all relative. There are short-priced payoffs that are actually generous, and long prices that aren't all that good. Understanding the exacta and knowing what situations to avoid create golden opportunities with this exotic.

The Exacta Primer

Here are four overall rules for managing exacta play.

— ***Rule #1***: As a quick rule of thumb to estimate value, ***if*** the favorite over the contender offers fair value, ***then*** the contender with the favorite will consistently be a value as well—usually at least 1.5 times what the favorite on top pays. Generally assume that if the exacta one way is a value, the other way is a value as well. If one isn't a value, the other often won't be either. (While this approach works very well for two horses, avoid boxing three or more horses. See Myth #1.) If this approach seems cavalier, keep in mind that these judgments are being made with only X minutes to post and an odds board that will continue to fluctuate after your wager is placed. Therefore your estimates will always be of limited accuracy. Late money impacts payoffs, so part of accepting the risk for expected return must include acceptance that payoffs are not known, and quick computations are close enough to evaluate and make a decision on risk and return. Quick computations are useful and you don't have time for a math exercise with two minutes to post.

— ***Rule #2***: If you think the favorite will win, discount other horses in the race with the same running style as the favorite. If the favorite is superior at what he does, then others running the same way are likely to unravel. A superior frontrunner should wreak havoc on the other frontrunners. A strong closer should leave other closers in his wake.

— ***Rule # 3***: If a horse can run second, it can win. With few exceptions, fit horses hit the board and unfit horses don't. A horse that runs second has the potential to win as well. Stubbornly betting exactas over and over with contenders only in second is bound to lead to anguish.

— ***Rule #4***: If you prefer one runner and no other entry sparks interest, forget exotics. You'll only overthink it. Strong opinions are worth betting on; don't ruin it by looking for more when it just isn't there.

For example, if I like a favorite and see only one other contender, then I run through the following decision process:

- — Do my two contenders have the same running style? If they do, I assume that one will ruin the other. Although a speed duel may be the undoing of the weaker contender, it does not necessarily translate to the undoing of both pace horses. The stronger pace horse often prevails, without succumbing to the rest of the field. I'll bet the stronger horse to win. If it's a toss-up on ability, I'll bet the one with longer odds.
- — If they do not have the same running style, there's a good chance they will run 1-2. If the exactas appear to offer value, I'll bet an exacta box of these two horses. I will usually place a win bet as well on the higher priced horse, especially at 4-1 or higher.
- — If the exacta combinations do not exceed the fair estimate of value, I will either pass the race or only make a win bet on the longer priced horse.

The exacta is one wager worth understanding and incorporating into your betting strategy, and is a great bet in many situations. Adding to its attractiveness, the exacta is often misplayed by the public. Understanding the common misconceptions regarding the exacta is key to knowing what to avoid. Here are some common myths and alternative betting approaches.

Myth #1: Wheeling and boxing

First, the myth: Wheel and box, it's the best of both worlds—the big payoff of an exotic bet, the guarantee that your top selection hitting will not be spoiled by not picking the right combination.

Bettors fear they will put the wrong runners under their top selection, so they eliminate the risk (wheels). Or they are afraid they will identify the top selections correctly, but they might finish in the wrong order (boxes). Lots of combinations, lots of opportunities to score! Unfortunately, lots of losing bets as well. Here are the cold hard truths behind why wheeling and boxing will slowly chisel away at your bankroll:

— Wheeling or boxing exactas guarantees that *at best,* all but one combination you bet is guaranteed to lose.
— When wheeling or boxing exactas, the bettor is wagering an equal amount on all combinations. For exacta wheels, this means you are putting just as much money on the prospect that the horse *least likely* to run second as on the horse *most likely* to get the place spot. The same lack of preference occurs when betting a 3 or more horse exacta box. The least likely outcomes get the same share of your bankroll as your most likely combination.

The logic behind wheeling seems sound to the novice. "If my longshot hits, I'm going to *make sure* I have the exacta." The bettor ends up with $22 in exactas on a horse in a 12-horse field. Compare the probable exacta will-pays to the payoff the same $22 bet to win instead. Unless you have strong convictions that the 1st, 2nd, 3rd and 4th choices (excluding your choice) in the field are likely to finish worse than second, you are *much* better off betting your choice to win than betting an exacta wheel.

The Breeders' Cup races are perfect evidence of why wheeling exactas rarely pays off. Through the 2004 races, there have been 142 Breeders' Cup races where exactas were offered. Just about every race has been loaded with contenders, making it hard to eliminate large portions of the field. Let's compare whether it would be better to bet the favorite to win, or on top of an exacta wheel. We would lose our bet either way in 90 races when the favorite lost. The favorite won 52 times. Of those, only 20 times did the exacta wheel pay more than betting the same amount on the favorite to win.

In situations where the exacta wheel paid more than an equivalent win bet, the second place finishers were always longshots.

Of those 20 races, 19 of the second place finishers were at odds between 13 to 1 and 78 to 1! The remaining second place finisher was still a longshot, at 8.7 to 1. Betting exactas in the Breeders' Cup is usually attractive, in hopes of hitting a home run even if the favorite wins. But how much would those successful exacta wheels actually ***profit***? Only 7 of the 20 wheels would have netted more than $200 profit (the highest profit being $613 in the 1998 Juvenile). Twelve of the 20 produced less than $100 in profit—little reward for hitting an exacta in a highly contentious, premier race.

In the other 32 instances where the favorite won, it paid better to make a win bet. (The comparison is betting the same amount to win that the exacta wheel would have cost.) In 11 of those 32 events, the exacta wheel even showed a loss.

The Breeders' Cup is a strong example of the "best case" for wheeling exactas, because each race has many contenders and, with 20/20 hindsight, the exotic payoffs always seem appealing. But even in these super-contentious fields, wheeling only makes money when the longest shots in a field find their way into the exacta.

If your only opinion is that your horse will finish in the top two, and you lack any insight into which other runners are most likely to finish in the money, wheeling is a poor substitute for handicapping! Avoid the many losing tickets with more attention to handicapping the race. Narrow your list of contenders, but be willing to use longshots with a realistic chance to run second or better.

Myth #2: Bet the favorite on top of the other contenders in a field.

It should be obvious that the favorite over the 2nd, 3rd and 4th choices would almost always be the most underlaid combinations in the exacta. Nevertheless the betting public finds it hard to resist using the favorite over every other horse receiving action at the mutuel windows.

If you really like the favorite to win, but feel the exacta will offer better value than the win pool, look for a single exacta combination with the favorite on top rather than covering several contenders. Every additional combination you bet chips away at your profit margin.

If a 2-1 favorite is paired with three other contenders, the $6 in combinations must pay substantially more than the $18 that a $6 win bet on that favorite will pay. The added risk that another horse will finish second should steer the bettor towards the win pool unless the exacta pool is offering exceptional value.

The "underlaid favorite" causes a dilemma for many bettors that like a non-favorite but want to bet some form of "saver." If you like a horse at 6-1, the logical exacta bet would seem to be the favorite over the 6-1 shot as a saver bet. It might hit fairly often, but the payoff will be paltry. The favorite gets a lot of action in the win spot of the exacta pool. Bettors should accept that and adapt their wagering strategy accordingly.

But what other options are there for the smart handicapper?

Option 1: Cold exacta with the favorite

If you like the favorite to win and have also identified what you consider to be a "best of the rest" contender, bet a cold exacta of the favorite over your second choice. The favorite on top will frequently generate an underlaid exacta payoff. If you can isolate a horse to run clear of the rest, you can focus your capital on that exacta. A $20 exacta would return more than $20 to win on the favorite. You are conceding the win spot to the favorite, and betting your second choice to beat the remainder of the field.

Be aware that every other bettor is looking for a cold exacta with a 1-5 favorite as well. If the favorite is an odds-on underlay in the win pool, there is probably no value in the exacta pool either.

Option 2: Matrixes

You don't think the favorite will run first (or even second), but find it hard to separate several other runners? The exacta is an opportunity to capitalize when you have isolated several contenders. Box two medium-priced horses, or bet an exacta of a longshot over and under medium-priced horses. If you like a longshot to win, even using the favorite in second will usually offer value.

Myth #3: Box the top jockeys in exactas and watch the money roll in.

The logic here is that the top jockeys win the most races, they run second the most times, therefore the exacta box should be profitable over time, without all the fuss of deciding which runners are contenders and which are just participants.

Actually, the top jockeys do not run 1—2 at decent odds often enough to make this bet worthwhile. The public bets jockeys to such an extent that the top jockey in a race may be overbet relative to the horse's actual odds of winning. This imbalance naturally affects the exacta pools as well. Following this method is perhaps the easiest way to guarantee that you will cash winning tickets at consistently undervalued prices.

A simple way to demonstrate this is to look at a small bottom level meet where the few decent riders get all the "live" mounts, and therefore win the vast majority of all races. The 1999 Northampton Three County Fair ran 54 races over the six-day September meet. M. Santiago, H. Lanci, and Al Howarth Jr. won 39 of the races. That's three riders winning 72% of the races. A $2 exacta box of all three riders (or of two when all three weren't riding in the same race) would have led to a bettor cashing 18 exactas in 54 races, an incredible 33% hit rate! That's a success rate many professionals would be satisfied with in the win pool! Unfortunately the payoffs would have totaled a mere $561.20 for $576 bet. Despite cashing tickets again and again, you'd be getting nowhere fast on the road to profit.

Understand that this minor league meet is not just an obscure example. I chose it because it is a best-case scenario for applying such a system. All three jockeys rode just about every race on the card, and the field size was consistently six to eight runners. I have run this trial on major circuits, such as the entire 1998 Saratoga meet, and the results are even worse. Increase the study to the top four or even five riders. The hit rate goes up, but the losses get worse and worse. Underlaid combinations, plus lots of losing combinations in every exacta box, and your bankroll is sure to slowly grind down to zero.

Myth #4: Betting exactas in small fields never pays fairly.

Fair payoffs are relative to the actual probability of winning and the payoffs being offered. An exacta combination in a small field can be an overlay, and an exacta in a full field can just as easily be an underlay. A number of formulas of varying complexity can be used to determine what a "fair price" for an exacta combination will be. These formulas multiply bet size times the odds of the win horse times the odds of the place horse, divided by the percentage that the track returns on dollars wagered. This generates a number that is then multiplied by a factor to produce a "premium" to guarantee value, such a 1.2 for a 20% premium.

These formulas generate accurate numbers, but for most handicappers it involves too much math to realistically perform these calculations as part of an on-track handicapping routine. Yet some simple arithmetic should help bettors see the relationship between field size and probabilities of cashing a winning exacta ticket.

There is a better chance of hitting the exacta in a 5-horse race than a 12-horse race, even if the two runners you use in the 5-horse field leave the gate at the same win odds as your top two selections in a 12-horse field. Why? As discussed earlier in this book, in a 5-horse field, there are only 20 possible combinations. In a 12-horse field, there are 132 possible combinations.

To put it another way, if in both situations you were "sure" your top selection would win, your chances of picking the correct horse to run second in the 5-horse field are 1 in 4. Yet in the 12-horse field your chances of picking the place horse plummet to 1 in 11. Add the reality that every additional runner in the field means increased potential for a troubled trip for your selection. More traffic, more chaos, more jockeys on the track trying to maneuver for position, and more and more unknowns than can be listed here. It doesn't take a mathematics degree to understand that bigger field size = more risk = you deserve a higher payoff!

True, the payoffs in a 5-horse race are small enough that they aren't really an "exotic" payoff. There are good and bad points to large and small fields when betting the exacta. The 5-horse race has fewer entries to study, possibly a clearer pace scenario to envision, and far less combinations to consider. You are more likely to be correct in your wager, but less likely to hit a big payoff. The 12-horse race has more entries to consider, and far more possible combinations. But it also will usually have a greater number of runners you can safely eliminate from consideration. And money (other people's money) will be bet on every combination. If you can handicap the race and identify a few solid contenders, the payoff will be more generous if for no other reason than all the money dumped on "dead" combinations.

Myth #5: The public's second choice is the horse most likely to complete the exacta.

Other than the favorite, the second choice *wins* more often than any horse, but the horse that runs second the most often is the *favorite*, not the second choice! The betting public still fails to understand that the "Place Horse" in an exacta combination should be selected based on its likelihood to run *second* (predicting a runner will lose but beat all but one runner in the field) and not on its chances of winning.

The most likely place horses are:

— **The favorite.** They win 33% of the time, but they also run second about 20% of the time. Despite being underlaid when played in the win spot, favorites consistently offer value when played underneath other contenders, especially longshots. Back to the Breeders' Cup, 13 of the 126 times an exacta was offered, the favorite has run second. The payoffs have usually been generous—and not just for the handful of people who caught the Arcangues/Bertrando $1,015 exacta in 1993 or the Volponi/Medaglia d'Oro exacta for $463.60 in 2002!

— **The "seconditis" or "sucker" horse.** This type of horse must have unlimited talent, because it can follow the winner and hold the rest of the field at bay, no matter how tough the competition is. A horse with 25 lifetime starts achieving 1 win, 9 seconds, and 7 thirds may be a sucker's bet to win, but should be an obvious horse for the place spot in exactas. Horses like this often give terrific value in exactas, because they tend to be judged by their win odds. If such a horse is 12-1 on the board, in all likelihood the public will use him like a 12-1 shot in the exacta. Such a horse actually should be considered more like one of the favorites to run second.

— **Horses with a running style contrary to the other contenders in the field.** If a field is loaded with frontrunners, a closer stands a better than usual chance of running second (or better). Likewise, a lone frontrunner has an awfully good chance to run no worse than second.

— **Horses that appear to have the most ability, but will be hindered by a poor post position or a running style that doesn't fit the track bias.** This is the most subjective criteria, but it pays to know when a horse is the most capable but compromised. They can be paired with runners better suited to the day's conditions.

Identifying these kinds of horses and using them in the place spot on your exacta tickets will both increase your chances of cashing a ticket, and make sure that ticket is a fair value.

A Better Way To Play Exactas

Depending on your personal goals and risk tolerance level, the way you bet exactas will vary, as will the percentage of your bankroll you set aside for exotics as opposed to "traditional" W/P/S bets. You may want to bet exotics, including exactas, in a way that supplements your win bets on key selections whenever additional value is offered. But you may not want to risk turning a winning opportunity into a losing one if your contender hits but the other runners you paired it with in exactas don't pan out. To find more return, you may accept higher risk and bet heavily in the exotic pools, understanding that your key horse may romp but you may still have zero to show for it, because you were accepting the higher risk in an effort to hit a real jackpot.

To Summarize:

— Play "value" contenders ***over*** the favorite.
— Bet pairs of mid-priced horses, and contenders paired up with reasonable longshots.
— Find the "Place Horse."
— Avoid the temptation to box and wheel, especially with favorites.

Whether you are content to come out ahead by a few dollars or your goal is to break the bank, remember the goal is to make a profit. When you have a lot of confidence in your expected outcome of a race, capitalize on it. It should be clear that the exacta remains one of the best opportunities for profit due to the public's misunderstandings about how to properly play it. If you can incorporate these guidelines into your handicapping routine, and avoid the common exacta myths, you should see your long-term profits grow.

Trifecta Matrix Construction

Trifectas are similar to exactas in a few key ways. Horses that are unlikely to win but likely to run second or third (the "sucker" horses) are often used in proportion to their longshot win odds instead of good place or show chances. Also, the public bets the favorite heavily over other horses receiving action at the mutuel windows in trifectas. This section briefly outlines a method to constructing a "matrix" to help capitalize on trifecta opportunities.

Construct a model for placing horses in trifecta combinations based on:

— The probability of winning,
— The probability of finishing third or better, and
— Value with respect to odds.

Base the matrix on:

— Win contenders (belong in win, place and show).
— Place contenders (longshots that could win but at best, will most likely only hit the board).
— Show contenders (fringe players that could ruin everything by getting in trifecta).
— Non-contenders (no chance to hit the board in any foreseeable scenario).
— "Vulnerable favorites" (favorites that you intend to play against in the win pool, but can be used in second or third, although not as a single because if they finish up the track the payoff can be stupendous!).

The Trifecta Matrix is as follows:

A, B with A, B, C with A, B, C, D, E
(12 combinations)

— ***Rule #1***: Both A and B cannot be the favorite.
— ***Rule #2***: C can and should be the favorite, as favorites hit the board more than any other runners even when they do not win. To not use the favorite is to guarantee long dry spells without cashing tickets. If the favorite is deemed a *complete* throw-out, however, it should not appear on the ticket at all.
— ***Rule #3***: D and E should include longshots that are unlikely win candidates, but can hang on (or plod up late) for third at a price.

A strength about this matrix is that two horses are used in the win slot but both do not have to finish in the money to win. Runner A can finish dead last while B goes on to victory, and you still have an opportunity to score. If A and B run 1-2, you have three runners covered in the third slot, including two longshots.

Suppose the following horses are our Matrix selections:

A: 9/2
B: 6-1
C: 8/5
D: 12-1
E: 20-1

The A and B horses are two medium priced contenders. Either one may also be a great win bet candidate, but if one of them topples the favorite C, it will generate a real score.

If C wins as the favorite, all is lost, but the payoff on the trifecta is very likely to be underlaid.

If either A or B beats the favorite and the favorite runs second, there are three possible show runners. This won't make a killing but a lot of decent trifectas will be cashed this way. Is a $200 trifecta merely a "saver"?

If A and B run 1-2, and the favorite C runs third, again this is a decent hit. But if A and B run 1-2 and one of the longshots D or E gets third, then it is certain to be a real score. The favorite is out of the money, ***and*** longshots are on the ticket!

This matrix allows the use of five horses without betting the 60 combinations necessary to box all five of them. Betting 12 combinations instead of 60 means far less losing tickets—whether or not the trifecta is hit. Yes, only two horses instead of five are covered to win, and only three of five can run second, but the decision to bet was based on a preference for A and B, and therefore they should be weighted more heavily in any betting scheme.

One more note on trifectas: The number of runners entered in a race is an important factor.

- In a 12-horse field every runner has a 25% chance of hitting the board.
- In a 10-horse field every runner has a 30% chance of hitting the board.
- In a 8-horse field every runner has a 37.5% chance of hitting the board.
- In a 6-horse field every runner has a 50% chance of hitting the board.

With larger fields, there are more combinations, and a decreased chance of selecting the correct three runners to hit the board. Therefore regardless of the final odds, the payouts should be higher in a 12-horse race than in one with only six entrants. It is the difference between 1,320 possible combinations in the field of 12, and 120 possible combinations in the 6-horse race!

Investment Strategy Advice

All discussions about value aside, when it's time to pull the trigger, how do you decide to bet?

First, win pool value on a lone contender calls for betting to win with the majority of the money you are prepared to bet in the race. If you think you have a key horse with generous odds, take advantage of this opportunity. The first priority is the win bet.

If you also want to bet exotics in this situation, so be it, but the exotics money should be much less than the win bet. If the odds are generous (4-1 and up is concluded here), don't forget a win/place bet.

Positive Win Strategies

— 50% overlay rule applies (3-1 for 2-1, 6-1 for 4-1) and means NO exactas or trifectas. Go for the win profit, not a 3-pool spread.

— Two horses to win if both are contenders at over 4-1 (60% hits on this bet requires $10 mutuels to give the 50% overlay needed).

Positive Win/Place Strategies

— Vulnerable favorite makes place overlays possible.

— Contenders over 5-1 that are legitimate best bets.

Positive Exacta Strategies

— Pairs of non-favored contenders at less-than-longshot prices.

— Favorites underneath contenders.

— Chronic runners-up in bottom of exacta with contenders on top.

Positive Quinella Strategies

— Overbet favorite with underbet contenders and longshots.
— Pairs of low priced contenders that are ***not favored.***
— Pairs of longshots that are also both bet to win.

Positive Trifecta Strategies

— Legitimate favorite in first over two or three contenders, several times.
— Contender keyed over two longshots and the favorite.
— Contenders combined when favorite is vulnerable, at least $1 box.

Favorite-itis—Hard Lesson Learned

Sometimes a race seems to be fairly predictable, yet turning this into an opportunity can be a whole different story.

Belmont Park, Mid-June, Thursday afternoon feature race, 1 1/16 ALWNX2

This race featured horses who have won a maiden race and one other non-claiming race in their careers.

You would expect a race like this to contain:

— Some claimers taking a shot at allowance conditions,
— Inexperienced runners that have managed two wins in relatively few starts,
— Habitual allowance runners who never seem to get through conditions, and
— A young stakes horse or two that still qualifies for this condition.

This race had runners in all of these categories, but only one stakes runner, Unbridled Jet.

Unbridled Jet was a late-blooming Bill Mott trainee that managed a good maiden and allowance win before trying the Peter Pan Stakes (GR II 1 1/8). In that race, he was the surprising favorite in the early betting and left the gate as the 7/2 second choice. He was in contention the whole way and finished within a length of third place finisher Lemon Drop Kid who would win the Belmont Stakes just 12 days later. Off such a strong effort, today's race would seem to be an easy tuneup for one of the big 3-year-old stakes in July.

Unbridled Jet faced an fairly ordinary field. The three other contenders included King's Crown, Crafty Man, and Qurman. King's Crown, a closer, had won two races at Belmont Park but failed in a turf race on Belmont Day in his most recent start. (The switch back to a dirt allowance made sense.) Crafty Man and Qurman were both lightly raced, have shown ability but lack stakes experience entering today's Grade II event. Both probably have good futures but are facing the toughest field yet in their careers. The remainder of the field appears overmatched against these top four contenders.

At 2-1 or more, Unbridled Jet would merit a serious win bet. I was not enthused with the 32-day layoff following a good stakes effort but with Bill Mott as the trainer, I assumed he was being his usual conservative self. The more I looked at this race, I was sure Unbridled Jet would not be 2-1 but would open somewhere around even money and probably continue to drop in odds.

I decided the race was going to be all but unplayable except maybe for the exotics. I looked at the three challengers to Unbridled Jet and decided that of the three, Crafty Man had the same running style as Unbridled Jet and thus was the least likely to fare well. Qurman was somewhat of a frontrunner, and King's Crown was a closer exiting a turf race so he figured to lack early speed today.

I bet Unbridled Jet in exactas and trifectas over Qurman and King's Crown. I thought that $8 bet gave me the chance to hit a short-priced trifecta and the exacta should pay around $12, at least breaking even if it won.

Unbridled Jet ended up 3-5, and after a quarter mile, rushed up to fight with Qurman through a very fast opening 6f. Turning for home, King's Crown had moved up on the outside to join the two on the lead, but I was not smiling. It didn't look like Unbridled Jet was ever going to pass Qurman, and King's Crown had a lot more momentum than either of them. On the far outside, Crafty Man, who unlike Unbridled Jet had stuck with his pressing running style, was running right by all three of them.

At the finish, it was Crafty Man, King's Crown, Qurman, Unbridled Jet. The trifecta paid $211 and I missed an opportunity where I had accurately identified the four contenders by relying on an underlaid favorite.

Epilogue

Unbridled Jet next skipped the Dwyer Stakes, another Grade II 1 1/8 mile $150,000 stakes at Belmont, and opted instead for the Long Branch Stakes, a $75,000 1 1/16 mile stakes at Monmouth Park. He ran second as the 2-1 second choice, beaten by a horse making its stakes debut after winning its MSWT and ALWNX1 races in fine fashion. One late bloomer beaten by another.

Handicapping Humor: Schizophrenic Handicapping

Sometimes I feel like ten handicappers in one, and none of them see eye to eye.

There's the **paranoid odds-board watcher** that sees conspiracies unfolding with every flash of the tote board. He knows there are no such things as coincidences. The opening odds, the big changes, the disparities between win and exotic prices, late money, early money—the X Files have nothing on this guy. And it's not just the odds board he watches. He thinks everyone is up to something—the superintendent is making the track biased on purpose, the pony rider is working the favorite into a frenzy, the hot dog vendor has the inside info and is secretly laughing at him. And they're all betting—he just has to figure out the Fix.

There's the **speed figure freak**—what an evolving personality that has been. Always looking for the horse that has "the number." Top figure horses, best last figure horse, best figure at the distance horse, best average figure. Par figures led to above par horses and sub par horses, weak fields and strong fields.

Then came pace figures, then pace pars and race shapes! Suddenly there are horses with superior pace figures but weak overall figures, weak pace figure horses with good overall figures. Fast-slow, slow-fast, average—average, and a never-ending quest for the "omni-figure" horse that is above par in both pace and speed figures, and every race it has run produced a higher number than the career best of every other runner in the race.

I think **Pulpit** was the last well-known runner to fit this bill back in January 1997. He paid $2.80, I think.

The **genealogist** has all but gotten a master's degree in genetics to help study turf pedigrees, mud pedigrees, average win distances, first time starter win percentages, and dosage. Hours and hours are spent poring over Stallion Registers, sales information, dam histories. When all else fails, this guy has a default excuse to explain why a runner did something his parents couldn't do—"He's a throwback!"

Next is the **mind reader**. His specialty is trainer intentions. Why is the horse in this race? Why is he adding blinkers? Why the jockey change? Why the move up in claiming price following a poor effort? Is the horse actually suited for grass or is the trainer desperate? Is this a prep race or an all-out try? Has he told owners, "It's a go?" Is he betting *his* money? *The mind reader has answers to every one of these questions.* Well, not exactly answers. But logical, plausible, reasonable rationalizations that would explain why the trainer is doing this and that.

The mind reader is even learning to read lips so he can watch the trainer talk to the jockey and owners in the paddock. That way he can see the trainer move his mouth to the words, "Don't push him this time" or "Win at all costs!"

The mind reader has tried to read the mind of the jockey for years without much success. He's not sure the jockeys are ever really thinking out there. But the responsibility of understanding jockeys falls to another personality . . . .

The **race analyst**. The classic "trip handicapper" in every sense. He's part football coach analyzing play-by-play films, and part NASCAR race commentator. He likes to imagine he has his own Jockey-Cam and can watch the race unfold. He also wishes he had a blimp cam, rail cam, head-on cam, rear-view cam, and maybe an EKG readout of every runner to know which ones are working hardest.

He believes that every horse with a poor trip will get a clear path to the winner's circle next time, and every runner with a fortunate trip won't be so lucky. The race analyst looks for every mistake, every misstep, every inch of ground lost on the turns and every lucky break a horse gets.

He sees it all. Too bad he can't see into the future.

The **geologist**. The track conditions guy. He is looking for track biases. How deep was the track harrowed? How hard is the turf course? No one else wants to hear about the details of soil and sod. All they really want to hear from him is "Rail good" or "Turf favors closers."

The **mathematician** knows all the percentages. Overlay, underlay, probable payouts, post position stats, stats on trainers, jockeys, layoffs, turn-backs, stretchouts. You name the situation, he'll tell you the statistical chance of it leading to a win.

He believes in a theoretical number called "o'fer" meaning something between a zero and ten percent chance. O'fers are not supposed to win, are not supposed to have any real chance, and are not supposed to ruin the best laid plans as often as they seem to.

The mathematician is always working with the speed figure guy and the genealogist, trying to assign a percentage to everything and everyone associated with the race. This drives the speed figure guy and genealogist nuts. They each think there's one predominant factor. The mathematician thinks there's a gloriously infinite number of factors.

Often the mathematician is the skeptic when the others are talking in terms of trainer intentions or poor trips or equipment changes. If numbers can't support the claims of supernatural—it's bunk.

The **veterinarian** studies the animals. He looks for positive and negative signs. He *hates* going to simulcast facilities, and would feel better examining $2,500 claimers in person at the county fair than watching Saratoga from an OTB. He studies equipment changes. "Blinkers on" is a good thing, but not sure about "blinkers off." Therapeutic shoes and pads are bad—they just bring to mind Unbridled Song wearing bar shoes in the Kentucky Derby, spinning 8-wide turning for home and losing a 4-length lead.

The paddock and post parade—he looks for sweat. Sweat is bad, white foam is worse. Unless it's hot or the horse does it all the time. Then it's not bad, but it's not a plus either. It's hard to factor in "sweaty" going to the window with 2 minutes to post. How sweaty was he really? "Just getting warmed up" sweaty or "might finish up the track" sweaty?

The veterinarian has one critical role. He is the guy at Mission Control with his finger on the ABORT button. If it doesn't look right to him—no bet. He takes the wind out of everyone else's sails, but that's okay as long as he's right more often than not.

Then there's the **junk bond trader**. He's bored by win/place/show betting. That's not where fortunes are made. He wants action in at least five pools a race—the more complicated the better. If they had a bet to pick the correct order of finish for an entire 12-horse field, he'd be first in line.

He's never embarrassed if a horse the rest of the crew liked wins, but no bet gets cashed because he talked them into going with exotics (that didn't hit) rather than betting to win.

He sulks when he loses out and the bet is to win or (gasp!) win/place. To him that's like buying a government bond.

The junk bond trader is the most dangerous character in the bunch, dangling the Huge Exotic Hit like a carrot. And he is shameless, presenting his schemes no matter how far-fetched, and always in a confident voice that makes you want to believe.

And finally there's the **banker**. He's the one that knows what's in the wallet. He knows what's left on the voucher. (He knows the limit on the ATM too!) He knows how much time is left to bet. He knows how much the tolls, admission, parking, *Racing Form*, program, hot dogs, and souvenirs cost. He knows a trip to the track gets surprisingly more expensive when family and friends come along.

He tallies the winnings when the daily double, exacta, and trifecta all hit in one race. He ruins the fun when he decides the losses are enough for one outing. When times are good, he's everyone's best friend. When times are bad, they all think he's a spoilsport and a miser.

The voices get awfully noisy at times, but sometimes they actually get along well enough to cash a ticket now and then. Someday I hope to find a way to handicap that dictates which voices to listen to and when—and that works every race, every time, of course. It'll sure be quieter around here.

SECTION 2

Time Management

The Two-Minute Handicapper

When your novice friend asks you with 5 minutes until post time what you think he should do for the race, what do you tell him?

Do you give out what you think is the most likely outcome? Or do you tell him what the biggest payoff might be? When there are only a precious few minutes to make decisions, *what's going through your mind*?

There are things a handicapper should study before the day begins, other things to study once at the track, and things that must be decided in the last minutes before each race.

The things you should study before arriving at the track/OTB:

— Which horses fit the race condition well
— Which horses are best suited to the distance
— Which horses can be safely eliminated from consideration
— What breeding information is notable

Take notes, use a highlighter, write it on a note pad. Whatever method works for you, draw your attention to the important data that you identify in advance. This is the kind of legwork that is much easier to do *before* going to the track.

The things you should study after arriving at the track/OTB:

— How are the track conditions? Does it help or hurt any particular running style or horse?
— How will late scratches affect the pace and post positions?
— Strong biases
— Early money or lack thereof when odds first get posted for the race

— Possible Double/Pick 3/Pick 4/Pick 6 opportunities that involve multiple races

The things you should study in the minutes before a race:

— Horse appearances (simply put, if the horse is an upset mess, hold on to your money—9 out of 10 times you are doing yourself a favor)
— Exotic will-pays vs. win odds
— Horses with heavy early betting that now have rising odds

If you are trying to review anything beyond appearance and payoffs at this point, you are overthinking it. Don't work yourself into a panic about other information. If you still hadn't noticed it 7 minutes to post, it probably wasn't that important in the overall scheme of the race.

If you bury your nose in the *Racing Form* or program right up to 3 MTP, you missed the post parade and the warm up—your only real opportunity for first-hand inspection.

Seeing your horse happy and eager to run is more useful than print at this point in your race analysis. *And how else will you know if your horse has subtle black bandages unless you're actually watching?*

Non-Math Lessons About Horses

To state the obvious, horses are animals. They have personalities. They have quirks. They have good days and bad. No amount of statistical analysis or handicapping prowess can estimate what is going on in a horse's head in the minutes leading up to a race. There is no good way to numerically rate how a horse "feels." The best you can hope to do is know whether or not there are reasons to question a horse's readiness to give a solid effort.

Whenever possible, inspect a horse before betting it. Although this isn't possible in the series bets like doubles and Pick 3s, it provides critical data that cannot be obtained any other way for races where you can see the horses and then make a wager.

Unlike other handicapping data, the most important aspect here is when ***not*** to bet—recognizing one or more signs that a horse is not ready for a good performance in today's event. Not only can that day's bet be avoided, but a poor effort can be explained, important to know if the horse "looks" ready and is better behaved before its next race.

There have been a handful of interesting and useful books written about what the "ready racehorse" looks like, things like pricked ears, eager movement, smooth transition between gaits, and so on. The thoroughbred is an athlete, and can have off days for a variety of reasons—too hot, too cold, doesn't like traveling, minor hoof injury, too fast of a workout last week, and so on.

Bad behavior can be a sign of a horse that doesn't want to run. If a horse throws a fit in the paddock or post parade (such as flipping over or throwing the rider), select another contender or preferably avoid betting altogether if that was the only horse you liked in the race.

Any pre-race incidents (having a fit in the paddock, flipping, or losing the rider) are good reasons to avoid betting. If the bad actor was one of two contenders you were considering, go with the other one. This is as good of a tie-breaker as you'll ever find. If you already bet on the bad actor, don't bet another horse to try to mitigate any losses. Also, note horses that behave poorly, run poorly, then return with much better disposition. A similar improvement in form can be expected.

Tantrums drain horses of energy, especially young horses or horses making their debut. You don't need to know if the horse gets injured. The energy expended in the incident already compromises its chances.

The rare exception to this rule is the chronic delinquent that throws fits before each start but it never seems to affect the way he runs. Lit de Justice went bonkers before every stakes race he entered, but that did not keep him from winning a slew of important stakes including the 1996 Breeders' Cup Sprint. Since Lit de Justice is retired, though, don't expect to see bad actors win.

If a horse throws its rider, runs off, but is not scratched, that horse is now a losing bet. There are rare exceptions, but you'll save money if you avoid all of them. If you have not bet yet, save your money. If you have already bet, don't rush up and bet other horses to try to hedge. Your plans have already gone awry. Don't throw more money away in an ill-thought out panic.

Another consistently negative sign is visible sweat. If the weather is warm and all or most of the horses are sweaty, this doesn't apply. But if the horse you like is the only sweaty horse, that is a bad sign and indicates anxiety and nervous energy. This can be a difficult sign to notice over televised signals as trainers often hose down washy horses in the paddock before saddling them.

Make note of horses that act up and observe how they run. When they return to the track, if their attitude is much improved, excuse any bad performance when the horse was not on his best behavior. Coronado's Quest won his first two races, had a fit before the Hopeful, and finished out of the money. He then pulled himself together and managed to behave for three straight stakes wins. The following spring, he raised havoc twice at Florida and was beaten badly both times, but upon returning to New York, was a cool customer and resumed his stakes-winning ways.

The Final Three Minutes To Post

The odds change dramatically as the horses are loading, racing, and even headed back to be unsaddled. Many systems and methods of analysis depend on accurately determining the final odds. When the odds continue to change after you can no longer place bets, the accuracy of a bettor's decisions will be compromised.

Anyone that has ever had a minimum odds level in mind for betting a given horse can recall a situation like this:

You like a contender but expect a minimum of 3-1 to consider the horse worth betting. The horse opens at 7/2, bounces up to 4-1, back to 7/2, then seems fixed at 4-1 as post time draws near. In your mind, this is perfect. You happily head to the windows and bet the horse to win. As the horses are entering the starting gate, your horse's odds flash down to 5/2. As they race around the far turn, the odds click again: 2-1. As the horses are pulling up, the "final odds" show 8/5! If you are lucky, your horse won and at least you get $5.40 or so. If it lost, you are even madder, because had you known it would go off that low, you would have avoided betting it as an underlay.

Here is another variation of this situation. You like the same horse as in the previous example, and want 3-1. But you also give a long look to a "live longshot" who would be worth a bet at odds above its morning line 8-1. When the odds open, your "primary" contender is 7/2, and your longshot is at 6-1. You focus your attention on the primary horse, because your "live longshot" may be live, but is no longshot!

When you bet with 4 minutes to post, you see the odds on your primary contender are at a steady 4-1 and your other horse is at 7-1. After you get the bet in on the 4-1 horse, you return to your seat and check the odds. Your contender is now 5/2, the longshot is 9-1. Another click and they are 2-1 and 11-1. Now you start to feel uncomfortable. At some point in the race, your horse drops to 8/5 and the other is 14-1.

It pains me to recall how many times the longshot has gone on to win from this point in the story. The number of wins is surely nowhere near the number of times the longshot quietly finished out of contention. But every time the longshot wins paying $30 while your contender and money go down in flames, it stings enough to stay with you for a while.

So, how do you adapt to this insanity? Is there a better way?

Dealing With Early, Late, and Really Late Money

I am firmly of the opinion that the odds board has nothing to do with handicapping winners. But it has everything to do with value, a critical part of the decision to bet or not to bet. So, for better or worse, odds matter.

What escapes the thought process of most bettors is that, ultimately, the only odds that matter are the Final Odds. That's what the payoff will be based on. If the final odds on a winning horse are 3-1, that's what the payoff will be. It doesn't matter if the horse started at 8-1 and steadily dropped to 3-1, or if the horse began at 4/5 and drifted up to 3-1.

Look at it another way. When you look at the results chart and see what odds the horse went off, you don't wonder what odds the horse was at with 5 or 10 minutes to post. When all is said and done, it shouldn't really matter how the odds arrived at their final resting place. ***But everyone knows that isn't how handicappers really deal with the odds.***

There are three types of action worth discussing:

Early Money: A horse's opening odds are well below its morning line.

Late Money: A horse's odds steadily drop between the post parade and post time.

Really Late Money: A horse's odds significantly drop from the time the horses reach the gate and begin to load, and when the race is over and the final odds are posted.

Early Money

When the initial odds are posted, the entire win pool may be only $1,000 or less, depending on the size of the racetrack. When the pool finally closes to betting, the win pool can contain $50,000 to $250,000 for tracks that simulcast their signal. The pool can be dramatically larger if it is a weekend or nationally simulcast stakes race.

Early money shows when only 5 to 10% of the money is in the pool. A $500 win bet placed early will make a huge impact in the pool early, while the same $500 bet to win with 3 minutes to post is just a drop in the bucket.

Just how much money pours into the pool in the final flashes of the tote board? The money that gets bet up until the post parade often accounts for only 25 to 40%. With 20 minutes to post, a single $2,000 bet at Keeneland could be 40% of the win pool and will substantially change the early odds. When the odds are final, that $2,000 bet will be a mere 1% of the pool.

On the other hand, the amount of money it takes to drop a 2-1 shot to 3/2 with 0 minutes to post is approximately a $20,000 change in the win amount bet on that horse between tote board updates!

Imagine the difference between betting the $20,000 with 20 minutes to post, making the horse 1/9 on the board, compared to holding out until the last possible minute. An early 1/9 shot will get a lot of dumb money and is unlikely to drift above even money no matter the circumstances. So for the heavy hitter, trying to bet as late as possible is important, and often the difference between getting 3/2 and 2/5.

Keeneland Saturday

MTP	Win Pool
20 min	$ 5,000
15	$ 8,000
10	$ 25,000
5	$ 40,000
4	$ 55,000
3	$ 75,000
2	$100,000
1	$125,000
0	$150,000
0	$175,000
final	$200,000

Pimlico Weekday

MTP	Win Pool
20 min	$ 2,000
15	$ 5,000
10	$ 10,000
5	$ 18,000
4	$ 25,000
3	$ 32,000
2	$ 40,000
1	$ 50,000
0	$ 60,000
0	$ 75,000
final	$ 90,000

Figure 2: Betting Action—Keeneland Saturday vs. Pimlico Weekday

The notion that early "big money" is big insider money is probably a myth. It is probably a heavy hitter that had to bet early and leave. But make no mistake, early money hypnotizes the betting. It draws dumb money like a bug light draws insects on a hot July evening!

It can make your selection a hammered underlay, or a generous overlay. It's not your fault—the action is not likely to be a true indicator of a pending top effort. But it will affect the odds.

Late Money

When a horse's odds drop noticeably from the time of the post parade until the horses reach the starting gate, people take notice. It can start a stampede at the windows that only drives the price further down. But when, if ever, does this late action mean anything?

If a horse figures to be an obvious contender, say a 3-1 morning line runner from good connections, and its odds fall throughout the final minutes to post, it's just the public landing on a logical contender and getting their money down. There is no reason to expect anything different. And if that horse wins, many will think that it was people in the know who pounded the horse late. But that is not the case. If a maiden race loaded with firsters has a horse drop in odds, again if the connections are good with firsters and the horse is precociously bred, then you should assume the late action is nothing more than the public arriving at a logical selection.

Another late action phenomenon that can be ignored is when a 1/5 or 1/9 shot is entered. If a horse opens at 1/9, all the other contenders are likely to be 10-1 and up. As post time nears, the 1/5 shot may click up to 2/5, and suddenly the 2nd, 3rd, and perhaps even 4th choices will drop to the 3-1, 5-1, and 8-1 range.

This is the combination of the public looking for anyone but the favorite to bet, and the parimutuel system blending the early money that made the favorite 1/5 into an ever increasing pool where few people are eagerly pouring money on a 1/5 shot. This is important because if you think the 1/5 horse is beatable, and early on you see your contender at 12-1, you may see its odds plummet to 4-1. This could change your view on betting against the 1/5 favorite. Don't assume you are getting an overlay in this situation—expect the odds to shrink. If 4-1 is still fine with you, no problem. If you expect double digits on the 2nd or 3rd betting choice, guess again.

Now, when does late money need to get noticed? When the horse taking the late action does ***not*** make sense. Horses that appear out of form, outclassed, or from low percentage connections are not entrants that would attract loads of betting public money. When runners like this are 15-1 with 8 minutes to post, it would make sense for them to steadily drift to 30-1, not drop to 8-1 in one click, 6-1 in the next, 9/2 in the next. When *that* happens, people scramble to their forms to see what they are missing.

How does one react? If the horse should be 15-1 and is 9/2, it's an underlay no matter how you look at it. If there is some inside info that you are not privy to, the runner may have a better chance than you think, but how much better you cannot assess. Can a horse improve enough off bad form or slow times to win? Certainly. Is it likely? No. Is it worth betting at low odds because someone presumably knows something the rest of the world does not? Not for me.

Really Late Money

It should be no surprise to the reader that money gets bet right up until the moment the gates open. Additionally, despite the miracles of the information age, there is at least a 1 to 2 minute lag time for the computers to total up all the money from all betting locations and post the final odds. If a horse was steadily moving up or down in odds as post time approaches, then it is no surprise to see the trend continue and push the odds up or down another tick by the time the final odds are posted.

But in early 2000, a disturbing trend of dramatic late bet-downs emerged that continues to persist despite a variety of investigations and new policies. Horses that were logical contenders would receive last-second huge bets of $20,000 or more. A 2-1 shot became 6/5, 6/5 became 3/5. The cause was traced to simulcast bettors with deep pockets and direct access to the betting lines.

Whether or not it was an unfair advantage, and whether or not anything should be done about it, dominated racing discussions for months. As a handicapper, the impact was severe. You demand 2-1 on a horse if you are going to bet it. At post time, the horse is 3-1 so you bet $20. The horse wins and the final odds show 7/5—below your criteria to bet. You collect $4.60 and feel robbed. Or, two horses are 5/2. You bet one and the other one wins, showing final odds of even money while you hold losing tickets on a 4-1 shot. You feel victimized even if there was no foul play. What to do?

The answer was to study the betting pattern. After a while, the pattern became more or less clear.

Big bet-downs occurred most often on horses that A) were logical contenders and one of the top three favorites, B) were likely to be setting or contesting the early pace, and C) were from barns with fair win percentages using capable runners.

Such horses could be noted as "vulnerable" to the late odds drop. If the horse was my pick, I passed the race. If I thought the horse was unlikely to win, I anticipated the odds on whoever I did bet to rise after the race began. I passed on a lot of horses that I liked that won and paid miserably. I bet a lot of horses that ran while their odds soared and some won at generous prices. When I got beat by a bet-down horse, I was comfortable that the pattern was known so it took the mystery out of it. The pattern kept me from betting logical contenders that the public already recognized. The horses were underlays and would likely have final odds below my value line.

Understanding the "Drift" and Anticipating the "Slide"

Most systems and decision making criteria expect the user to make plays based on odds. Examples are based on final odds, as if what you see with 10, 5, or even 1 minute to post time will be the final odds. When it comes to odds and payouts, you need quick decision making that does not depend on precision. Radical changes in the odds board are just another challenge to the modern handicapper.

The best way to avoid being disrupted by late changes is to understand when such shifts are most likely to occur. The Drift and the Slide are two ways to understand betting action during the critical moments just before post time.

The Drift

Look for contenders that get notable early action and are now drifting up to more valuable odds as post time approaches. If you observed that a horse you identified as a possible play received heavier than expected early action but is now drifting up in odds, you have some positive indications along with possible value.

The early action is not necessarily "smart money." But one way or another, it indicates that somebody agrees with your assessment that the horse is live. If the horse remained at these low odds, it might offer poor value. The drift up in odds now gives you the opportunity to get a fair price in spite of the positive signs you see.

As post time approaches, the horse's odds should continue to rise as late money predictably drives odds down on favorite(s). Bet as close to post time as possible. Don't be surprised if the price continues to climb upward even after the gate opens.

Horses that are likely to drift up in odds:

— Morning line longshots that open well below their morning line odds

- Low profile shippers, especially if there is money on them when the odds are first posted
- Mid priced horses when the favorite is not odds-on; the late money on such favorites usually balloons odds on the other contenders

This angle applies especially but not exclusively to maiden races. In maiden races, the late money tends to gravitate towards horses with experience, particularly those with in-the-money finishes.

Remember that the degree to which a horse's odds "drift" will be relative. A low to medium priced horse that drifts from 4-1 to 6-1 is just as attractive an opportunity as the 10-1 shot drifting to 15-1, or the 20-1 shot that may climb to 30-1. More 6-1 overlays will find the winner's circle than the 15-1 or 30-1 overlays, and they are a generous payout all the same.

The Slide

The Slide is the often-predictable drop in odds on the favorite as the horses enter the gate, leave the gate, and even after the race ends. Over half of the win pool money registers on the odds board in the final minutes of betting. The computer systems that totalize the betting lag a minute or two behind, so the final odds aren't posted until the race is underway. As favorites get bet down in these last minutes, the effect is often seen after the bettor can do anything about it.

Avoid favorites hovering at odds on as post time approaches unless you will be satisfied with final odds 2 to 3 ticks lower once the race is official (the pig-pile-on-the-favorite effect).

This has happened to anyone who has played the races in recent years. Placing a bet as the horses approach the starting gate—in the final moments that betting lines remain open—sometimes means watching late money subsequently pour in on your choice until the odds are no longer appetizing, regardless of the outcome. Even if you win, there's a bittersweet feeling that you got less than you bargained for.

Horses that are likely to be bet down:

- Morning line favorites that remain above their morning line odds by the time the post parade is happening
- Horses trained by the leading trainer or a "hot" trainer at the meet
- Horses ridden by the leading rider(s)
- Second and third choices facing an odds-on favorite—Bettors will take any alternative to have some action on an otherwise unplayable race
- Favorites that are between 4/5 and 6/5—Gamblers that think an even-money horse is a lock will often wait to make sure they're getting even money, then they join a stampede that ultimately drives the entrant down to 2/5 or worse
- High profile shippers that attract attention due to name recognition

As much as half of the final win pool may be wagered during the final moments a bettor has to place a bet. Odds will fluctuate even after the race begins and sometimes after horses cross the finish line. A consistent trend is that the favorite will receive a disproportionately heavy part of the action in these final moments. Generally the top contenders and morning line favorites will drop in odds, and longshots will go up accordingly.

A 3/2 favorite entering the starting gate may cross the line as the 4/5 favorite. A potential $5.00 payoff is reduced to a $3.60 payoff if the horse wins. The already narrow profit margin can be eliminated by the late action.

Without keeping your eyes glued to an odds board, try to be mindful of plummeting odds, particularly on favorites. If a runner's odds are dropping minute-to-minute, expect the trend to continue until the odds are finalized. I generally avoid "Slide" horses because it is difficult to guess final value. Especially when playing favorites, be prepared to accept the worst case scenario of receiving a payout below what you see when betting. If you are not going to be satisfied with the lower payout, avoid the bet altogether.

Time Management In Simulcast Venues

Six tracks, $300 in the wallet, and it's high noon.

What ruins simulcast bettor bankrolls? It's certainly not a lack of information. Even though you are not live at the track gaining shoe information and late changes on track conditions, these are annoyances but not insurmountable obstacles. The problem is not a lack of good information, but a lack of time to evaluate the available information.

Breaking Down the Typical Day

Six tracks and an average of nine races per track offer options something like the following:

— 54 Win, Place and Show opportunities
— 54 Exactas
— 18 Quinellas
— 6 'early' Daily Doubles
— 6 'late' Daily Doubles
— 30 Pick 3s
— 30 Trifectas
— 12 Superfectas
— 12 Pick 4s
— Multi-track Pick 3s and Pick 4s
— 6 Pick 6s

The first obstacle has nothing to do with the wagering menu. The 54-race card means that for every hour spent handicapping, about a minute can be devoted to each race if all are given equal consideration. Spend 3 hours handicapping and that allows an average of 3 minutes a race. A thorough handicapping job is out of the question—or is it?

The solution, of course, has to be to reduce the number of races under consideration. If you favor maiden races, seek those out and handicap them above all else. If you like to exploit speed biases, focus on the tracks that you think are the speed favoring ovals. Regardless of what your specialty is, give yourself time to focus on your strengths.

If you love a graded stakes feature and want to exploit your opinion in the daily double and Pick 3 pools, look at the races before and after the feature even if they are not your specialty. Maybe something will jump out at you, maybe you'll focus back on the win, exacta, and trifectas in the feature, but give yourself the opportunity to develop intelligent opinions. Once you have studied the handicapping factors, then you can get down to the equally overwhelming task of handling the wagering options.

The Six Track Shuffle

Advance preparation lets you identify your best opportunities ahead of time, then adapt your plan throughout the day. The day starts with six daily doubles from six various locations in North America. You want to play daily doubles because they offer greater value than win betting. But you won't want to bet six daily doubles (or will you?). You could bet $2 on doubles covering two contenders in each leg ($2 x 2 x 2 = $8 x 6 tracks = $48). If you spent $48 on all these $2 doubles, with only 6 possible winners out of 24 combinations bet, you'll either have to hit several of them or hit one paying $50 or more just to break even. But you're not here to break even! You're here to make money.

You would be better off picking the best of the six doubles, and betting four $12 combinations on it. That way even a $16 double payoff would pay $96—doubling your money on a pretty chalky venture. The point is doubles generally offer good value. Rather than playing all of them, focus your capital on the best opportunity, or two if you must, and take your shot.

Of the six daily doubles, there will be ones that look good and ones that look better, and ones that look awful. Do you also bet win, exactas, trifectas, and start Pick 3s? Adapt, decide and execute!

On to race two (at six different tracks). If you are live in the double, do you hold your breath and hope, cover some savers, or assume the horses you used will run like you planned and bet them in exotics?

Well into your day, the races are going off every few minutes. Patience is the order of the day. *Trying to explain where the day leads you from here is like trying to describe where all the balls on a billiard table will go when the rack gets broken up.* The answer is different every time, and the variables are too great to map out without the assistance of NASA engineers. Nevertheless the key to success is mapping out your day, and then remaining mindful of your plan.

You place a bet. If you lose a bet, there is another race going off within minutes. It is easy to grab the program, glance through some information, and put a bet down. If you are going to do this all afternoon, don't waste your time handicapping in advance. Don't kid yourself into thinking a fly-by-the-seat-of-your-pants style will enable you to prevail. All the best laid plans will be undone by your indiscretion with your bankroll.

Late decisions can be made, even for serious, well intended wagers. Suppose a race has two frontrunners, and you decided the night before that an inevitable speed duel will ruin both runners' chances, but no other horse stands to clearly benefit. Planning to pass the race, you notice one of the speedsters runs off in the post parade, and is a late scratch. Now you have a lone-speed horse. The late scratch will change the odds of every other runner, but when the dust settles the remaining speedball may be a value.

If you gave the horse only a 6-1 chance because of the speed duel prediction, now you may assess the horse as even money to wire the field. At 3-1 odds, what was an underlay minutes before is now an overlay. This is not a hasty decision but a thoughtful one based on a study of pace and an assessment of value. Yes, buying a win ticket on the horse was a last-minute decision, but this does not mean it was an impulse buy!

So with a menu of races and a menu of wagers, the possibilities are endless. But you can remain in control if you have a framework planned out in advance, and only deviate from it when additional information is compelling enough to make an intelligent adaptation.

Make a plan ahead of time for the day, but adapt based on data, not on emotion. *That is the key to surfing the information tidal wave.*

Belmont 1	Daily Double 1 w/3,7 and 13 (if in). 1 is 1st time claiming
Bel 6	MSWT. 4, "to watch" horse, watch board w/1, 7, 11 - for action, consider exactas & tris
Bel 10	Left Bank, trip horse faces a lone frontrunner, demand 3-1
Del 2	1 1/16 MSWT. 3 will be odds on and not bred to rate, look at 2,6 to repeat
Del 8	1 3/8T. 2,4 shipping from Saratoga, tower over the rest.
TP 2	MSWT 6f. 11. 2nd time starter should improve, not good doubles to use
TP 9	6 makes sense, 2 could be odds-on and looks vulnerable to speed duel. Start Pick 3s.
TP 10	1 may wire field, 5 logical contender.
TP 11	Wide open, use 1,4,7 in Pick 3s. Look over race again for overlays if Pick 3s not alive.
SAX 6	4, Drysdale turf layoff invader from Europe, adds Lasix.

Figure 3: Sample Day Plan

SECTION 3

Data Management

Tools and Data

Selecting contenders takes information as well as tools to analyze the available information. How much information do you need to analyze a race? You could gather and review all of the following for virtually every race:

Post Position info
Track bias info
Running style info
Distance profiles
Shipper stats
Workout data
Track condition, track maintenance reports, and weather
Connections info: Trainer stats, jockey stats, jock/trainer combo data
Breeding: Sire info, dam info, and sibling info
Figures: Pace figures, speed figures
Times: Turn times, final fractions, Par times

The information that "matters" is very situational, very subjective, and will vary with every handicapper you meet. So, how do you not go crazy?

Develop a profile for a given race, prioritizing what information matters most. Once you have defined this "winner's profile," use it as a measuring stick to evaluate the field.

The Data Management section will give you a practical way to prioritize your information needs, and discuss what that information helps a handicapper learn. A brief outline of the relative value of information is below.

Critical Information:

— Race conditions—What kind of horse wins this kind of race?
— Distance/Surface—What post positions, running styles, quality of horses win?

- Track condition—Does an off track change the winner's profile? Who is proven in the off going?

Recommended Information:

- Par Times/Figures—How fast do these races usually go and who can do that today?
- Pace scenario—How fast will the likely pace be? Will that help or hurt any horse in particular?

Nitty-Gritty—The more of this information you gather, the better:

- Trainer info—What trainers can win with regularity, in general and in these specific circumstances?
- Jockey info—Can the rider win for this trainer, with this animal, with this race setup? Is this a specialty setup?
- Breeding—What runners may improve because today they are trying something that they are bred to do but haven't gotten the chance to try yet?

Managing Expenses Using On-Line Resources

To gather the information needed to assess a particular race situation, use on-line resources to manage your expenses. The Internet offers a great deal of information, some for free and some for a fee. On-line handicapping data constantly changes and provides opportunities as well as time savers. Using the free resources along with a well-structured budget can help you manage the expenses associated with handicapping.

What must be paid for:

- Past performances, with speed and pace figures depending on the provider
- Handicapping picks (e.g. Wizard, Kentucky Handicapper)

— Detailed stats and ratings of trainers, jockeys, and breeding info

What is available for free:

— Daily entries with trainer, jockey, morning line odds, conditions
— Daily news and columns from racing's premier writers
— Scratches and changes
— Complete Equibase result charts
— Live updated track odds (for example, Supertote at www.brisnet.com)

The tools of my handicapping world— Where I get my information:

1. *Daily Racing Form*

Still the most economical way to grab a lot of info, the downside is that what you read, everyone else can read too. Not at all a source of inside information.

Note: If you can't explain heavy action on a horse, look to the *Racing Form* handicapper's selection, the first page of each track's past performances. More people go by this than you would think and the influence on the betting is often significant. If you like a horse as a betting opportunity but the Form handicapper picks it as a Best Bet, kiss value goodbye. As a result, the Best Bets aren't really the best bet because betting should take value into consideration.

2. *Speed Figures*

An essential measure of capability. Realize that figures are generated by a mechanical system and adjusted based on the opinions and research of the person making the figures. The more you understand the methodology, the more you can accurately factor the information into your handicapping. If the methodology is sound, you can better trust the figures you read.

Beyer speed figures, found in the *Daily Racing Form*, are a reliable, readily available source. The figures are, however, sometimes adjusted for subjective reasons. Not a scientific reading or prediction of future effort, they provide a way to quantify demonstrated ability over given distances.

3. *Par Times/Par Figures*

Knowing how fast the competition is at a track is key to discerning ability. Whether using average finish times for a given class of horses at different distances, or using average speed figures earned by the winning runner at a given class and distance, knowing what kind of effort is normally required to win is very important.

You can get this data by keeping notes on times, looking at the "Beyer Speed Figure Pars" table occasionally found in the *Daily Racing Form*, or buying a Par times product. This is something you really need to know about a track. It's up to you whether you want precise Par time charts or just want a general feel for what's considered fast and slow at a track. Knowing one or the other (and knowing which type it is—precise or general) is important.

4. *Pace Figures*

Pace analysis is a key element of handicapping. Measuring a horse's ability to run the opening fractions of a race can help identify potential advantages or weaknesses, and help predict lone frontrunners, speed duels, etc. Pace can be measured using times or fractions. You can make your own notes or pay for someone else's. At the very least, your knowledge should include an understanding of what is considered slow, moderate, fast, and suicidally fast at your favored track.

If a horse led until the stretch and faded, it helps to know whether the early fractions were fast or ordinary. If it was a fast pace and the leader faded, no surprise and no real negative on the horse. If it was an ordinary pace and the leader faded, it was probably a poor effort.

5. *Breeding Information*

It's useful to know if a sire or dam excels with young horses, mud runners, turf runners, long distance runners, first time starters, etc. More and more of this information is showing up in the *Racing Form*, which means everyone else reads it too. You can supplement that info with publications like *Maiden Stats* or Tomlinson's *Sprinters and Stayers.* Some sources of past performances regularly include mud and turf figures.

Keep in mind the useful information is when there is something extremely good or bad about a horse's family tree. High percentages (over 15%) or low percentages (below 8%) can help decide if a horse is a good or bad bet. Any percentage between 8% and 15% means little. Why? An average field is 8 horses, so the blind win percentage should be 1 in 8, or 12.5%. In many categories, that is the more or less random win percentage chance that any horse has. The 8% and 15% range is a good guideline to rule out apparent trends that could be completely due to randomness.

The following is a sample sires list. Handicappers would be well-served to develop and periodically update a similar list.

— ***Debut Sires***: Avenue of Flags, Boundary, Danzig, Elusive Quality, Forestry, French Deputy, Smoke Glacken, Theatrical, Carson City, Gone West
— ***First Routes***: Kris S., Go For Gin, A.P. Indy, Seattle Slew, Unbridled, Broad Brush, Awesome Again
— ***First Turf***: Danzig, Kris S., Go For Gin, Kingmambo, Theatrical, Polish Numbers, Lord of War
— ***Sloppy***: Carson City, Kipper Kelly, Mt. Livermore, Conquistador Cielo, Mr. Greeley, Mr. Prospector family
— ***Muddy / Good***: Saratoga Six, Runaway Groom, Jade Hunter, Broad Brush, Pleasant Colony, A. P. Indy, Mr. Prospector family

6. *Trainer Stats*

The same rules apply here as with breeding stats. It's useful to know what kind of conditions that a trainer excels at, such as maidens, mud, or routes. Past performances include more and more of this type of stat, which means everyone else reads it too. Other publications can help find stats that are not common knowledge, like Mike Helm's debut trainer guide, *Track Stats* from TSN Publications, and Jim Mazur's meet-specific "The _____ Handicapper" book series.

The useful information is when there is something extremely good or bad about a trainer's moves. High percentages (over 15%) or low percentages (below 8%) will again eliminate apparent trends that are similar to the random win percentage chance that any horse has.

7. *Jockey Stats*

At any track there may be 40 or 50 jockeys riding, but the top 6 to 8 riders account for huge percentage (often 80% or more) of all race wins. If one of these top jocks is on a horse you like, you probably don't have to overthink the jockey stats.

"Nice to know" info includes whether a jockey excels on turf but not dirt, or sprints but not routes, with certain trainers, etc. Some of this is covered in the Racing Form where the world can see. If you watch a particular track, consider spending some of your research time looking for these niche statistics.

High-Tech Tools For Trip Handicapping

There are tools out there to help you evaluate horses, rate them, and analyze their performances. A "trip handicapper," by this book's definition, closely watches races and takes note of horses expected to fare better next time out. The trip handicapper sees some reason to think the horse will run better next time. The biggest challenge has often been knowing when and where the "horses to watch" will run next. Useful tools are now available to help bettors know when the horses they like will run—and these tools are not just for the "trip handicappers."

Seeing a horse run well enough to merit consideration the next time it races can take on several forms. The horse can have a troubled trip. It may have made a bold move sometime during the race. It may have finished well. It may have been caught in a speed duel. Whatever the reason, it caught your attention.

There are several factors that will dictate how well "trip handicappers" do in profiting from their observations. The first plight of trip handicappers is guessing how the "trip horse" will fare against the field the next time it runs.

If you see a horse get into trouble, when it next runs, it will either:

— Improve and show its real ability or,
— Fare no better than the last time it ran (due to the trauma of the troubled trip, tired, etc.).

If the troubled trip horse ***does*** run okay, he may either:

— Face a field he can compete with under conditions that suit him or,
— Face a field he is outclassed by, negating any improvement that may be forthcoming.

Making an educated guess which conditions apply is challenging under any circumstances.

But the second challenge for trip handicappers is that they are not alone in their quest to spot troubled trips or good middle moves. Video replays, results charts, nightly recaps on cable TV—if a horse gets into trouble and recovers to finish well, *it will get noticed*!

Such horses get bet below their fair odds in their next starts all too often. Oddly enough, trip handicappers love to rationalize that the depressed odds are a positive sign. "They know this horse is set up—the stable is really trying." The reality is, the low odds are probably the result of like-minded trip handicappers getting their money down early.

Finally, we've all heard the story of the bettor who saw a horse get into all sorts of trouble but finish well. He waits for weeks for the horse to be entered again and just when he's given up all hope, he discovers that the horse ran and won at huge odds—at another track.

There are now services available to eliminate this nightmare. If a horse enters, you are notified. If your horse has a workout, you are notified. The services don't tell you who it is entered against. They don't analyze its chances of winning. But they do save you hours of research time every week.

A Better Way to Trip Handicap

Tools are now available that provide a better way to keep track of this information and the resulting betting opportunities. Entries and related data are easily accessible through the Internet. Allowing tracking of individual horses was a logical next step that some websites have taken.

Situational "To Watch" List

Keep a list of 20-plus horses with one of the on-line entry notification services (e.g. StableMail at DRF.com, Stable Alert at Brisnet.com). You don't have to buy a *Racing Form* or program to "see if anything is in"—they'll tell you. Update often with your key horses.

This approach can also be used to take advantage of trainer stats you discover through your research. Add horses that fit certain situations that should be profitable in the long term, such as:

- — Trainer excels with maidens making their second career start—put them on the roster after their debut. Wait, bet on their second start, then remove them from the roster.
- — Trainer does great with layoffs. Take horses that haven't run in a while, load them in, and wait until they run. Once they run, drop them from the list and go with something else.

If you identify key situations, you can then wait for the computer to report to you that the situation is underway. If you know a trainer hits 40% of the time with dirt-to-grass or route-to-sprint moves, you load in the dirt runners or route runners you know of, and wait for them to show up. If they do show up, you can see the race conditions along with post position, jockey, race number, and track. You then have enough info to decide if they roughly fit your criteria.

By highlighting horses that qualify for long-term profitable situations, you have already done half the handicapping without picking up the *Racing Form*. You can avoid trips to the track/OTB parlor when there is nothing of interest. If only one "situational bet" arises, you can use it for a phone account bet and save the trip. Not only does it save you time, but it might keep you from getting sidetracked from those profitable situations on an otherwise bad betting day.

The greatest "trip horse" in recent years was Touch Gold who had the worst trip ever seen in the Preakness, and who, with the backing of every racing enthusiast in North America, came back to win the Belmont Stakes. He paid $4.50. You can get just as much satisfaction, certainly more value, and probably more profitable results, if you develop your own "to watch" list, based on proven situations and trainer maneuvers, instead of things you and the whole world watched.

Handicapping Humor: The Top Ten Trip Notes From The Absolutely, Positively, Ultimate Bad Trip From Hell

Anything short of this, and at least your horse's trip "could have been worse." Unless, of course, the horse dumps its rider leaving the starting gate or is pulled up during the race.

10. Left at the start.
9. Pinched shortly after the break.
8. Shuffled back.
7. Taken up entering the turn.
6. Checked wide leaving the turn.
5. Sent way too soon.
4. Blocked in traffic throughout the stretch.
3. Hit with other rider's whip.
2. Found his best stride way too late.
1. That no-good (fill in name of least favorite rider here) "wasn't even trying."

Home Betting Fact and Fantasy

Home betting appears in this chapter because a home wagering account is a tool of the trade. This is a chance to describe my own experiences with some of the home betting options. After a decade of using phone accounts, some real limitations remain hindrances to converting my home into a betting parlor. It is getting better and better, but accurate live odds and late changes in surface condition, equipment changes, or weather really are tougher obstacles at home (or on the road) than at a betting facility.

Sitting at home on the couch calling in bets and making a sizable living is a fantasy. If you live in a place with access to TVG, HRTV, or other cable/satellite live racing simulcast channels, the difference between home and OTB betting is minimal. But for everyone else, a phone wagering account is not the key to self-employment in your family room. Its primary asset is as a tool when there are horses you want to bet, but can't get to the track.

On the plus side:

— If there is a horse you like that is running and you can't go to the track or OTB, you only need a phone or Internet access. This pretty much puts bookies out of the horse business—you can bet directly into the track pool.

— You can call and get scratches, track conditions, and equipment changes.

On the minus side:

— The temptation to call in bets just to have something "live" is always there.

— Mistakes over the phone are impossible to fix. No tickets to look at, if the teller reads back to you what you just said like a parrot, but keyed in the wrong bet—you are out of luck. There is no way to prove whether you told them the wrong number, or if they made a mistake. Of course, you only become aware of the problem if the bet won and you don't receive credit to your account.

— Although live odds are available via the Internet, if you are relying on a phone wagering service, "buyer beware." Odds read to you by the phone teller are often WAY OFF the actual current odds. Some just read the morning line, some read from the wrong track, and some seem to just make it up. I've called and asked, "How many minutes to post?" The answer, "3 minutes, sir." I say, "Can I have the odds on Number 4?" The answer, "8-1." (Morning line was 4-1.) I see a value and bet, then watch the replays at night and see the horse went off 6/5. To seal it, the commentator remarks that the horse opened at odds-on and was heavily bet right up to post time. I have also had the opposite happen—a horse I expected to be a longshot (morning line 15-1) was quoted at 3-1 with two minutes to post. I passed. The horse actually went off 12-1 and won, paying $28.40. Odds can change, but not *that much* at a large racing venue.

— Late changes do not get updated frequently or accurately. Examples are half an entry scratching, a late jockey change, or a race taken off the turf. Changes can occur with hours to post and the information still not be recorded on the phone account system.

— You miss the pre-race analysis and visual inspection of a horse going to post. I underestimated how important this was until I closely studied my phone bets. You can't ask the phone clerk if the Number 3 at Churchill Downs "looks washy." I did that once, just to be funny, and was forwarded to customer service!

A Better Way to Bet From Home

If it's not a question you would ask in person to a teller at the track, don't ask on the phone. You have no idea if the answer is accurate.

Use a home wagering account as:

— A last resort when you can't be at the track and no one you know can be there to check final odds and bet for you.
— A situation play for a lone runner that you will bet regardless of other circumstances and factors—if the price is right, considering the dubious odds information you might be given.
— An opportunity while watching feature races live on TV from home. If the race is on national TV, expect phone lines to be busy. Be careful not to go nuts and bet in the thrill of the moment—or worse, to show off your phone betting account to your friends.
— A way to bet solid win and simple exotics (daily double, exactas) when you feel confident you will get the value you are looking for, and again you can't (or don't) go to a betting facility to make the "play of the day."

Do not use a home wagering account to:

— Place bets on the entire card while on your lunch hour from work.
— Bet turf races when you know it's raining trackside.
— Bet 40 trifecta combinations on a race. Just imagine trying to explain to Customer Service that the 27th trifecta you called in was mis-keyed, costing you a tax form hit!

Giving do's and don'ts about phone betting without backing up each one with proof and justification is difficult. These are based on my own experiences. The best thing to do: Be fully aware of when you use your home betting account. What types of bets and situations lead you to use the account? More importantly, what is your success rate, especially compared to on track or at a simulcast facility? Keep track of trends when making home bets. It will help you to know when you should call, and when to resist.

Finding the Right Horse

With bankroll and money management behind us, you now have a huge edge over most of the people you are betting against. Of course, to cash a ticket, you still have to place a winning bet. There are many ways to pick winners. There are simple angles and complex systems. There are ways to yield a high percentage of low-priced winners, and methods to pick overlaid longshots. Every handicapper has their own way, and hopefully the next few chapters will help readers build on their own methods of picking winners.

This will always be a matter of personal preference. You may be salivating over a 5/2 shot that by your estimation has a 40% chance (3/2) to win. The guy next to you may be crazy about a 15-1 shot in the same race, that has a 1 in 10 chance of winning. You may both be right.

In theory, if this situation occurs 10 times, you would collect 4 times in 10 and pick up $7 for every $2 you bet. Overall, you gather $28 for every $20 you bet ($7 x 4 wins versus $2 x 10 events). He cashes 1 win in the 10 race series and gets $32. Both can be profitable. You might not be comfortable cashing 1 bet in 10, and he may not stay interested in $7 winners. You both will be wrong more often than right, and yet both approaches still make money.

Bankroll management can make or break any successful handicapper. Your "40% win at 5/2" method demands frequent tickets being cashed on a narrow profit margin. His 1 in 10 longshot method requires a bankroll that can weather long losing streaks.

Develop your own winner's profile in order to decide how the winners end up victorious. You need to know what kinds of horses win various kinds of races at different locations. (An example would be a database or recipe box full of winner profiles for certain conditions.) This is one reason that it is often easier to specialize in one favored track. However, in a racing world of increasing simulcasting, this is usually unappealing.

As a first step in this, survey the day's card for horses that stand out as contenders. Based on the available races, review and decide which will present good betting opportunities using a consistent method. Here is one general overview—how to quickly find contenders, key points to look at when comparing types of races, and when to automatically pass a race.

Finding Contenders

Contenders are horses which I can assume meet any combination of the following criteria:

- In a fair enough condition to perform on race day in a sound, solid effort, consistent with expectations based on past performance.
- Well enough suited to the race's conditions to be competitive.
- Talented enough to have a reasonable expectation of beating the other entrants.
- Consistent with a long-term pattern that leads to success a high percentage of the time regardless of other circumstances.

Differentiating Race Types

Different types of races present a variety of betting opportunities. Ongoing research at your preferred racing venues will help you stay current on trends. General things to watch for:

- What kind of races are dominated by favorites and what kind are not?
- What factors are most important in different kinds of races?
- What kinds of races are profitable for you over the long term?
- Which ones have outcomes too random to consistently predict?

Mechanical Pass Criteria

Finally, outcomes can be expected to be the result of chaos as much as any other factor; the morning line ***and*** post-time favorites win a mere 20% of the time or less. Pass races where:

— Half the entrants in the field are contenders,
— The only contenders have o'fer trainers and/or jockeys,
— All are proven failures at this class level, or
— None can run to Par.

Process Improvement

With this overview in mind, let's look at how to improve selections and betting success over time.

As stated earlier, this is a game where keeping score is quite easy. You leave the house with X amount of money. You bet all day, and return home with X, plus or minus profits, losses, and expenses. The "before and after" wallet check is the sincerest form of self-criticism for a handicapper.

To become a better handicapper, it is crucial to analyze what you do and take note of what worked and what didn't. On any given day this proves very little. Over time, however, trends will start to emerge. Recognize what worked and what didn't, and make notes. Your memory is made of paper! If you don't write things down, it is human nature to remember and embellish successes, and downplay and understate your losses.

I find it most helpful to break down my own analysis in several ways:

— The kind of race: Track, distance, surface, condition.
— How I bet it: W/P/S, exacta, trifecta, doubles, Pick 3.
— Why I bet it: What advantage I saw, how many contenders etc.

It doesn't hurt to record what would have worked better or what else you considered doing. Just remember that any one success or failure does not indicate successful or flawed methodology. Trends over time will show you what works again and again, then it is up to you to adapt your practices based on what you learned.

Sample Record Format:

Date	Where	Distance	Surface	Bet	Why	Result

2 year old races 1 Mar - 1 Aug:

Date	Track	Dist	Surf	Bet	Why	Result

Figure 4: Sample Handicapping Record

So Remember . . .

Predicting what a horse and rider will do is not possible in the exact sense, just like predicting tornadoes. We can't say exactly when a tornado will form, or what it will do. But we can understand what circumstances lead to tornadoes well enough to know when the conditions are right (actually, wrong) for one. Likewise, we can't be exact about what the horse and rider will do. But we can understand what circumstances make victory most likely, and what circumstances make victory unlikely. A bettor's own notes are the most valuable tool in this process.

Dealing With Tips

Relying on tips is like letting other people do your handicapping for you. First, what qualifies as a "tip?" Tips have to be examined in terms of where the source information is originating. If a fellow handicapper divines something from the *Daily Racing Form*, this is merely sharing research material. This is not a tip.

If the owner, trainer or other stable person provides the info, and it is information that could not be gathered in the *Racing Form* or program, then it is a tip by this definition. Tips from the stable heard second-, third-, or fourth-person rapidly become hearsay.

It also needs to be clear why the inside information is being shared. If you are friends with stable personnel that have a history of sharing reliable opinions ("We're ready this time," "We probably need a race," etc.), that is a world different from the connections that think that their horse is a can't lose proposition. Such people tend to tell anyone that will listen that their horses will win. This not only dilutes the price, but is little more than a rooting interest and high hopes.

Here are two valid examples of well-intended "tip" information.

The first example was gained early one fall morning during workouts at Keeneland. After watching several horses work from the starting gate, one member of the stable was excited and elated at one runner's effort. What looked like an ordinary breeze from the gate was making the connections very happy. I asked what was all the good cheer about, and the young lady said, "Didn't you see that? She broke clean and kept right in stride with the others. She's finally figured it out. You'll see tomorrow."

I noticed the filly's brass nametag on her halter and sure enough, the 2-year-old was entered in a 1 1/16 race at Keeneland the next day. She had two miserable starts in her past performance info, breaking last and next-to-last in the efforts. In each race, the horse had been 15 lengths back early, and made mild gains to finish mid-pack.

Now after 6 weeks off and a steady worktab, she was returning to the track at one of the most speed favoring ovals in the country. With her past performances, she was sure to be a longshot. The horse was listed at 12-1 morning line. The first flash of the odds board showed her at 5/2!

As a longshot, I loved her. As the favorite, forget it. But as the minutes ticked by, the odds slowly rose. 7/2, 9/2, 6-1 after the post parade. I headed to the windows. I should note at this point that having handicapped the race, nothing else stood out. I was not betting against horses that figured to easily pass through the maiden ranks.

The race began with the filly leaving the gate in good order, holding the lead and the rail path around the first turn, and never facing a serious challenge. In the end, she paid $17.30. On her past performances, she was still an underlay. But based on the inside scoop, 7-1 was a decent hit.

The second tip is the one that arrived too late, and cost me a Pick 6. In the 5th leg of a Saratoga Pick 6, I had used three contenders in a contentious 12-horse $50,000 turf route. After four consecutive miracles, I found myself live with the three favorites, and also confident that I had the final leg covered.

But a problem occurred.

In the paddock, I noticed a horse with some sort of wire basket over its nose and mouth. The horse was having a fit. I checked in the *Racing Form*, and the horse had been disqualified for attempting to savage competitors in two of its last four races. Then the nightmare kicked into high gear. The horse's odds dropped from 13-1 to 9/2 in one click!

Then over the loudspeaker, I heard the announcer say that the horse would be racing with a muzzle on! A muzzle! On a horse! Like a greyhound!

I felt butterflies in my stomach and the horse's odds continued to sink. I wanted to bet the horse to win to cover my Pick 6 investment, but didn't want to make money off the larceny I was sure was afoot.

The horse dueled head and head with one of my runners, didn't lunge at his foe, and won by a nose. My runners finished 2nd, 3rd, and 4th. My horse in the next race won and I picked up three 5 of 6 consolation tickets worth a couple hundred each. But I was sick.

The Pick 6 paid $32,000, and I was robbed by not getting the inside scoop in time to bet on it. I actually doubt the connections were sure that the muzzle would work, but they had an inside edge that was probably worth a big shot at the windows. Maybe the *Daily Racing Form* needs to include "muzzle on" and "muzzle off" as equipment changes.

Handicapping Humor: Six Characters To Avoid

For your entertainment or advice, here are types of tipsters I have come across and how they operate. The lesson in all of this is to trust your own judgment, not the convictions of others, no matter how fierce those convictions might be!

"The Play of the Day"

This is the person that always has at least one story. There are never any direct conversations to pass along, just "I hear they are shooting today," or "Word is this one's set up." Sometimes the info is blended with *Racing Form* details, such as a horse the Form lists as adding blinkers and Lasix translating into a tip like, "They're pulling out all the stops today, and think they can't miss. They're adding Lasix and blinkers and expect a big form reversal."

No real inside information, just some analysis wrapped around a vague reference to some inside scoop. Useless even when the horse wins.

"Pigs do fly, I've seen it myself"

Any horse who looks too awful to even entertain the possibility of an in-the-money finish is a chance to make a fortune. Each longshot could be a legendary coup with the greatest case of repeatedly stiffing a horse to protect its odds that the sport has ever known. A $50,000 claimer is eased, returned 6 weeks later for $30,000 wearing front wraps and was distanced at the finish, and now is entered for $17,500.

The tipster thinks the trainer is stealing money. "If he didn't look this bad, the trainer knows the horse would get claimed. This is a set-up." At the finish, the horse trails the next-to-last runner by 15 lengths, and the tipster walks away convinced that the rider was holding him back for better odds next time out.

"Then again, maybe not"

These characters will give you a conniption if you listen to them. First of all, they always see the toteboard as good news—regardless of what the odds are doing. Second, the horse's chances seem to get better and better with each passing moment. As the tip gets retold again and again, the story gets more and more convincing. If the odds are dropping, then it's "See! They're getting their money down." If the odds keep going up, it's "See! No one else knows."

The object of desire is usually a first time starter or horse returning from a long layoff, and the inside dope is that the horse is ready at first asking. Until . . .

The gate opens. The horse breaks mid pack ("I hope they're not just giving him a race") and looks to be struggling to maintain its position ("They might know the horse just needs one"). Then the horse begins to noticeably weaken with 1/2 mile still to run ("Yeah, they're just giving him one"). The tipster shakes it off as if events were all according to plan.

You'll never hear a "Gee, I really blew it—my information was way off!" Falling for this once with the would-be tipster is a lesson learned, ever listening again is inexcusable.

"The trainer told me to bet him"

I have a friend that tells me this about half the time a certain trainer enters a horse. If the trainer didn't tell him to bet, then the story is, "Well, last time the trainer said to bet him, but I didn't talk to him today." The problem is that the trainer wins at a 12% clip and hasn't saddled a longshot winner in recent memory. Added to this, the trainer often says to bet $5 W/P/S. What trainer would tell a friend to bet $5 W/P/S if they thought the horse was headed for the winner's circle?

I soon learned that it wasn't the trainer seeking out our mutual friend to tell him to bet. It was my friend bugging his favorite trainer and the trainer saying something polite and optimistic.

"The Pollyanna owner"

My horse can do it, I know he can, you just gotta believe it like I do!

Who can blame an owner for thinking his or her horse is something special? Unfortunately, there can be only one winner in the race, leaving all other owners disappointed. Being a horse owner means understanding that you are going to lose more than you are going to win. Nevertheless, some owners are blindly optimistic about their runner's chances in any given event.

Sitting at breakfast outside Saratoga on the morning of the Hopeful Stakes, I overhead the connections of Pettit's Quest telling the people seated around them that they had a horse that should win today. They seemed ***very*** confident about the horse's chances and planned to bet him.

Pettit's Quest was entering a Grade 1 race fresh off a maiden win at Laurel in an ordinary time. He was the longest shot on the board in the morning line, went off at 45-1, and would have been the greatest tip had the story had a happy ending. He finished last, never reaching contention. In the owner's defense, the horse probably looked like a champion beating maidens several weeks before at Laurel. But the horse ran to form, not to the owner's expectations.

"Mr. Obvious"

This tipster picks heavy favorites and boldly, daringly declares them to be an inside trader's dream. For example, a horse at 8/5 in the morning line that looks solid on paper opens at 4/5. Only Mr. Obvious would stake his reputation on a 4/5 shot and act as if he's on to something special. Since 4/5 shots tend to win quite often, Mr. Obvious often struts around basking in the glow of victory.

It's hard to remain seated when someone slaps you on the back and says, "Didn't I tell you so? I gave you one!" when the horse pays $3.60. I remember a guy going bonkers like he'd won the lottery when Best Pal won the Cal Cup Classic, paying $2.80.

No, "Mr. Obvious" did not hit the Pick 6, or even the Pick 3. Just $2.80.

Quick Math For Handicappers

I don't bring a calculator with me to the track. If I can't complete a calculation in my head, I assume I am overthinking things. That said, understanding the percentages is knowing what it takes to win. The first time you walk into a casino and watch the action at a craps table, it seems chaotic and random. Once the odds and percentages are understood, the game becomes easy to play (although not necessarily profitable).

These days, more and more information is given in terms of percentages. The trainer gets 20% winners with 90+ day layoffs. The sire produces 8% first time turf winners. There is a 60% chance of afternoon thunderstorms.

How do you translate these into meaningful data? Which stats are valuable and which are not? Do you calculate all the percentages and ultimately compute a projected winner? Maybe, if you're using a computerized program written to generate bets based on mathematical expectations.

Do you ignore the stats and rely on other info to make your selections? If not ignored, are you weighting the stats too lightly and the other info too heavily?

You will encounter percentages in these categories more often than any others:

— Favorites' win percentage in various situations,
— Breeding,
— Trainers,
— Jockeys,
— Post positions, and
— Running style.

That covers a lot, so let's start with simpler percentages first.

Fun With Percentages For People Who Hate Math

An assumption will be made for the following discussion. The assumption is that the odds in any given race are a fair representation of a horse's actual chances of winning. In reality, this is rarely true. But for the purposes of this chapter, let's put decisions regarding value on hold and work with figures without worrying about whether or not an even-money horse deserves even-money odds.

Quick estimates can be amazingly helpful when looking for value, and the quickest estimate is one where someone else does the math for you. This is what happens with odds. Everyone bets, the track takes out 17%, and the resulting odds add up to 100%.

A horse has to win.

There is a 100% chance that an entrant in the race will be declared the winner if the race is run and subsequently declared official. Based on that assumption, all the odds are going to add up to 100%. If the betting public is doing its job efficiently, the odds on all the horses will be fair.

An even-money favorite will win 50% of the time.

A 2-1 favorite will win 33% of the time.

A 50-1 longshot will win a very small percentage of the time (2%).

The betting public is usually good at identifying the most likely horse to win and backing it with money. The second most likely horse to win will take money from fewer people, and so on.

As a quick estimate, we can assume that the odds in a given race are fair and that a horse's odds correspond to its chances of winning. In any specific race, you might like a horse that you think should be 2-1 that is 3-1 instead. You may be right or the public may be right—on that particular race. ***Overall***, this assumption is very accurate. If one horse's odds are too low, the odds on other horses will be too high. It balances out. So for the sake of quick estimates in this exercise, a horse's chance to win can be estimated based on its odds. The following shows approximate odds and the corresponding percentage of the time that the horse should win, given the odds:

1-1: 50 % chance to win

2-1: 33 %

3-1: 25 %

4-1: 20 %

5-1: 16.7 %

6-1: 14 %

7-1: 12.5 %

8-1: 11 %

9-1: 10 %

10-1: 9 %

20-1: 5 %

25-1: 4 %

40-1: 2.5 %

99-1: 1 %

If the betting pool is efficient, the win odds should be fair relative to each horse's chance of winning. An accurate understanding of a horse's chance of winning (obtained through solid handicapping) will help pinpoint *inefficiencies* in the pool and, as a result, good betting opportunities.

Simple Percentages and the 15% Rule

The average field size in racing today is about 8 horses. (Some circuits and meets average less than that.) Not knowing anything else, 1 in 8 = 12.5% can be used as the random average chance of any average horse winning any typical race.

Use 12.5% to judge data about past racing statistics, training stats, breeding stats and jockey stats. 12%, give or take a couple points, means the win percentage is *average*—not good, not bad, just normal.

A sire that wins with 12% of his first time starters gets a *normal* share of winners. This means that his runners aren't really helped or hurt by genetics when it comes to their inexperience. Any time you see stats about a trainer, sire, or jockey and the win percentage is between 8% and 15%, this is not info that tells you much more than that nothing extraordinary is occurring. It does tell you to look elsewhere for performance clues.

Below 8% in a category means you have found a weakness—good to know that not even a fair share is won. For example, it doesn't matter if a jockey with a win percentage of 5% has the low percentage because of bad riding skills or because their agent isn't very good and can't get the jock live horses. The jockey still only wins 5%, regardless. That's 1 win per 20 starts, and 19 losing tickets for each cashed ticket, producing a loss unless the wins pay more than $40 on average.

Above 15% in such categories indicates a strength—even better to know when ***more*** than a fair share is won.

Percentages are very important when they expose a strength or weakness. The 15% rule of thumb helps filter valuable stats from incidental information. This 15% rule works very well for all of the general statistics thrown at the handicappers. Most importantly, you can use your research time to go a step further.

The 15% Rule of Thumb

A typical field of 8 runners yields a random 1 in 8 chance of winning, which is to say the horse has a random chance of winning of 12.5%. When looking at longshots, you need some means to ascertain if the runner's chance of winning are *better than random.* But why 15% percent for longshots? The following are lots of reasons, but also remember that this is an EASY TO USE rule of thumb. This is something you can use at the track without paper, pencils or slide rule.

Look for horses with a legitimate chance of winning that are being overlooked. This means they are both contenders and underappreciated by the betting public. 12.5% is merely average, and you want to find better-than-average scenarios. Find those contenders based on statistics that support the notion that a horse has at least a 15% chance of winning. This means that in your estimates, you give a horse at least a 1 in 6 or so chance to win.

Now insist that the horse is at longshot odds of 9-1 or more. At 9-1 or higher, the horse returns $20 or more if it wins. You estimated the horse's chance of winning at 1 in 6. With accurate handicapping, this returns one winning ticket for a minimum of $20, for every six bets totaling $12 bet. Substantial profit—which sounds great, but is admittedly hard to find. When playing longshots, this is the kind of premium that bettors need to expect.

If information does not support that the horse has a 15% or better chance of finishing first, the horse should not be bet to win. Do this and value is more or less secure.

Why 15% Even For Longshots?

15% has been a long accepted threshold of being considered a successful trainer or successful jockey. In a field of seven or more horses, each horse has a theoretical chance of winning one in seven times. For ten horses, each has a theoretical chance of winning once in ten. The outcome in most races *is not a random event* by any measure.

However, if by our own approximations a horse has a smaller chance of winning than the random chance of *any* horse in the field, then this horse *is not a contender.* This is a practical, even-handed definition to weed out the unlikely contestants.

A thing or two about longshots in general. If you are going to place a wager involving horses at 6-1 or more, the following need to be considered:

Is this a horse:

— That has a legitimate chance to win?
— That could inherit a win if a lot of things go wrong with the other contenders?
— That once ran well enough to win this kind of race but lately has not shown that kind of ability?
— That can hit the board but probably has little chance of winning?
— That has no redeeming attributes other than great connections?
— That by all estimation looks the best and the high odds are completely unexplainable?

It is important to distinguish between picking longshots worth betting and betting on the best-looking longshot.

Many bettors look at each race, check the odds, and then try to make a case for every horse that will pay double-digit odds. The most convincing candidate becomes the bet—this is bad. When a horse figures to contend and is offering longshot odds, it is offering value as a bet. But when a horse is at longshot odds because it is legitimately an outsider, the scenarios that would enable it to win are unlikely to occur and the long odds reflect the slim chances of the horse winning. This is a distinction few longshot players are able to make.

The 15% Trainer

Finding the trainer that wins at least 15% of the time is a great way to find contenders. Even better is finding a 15% win trainer whose horses pay at odds of better than 5-1 over the long term. When a 15% trainer's horses rarely win at odds greater than 5-1, it will be difficult to produce a long-term profit betting his entries.

For example, from 1999 to 2001, trainer Bill Mott maintained a 22% win rate at Gulfstream Park. That percentage dropped to 4.6% with his 108 horses that went off at odds greater than 5-1. Shug McGaughey was a complete zero for 34 at Gulfstream over the same three-meet sample. That is a large sample of horses from two high-win percentage barns that could be safely ignored.

Trainer statistics will be discussed later in more detail.

The 15% Jockey

Most tracks have no more than six to eight regular riders in multiple races on a daily basis while maintaining a 15% or greater win percentage. Aside from those jockeys, certain trainer-jockey combinations can be found which do click with a high frequency. This will also be discussed in more detail.

Sire-Dam Statistics

The progeny of certain sires exceeds the 15% win rate in categories such as debut winners, first time on turf, running on an off track, at a route, etc.

Dam statistics often reveal small sample indications of a horse's ability. It is not uncommon to find dams who have had seven 2-year-old winners from eight starters. But, conversely, there are also regally bred dams that have produced numerous foals without any of them finding the winner's circle.

These are potent, small sample stats that should be taken seriously in any maiden or first-time-turf scenario.

More Clues For the 15% Statistic

Some more clues that a horse has a better than 15% chance of winning:

— The horse has won more than 15% of its starts in its career.

- — The trainer is making changes that have frequently led to success with past horses (blinkers on, fronts off, three works between races).
- — The horse has run to Par at this distance.
- — A horse that fits the winner's profile, even if it does not appear to be the fastest horse in the field.

A runner that is categorized by that last clue (fitting the winner's profile but not appearing to be the fastest horse) often offers a much better value than a horse who appears to be the fastest but lacks a favorable running style for the track, has drawn a poor post position, or is trying a distance that seems unsuitable.

A Golden Rule:

Any horse that can run to Par at the distance and has a running style that suits the distance *is a contender* and has a legitimate chance to win. Odds will help determine whether or not the horse is a value to bet.

Adjusting For Post Position

With post position percentages, it gets a little complicated. The win percentage for post #1 is based on every race run—every race has a horse break out of the #1 spot. This includes fields of 4, where the random chances of winning are 25%. It also includes fields of 14, where the random chances to win are 1 in 14 or 7%.

The win percentage of post #14 is only based on races where there *is* a full field of 14 starters. The random chance of winning (7%) is already pretty small, and post position has nothing to do with that. Post position might have a little to do with it since breaking from the outside of the track makes it difficult to get position. But the horse is racing against more competitors, no matter how it breaks or what its running style is.

Posts 9 through 14 tend to have anemic percentages at every track. Is it the post? Or is it that in big fields, every runner's chance to win naturally decreases? If you put too much emphasis on low percentages for outside posts, you would base your judgments on an illusion.

In comparison, if an ***inside*** post has a very low percentage, say only 8% wins, the average is based on every race run under those conditions and is a more reliable figure. At the 8% win rate, this is lower than the 12.5% the average horse in the average size field should win. Then you have something worth noting.

Going the other direction, a genuine rail bias at a track might be indicated if the win percentage out of both post positions 1 and 2 is 15%. If your choice was starting from the rail, you could feel more secure in betting him. If your choice starts from post 6, and the even-money horse is starting from post 1, you would weigh the post position factor to the favorite's advantage.

A Final Note on the 15% Rule of Thumb

The 15% rule should be revised in fields of six or less horses, because 15% is less than the random chance of winning in such a small field. In fields of six, a horse must have a 20% or greater chance of winning to qualify. In a field of five, this increases to 25% percent. In a field of four, to 33%.

Favorite Win Percentages and Opportunities

Overall, the favorite wins 33% of the time.

There are numerous systems that more or less depend on this lone statistic. Cashing tickets 1/3 of the time is enough to make any system appear successful, even if the payouts aren't enough to make a profit.

The other side of the coin is that favorites get beat 67% of the time. That's a lot of races where the favorite fails to cross the wire first. Of course, the favorite is only one horse winning or failing. If the favorite loses, it can be to any other horse in the field, so that 67% gets split amongst every other runner.

In some situations, the 33% rule of thumb is not the correct assumption for long-term favorite win percentages. Here are some useful numbers to digest:

Favorites win approximately:

______% of the time	In the following condition
55%	2-year-old allowances and stakes
50%	Older horse allowances beyond, "non winner of" level (includes open money allowances, overnight handicaps)
40%	Steeplechases
40%	2-year-old MSWT races
—33% average*—	
25%	State-bred or restricted allowances
22%	3-year-old claiming
18%	Older maiden claiming

*Above the line: Conditions where favorites fare better than 33% average
Below the line: Conditions where favorites fare worse than 33% average

Figure 5: Favorite Win Percentages

The percentages given above will naturally vary based on field size. Also, note that odds-on favorites win more often than lukewarm favorites. Below 3/5, the win percentage exceeds 50%. Above 5/2, it drops below 25%. All of these variations even out into an overall 33% for the long term.

What can be learned from this? In certain situations, the favorite is very solid. In other situations, the favorite is much more vulnerable. This means that the public is better or worse in different situations at picking the winner. It also means that the information used by the public is a more reliable predictor of performance in certain situations (the true meaning of "running to form"). For example, in 2-year-old stakes, the horses perform as the public expects upwards of 50% of the time. The public is very good at picking the winner in this kind of race. But in older maiden claiming races, horses seldom perform as the public expects.

Betting favorites might seem like good advice to a friend tagging along to the track since they'll probably have fun cashing a few tickets during the day. But the goal for the handicapper is to make a profit, not to cash tickets. Knowing which favorites are worth betting can make the difference.

It's Unanimous—Not!

It's hard to disagree with your peers. When handicapping leads to a seemingly obvious choice, everyone may be in agreement that the horse is the most likely winner. This does not mean that odds-on is a good value to bet. If all of the trackside commentators agree that a runner is all but a sure thing, it's time to start looking for upsetters.

Key to this is distinguishing legitimate favorites from vulnerable ones. There is little point in ever betting a 1/5 favorite to win. There is also no reason to bet against a legitimate favorite if there is no apparent weakness. Keep in mind the actual chance of a favorite winning versus the return you'll get for your bet. A 2-1 favorite must win at least 1 time in 3 for you to break even. An even-money favorite must win 1 in 2. A 1/2 shot must win 2 of 3, and so on.

Also, if favorites' odds drop, the other horses' odds must go up. If you think that two 2-1 co-favorites have equal chances of winning, and then the public bets one down to 4/5 driving the other up to 7/2, take the horse with the longer odds EVERY TIME.

Having the most ability or the strongest past performances does not equate to a sure thing in betting. In his 21-race career, Secretariat won 16 races but was also defeated 5 times. He was beaten in his debut due to gate trouble, in the Champagne Stakes via disqualification, in the Wood Memorial due to an abscess in his mouth, and in the Whitney Handicap and Woodward Stakes by racing luck, or as Tiger Woods would say "not having his A-game" on those days. Even legends have their off days.

Odds-On Favorites Trying Two New Things

Every race has a favorite. There are solid favorites and there are vulnerable favorites. Solid favorites shouldn't lose and shouldn't be played against. Vulnerable favorites should be played against with gusto. What makes a solid favorite and what are the telltale signs of vulnerability?

Since speed figures were added to the *Daily Racing Form*, they have become the top indicators of betting interest. The horse with the highest last-race figure or with the highest recent figure will be the likely favorite. To be sure, figures are an expression of past ability. The horse showing the highest speed figures is likely to be a contender if today's race is under similar conditions as when the top figures were earned.

But in an unfamiliar situation, the race favorite is a riskier proposition. A favorite repeating an effort that previously delivered a win is a more reliable bet than a favorite in uncharted waters. When the public is assuming a horse can win a race even though there is no precedent for success, it's a good time to look for other contenders. Favorites venturing into foreign territory are consistently among the most vulnerable choices that the public selects.

Top speed figures from past performances or not, favorites trying *any two or more of the following for the first time* can be viewed with skepticism:

— Stretches out to longer distance for the first time
— New track

— New surface (turf or dirt)
— New class or graded stakes level
— First time on an "off" track (muddy)
— First time facing "real" pace pressure. For example, a maiden winner wired its maiden race by daylight with comfortable fractions. In an allowance or minor stakes, it will have pressure on the lead.

Until these horses reproduce their top figures under the new conditions, do not assume that they will reproduce their past success. The betting public will make this mistake, which will offer you value betting against the favorite in these situations.

Favorites and Exotic Wagering

Favorites in the win pool are usually over-used in exotics. Whether a horse is a heavy favorite or merely lukewarm does not change this.

In daily doubles and exactas, all favorites are used by the public as if they are 3/2 or lower, due to fact that people throw the favorite into most keys, wheels and boxes just because the horse is "the favorite." In the second leg of the daily double or in the second or third legs of a Pick 3, the morning line favorite ends up on a high percentage of tickets.

Without a live toteboard to see who the public likes, many will default to the morning line and add the horses at lowest morning line odds to their tickets. Readers can prove this to themselves after the first race is declared official, examining the daily double will-pays. The second race morning line favorite is likely to be the shortest price will-pay even if the live tote odds for race 2 are preferring other runners.

In trifectas and starting Pick 3s, all favorites are used as if they were 1-1 or lower, due to the fact that people throw favorites into multiple combination wagers.

Am I saying that a lukewarm 5/2 favorite will be on the same number of tickets in the trifecta as an even-money favorite would be?

YES!!

Why? Because the favorite, is the favorite, is the favorite. Deservedly so or otherwise. So high priced favorites pay like chalky ones in many exotic pools.

Think in terms of the typical schmuck deciding who to include in the final leg of his Pick 3 ticket. Be it a 3-1 favorite or a 4/5 chalk, it probably gets thrown on the ticket to make sure he has a chance to cash if he's right in the first two legs. It's human nature.

On the bright side, this means that low priced favorites often pay nearly as well as mediocre ones. So a heavy favorite is really a better bet in exotics than a higher priced favorite, in a backwards sort of way.

Be prepared for depressed exotic prices with favorites of both the post-time and morning line variety. Conversely, expect value whenever favorites of any kind are eliminated.

"Human Intelligence": Trainer Percentages

The first stop in seeking out some kind of inside information through Human Intelligence sources is the trainer. In looking for trainers that meet the 15% criteria, it is important to know how the trainer achieves wins.

Trainer Appreciation

It is easy to be critical of trainers that fail to achieve a high win percentage, or fail to get stakes quality horses into the winner's circle in marquee events. But it is important to understand the variety of disciplines a trainer must master to succeed in this game.

Animal caretaker: Up at 4 a.m. making sure each animal's diet, grooming, and veterinary care are properly handled.

Athletic trainer: Trying to optimize the ability of the equine athletes in their care—monitoring workouts, healing ailments, developing the horse to race at the distance and on the surface it is bred for, and increasing raceday speed and stamina without detrimentally affecting the runner's long-term development.

Logistics coordinator: Each horse must have a schedule of workouts, gallops, nominations, race entries, races, shipping arrangements, and jockey assignments. Some trainers simultaneously manage dozens of horses, each with its own preferred distances and surface.

Businessman: A trainer employs up to dozens of grooms, exercise riders, and assistants. The trainer must also arrange and pay for veterinary services, equipment, feed, stall space, stakes nominations, and race entries. Owners must be billed for their share of expenses, plus trainer fees and shipping costs.

If a trainer cannot effectively manage all of these roles simultaneously, he or she will not find long-term success in this business.

Regardless of how well a trainer manages all of these roles, however, the selection of jockey is one of the most critical factors. When the gate opens, it's just the jockey and horse. If the trainer cannot get an adequate jockey assigned to his horse, all the best laid plans can be undone.

Don't trust trainers to pick the right jockey.

Why would a trainer spend weeks, months, even a year getting a horse ready for a big effort, only to put a rider on board that can't handle the task? It happens all the time at every track in North America.

Sometimes a trainer uses an apprentice to get the 5-lb weight allowance and finds the apprentice unable to keep the horse out of trouble. In 1999, apprentice Inosencio Diego managed to get 88 mounts at Saratoga without winning a single race. These were not all longshots. Many were contenders from claiming trainers he successfully delivered for at Belmont and Aqueduct earlier in the year. Whether mounts were from loyalty or the persuasive power of Diego's agent (the legendary Angel Cordero), bettors that shared the trainer's faith in Diego burned a lot of money.

Over a 2-year period from January 1, 1999 to December 31, 2000, Shug McGaughey used jockey John Velasquez 63 times, winning 12 of the starts for a healthy 19% win rate. However, 29 of those starts were in stakes races and netted only a single win! The 11 for 34 mark in non-stakes events is as solid a jockey-trainer combo as a handicapper will find. The anemic stakes record is equally important to the bettor. Both of these short-term examples are not to be taken as "the jock's fault," but when a jock/trainer combo is not winning, it's worth noting.

Jockey mis-matches do not have to be so blatant to be recognizable to the handicapper. Every day, trainers put riders on horses in situations where they are clearly not the best rider for the job. As will be discussed later in the book, a jockey with a 15% win percentage overall but a 4% mark on turf will continue to get turf mounts from loyal trainers. Avoid deferring to the trainer's judgment and instead evaluate the rider as either well-suited or ill-suited for each mount.

If an otherwise contending horse is ridden by a jockey in a slump, or in a race category that the rider has a poor win percentage in, do not bet the horse. Do not anguish over whether or not the rider will come through. Pass the race and save yourself the ulcers. If your information shows that the jockey-trainer combination is questionable in today's conditions, passing the opportunity is sensible risk management.

Trainer Win Percentages

Prior to 1980, runners averaged more than 10 starts per year. By 1990, that average had fallen to 8 starts per year. This continues to decline, with the average starts per runner dropping in recent years to less than 7 starts per year. Most trainers have fairly limited stall space, keeping only a handful to 30 horses under their care at a time. With those horses starting less frequently, it is more important than ever for horses to deliver. Successful trainers follow patterns which usually produce wins again and again. Understanding those patterns will improve your long-term success.

If a trainer has a 12% overall win percentage, do the wins happen randomly? Is every horse the trainer starts equally likely to do well? Maybe not. Maybe in digging deeper, you may find that the 12% is made up of a lot of smaller, more specific samples. An example would be Trainer "Joe Bag-o-donuts" with the following stats:

— 4% with first time starters (awful)
— 8% with first time turf runners (not good)
— 12% with first time blinkers (doesn't really help the runners)
— 15% with sprinters trying a route first time (pretty good)
— 22% with stakes runners (really good)
— 28% with first time claimers (super)
— 33% with turf to dirt switches (which might explain why he bothers with turf runners if they only hit 8% of the time)

Some percentages within this overall 12% win rate are outstanding (turf-to-dirt). Some situations should be avoided at all cost (first time starters or turf). More detailed statistics can lead you to outstanding betting opportunities for this trainer in the right situations.

The more percentages you have, the more you know. If all you have is the overall trainer percentages, it may be enough if that win percentage is terrible or super. With the majority of trainers that fall somewhere in between, the more you can break out the percentages, the better. You may find some specialized weaknesses and strengths that will lead to excellent betting opportunities.

Handicapping Humor: When Trainer Quotes Should Give You Serious Doubts

Whether watching on TV or reading an article, any time you see a quote like this, you can draw a big red "X" through the past performances of the horse in question. You'll almost always be doing yourself a favor.

10. "We don't have him cranked up 100%, but he doesn't need his best to win today."
9. "The jockey did nothing wrong, it's just bad luck that he's been steadied in the stretch in each of his last four starts."
8. "Veterinarians worry too much."
7. "Breeding means nothing. Just because his sire, dam and their offspring have never won beyond 7 furlongs doesn't mean *he* won't go a mile and a quarter."
6. "What do you mean the bandages can't go above the knee?"
5. "No, nothing's wrong. We just wanted to give him some time off. A lot of time off."
4. "Horses don't read the *Racing Form*. He doesn't know those other horses have run faster than him."
3. "If we're lucky, that last race didn't take too much out of him."
2. "Well, she's lost some weight, but hopefully she can hold her form for one more race."
1. "Unless something completely unexpected goes wrong, I can almost guarantee he'll win."

Dealing With Trainer Cycles

There was a time in the late 1980s and early 1990s, just before mingling simulcast money with on-track wagering became commonplace, when one of the primary challenges for bettors was to figure out if connections were betting horses based on inside information. A horse could be receiving little action on track and be hammered in Las Vegas or remote simulcast locations. The on-track patrons would have no idea the horse was receiving heavy off-track action. Around the racebooks such money was referred to as "the steam."

Today's merged pools provide handicappers with a more complete picture of the betting action that is taking place, but the second-guessing of trainer intentions continues.

Workouts

Tracking certain trainers' preferred methods can help you identify contenders. Some trainers give horses fast works, others slow breezes. If a trainer like Bob Baffert, known for fast 4 to 6f workouts, has a horse with fast works . . . what does that mean? Very little—that would be "business as usual" for his runners. What if the works are slow? Is the horse unable to stick with the fast work program, or is it fine? Works should only matter if you monitor a trainer pattern that conclusively shows a correlation between a.m. activity and race performance. Without first-hand knowledge of the normal trainer pattern, it is difficult to accurately discern strong work patterns from weak ones.

The New Breed Of Wonder Trainers

There was a time when 20% wins was the mark of a top trainer. Horses raced in larger fields, and lots of horses meant lots of losing starters.

But as the shrinking field trend continued on into the 1990s, a new breed of claiming trainer emerged. Barns could bring a string of horses to a meet and win 25, 35, or even 45% of their starts. Streaks would defy traditional logic, and for extended periods of time, trainers would seem to have the Midas touch. What was going on here? Was foul play afoot or was it simply terrific horsemanship? What do you do when confronted by a race when a seemingly ordinary horse is entered by a trainer winning at a 40% clip? Is this an automatic 3/2 shot?

Let's divide this discussion into two theories:

1. That not everything is on the straight and level.
2. That the trainer is a master of the condition book and has a stable loaded for bear.

A brief discussion of medication follows, but handicappers will have little success betting races if they default to blaming chemicals for changes in horse performance. The game has far too many other variables at work.

Horses, like all other athletes, get treated for various maladies. These days, horses usually race on Lasix at some point in their careers. Either a horse needs Lasix or it doesn't. If it was performing at a given level, runs poorly, then returns with Lasix, it is safe to expect a return to the old performance level. Don't expect miracles—just a correction.

Drug testing in sports being what it is, it is clear that a number of performance enhancing drugs are in use, not just in racing but in other professional athletic events.

It is a cat-and-mouse game between the people developing the drugs and the people developing the testing procedures. In horse racing, when a trainer can figuratively turn straw into gold, at times overnight, suspicion arises that something is amiss. Drugs of interest in this chapter do one of four things to a horse:

— Improve breathing,
— Reduce pain and soreness,

— Build muscles faster than normal, or
— Stimulate or adrenalize.

Are medications, legal or otherwise, a part of the game? Yes. Are all connections playing by the rules? No. But it is unfair to jump to the conclusion that every time a horse has a positive upswing that something is amiss. The vast majority of trainers conduct stable operations with hard work and astute decision making when it comes to selecting races for their stock.

Indeed, proper placement of a horse when it is in top form is usually the difference between a win and a loss. As trainer Bill Mott once said, "What you try to do in training horses is keep yourself in the best company possible and keep your horses in the worst company possible." Proper race selection can make or break not just a horse's career, but a stable's bottom line. Trainers that figure out where a horse can win will have much more success than trainers that don't understand their horse's ideal conditions. It is an all-too-often overlooked aspect of the sport and, for the most part, a much bigger determining factor in face outcomes than pharmaceutical factors.

Revving Up For Big Meets

Few trainers can win at a 20+ percent rate year-round. Instead, they tend to decide which race meets are most important to their business, and train accordingly. Trainers hit high percentages by aiming for a specific meet. They rest and train horses to peak for that meet, then place each horse in a race it is most likely to win when the meet gets underway.

In 1999, Frank Brothers was ice cold at the Fairgrounds meet between December and March, then 14 for 22 at Keeneland!

Date	Track	Horse Name	Race	Distance	Surface	Jockey	FP
02Apr99	Kee	Good Night	Stakes	1m	T	Sellers	1
03Apr99	Kee	Cover	MSWT	1 1/16	D	Sellers	9
03Apr99	Kee	Conserve	Alwn2x	1m	T	Sellers	1
07Apr99	Kee	Grasp	MSWT	4.5f	D	Sellers	1
08Apr99	Kee	Samba Rhythm	MSWT	7f	D	Sellers	1
08Apr99	Kee	Stint	Alwn2x	7f	D	Sellers	1
08Apr99	Kee	Barrier	MSWT	4.5f	D	Sellers	1
09Apr99	Kee	Gibbs	MSWT	4.5f	D	Sellers	1
11Apr99	Kee	Land	MSWT	4.5f	D	Sellers	5
14Apr99	Kee	Freshbroom	MSWT	6.5f	D	Sellers	1
14Apr99	Kee	Pantufla	Stakes	1 1/16	D	Sellers	2
14Apr99	Kee	Free Mantle	MSWT(f)	1 1/16	D	Sellers	3
16Apr99	Kee	Good Night	Stakes	1 1/8	T	Sellers	2
16Apr99	Kee	Kaluki	MSWT	4.5f	D	Sellers	5
16Apr99	Kee	Buff	Alwn$m	1 1/8	T	Torres F	1
17Apr99	Kee	Liable	Alwn1s(f)	6.5f	D	Sellers	1
18Apr99	Kee	Convent	MSWT	1 1/8	D	Sellers	1
18Apr99	Kee	Devine	Alwn2x(f)	1 1/16	D	Sellers	1
21Apr99	Kee	Throw	Mdclm	6f	D	Sellers	--
22Apr99	Kee	Miner's Key	Mdclm(f)	6f	D	Martinez	1
23Apr99	Kee	Chill Seeker	MSWT	7f	D	Sellers	2
23Apr99	Kee	Intern	MSWT	7f	D	Sellers	1

Table 1: Racing History for Frank L. Brothers, 4/2/1999 to 4/23/1999

Source: Bloodstock Research Information Services, Inc. (*www.brisnet.com*)

Note that Brothers not only won 8 maiden races, but won 14 races with 14 different horses! That's having the barn firing on all cylinders.

Top trainers will often have a cold June and July, then have a big Del Mar or Saratoga showing year after year. The pattern is simple to understand: Take it easy on the stable, get the gang fit and rested, then thumb through the condition book and pick races that each horse is most likely to win. At the risk of making this sound easy, that's the gist of it. Aim for a particular meet, give every horse its best shot, then deal with each horse's future after the big meet ends. The stable goes cold, then red hot, then steadily cools off again.

Giving credit where credit is due, to accomplish this a trainer must:

— Have runners that can win at a premier meet (capability),
— Get these runners into peak shape (preparation),
— Match horse ability with race conditions to place them where they can win (knowledge of the competition), and
— Name riders that can deliver on horses ready to win (jockey factor).

There are but a handful of trainers capable of this, whether with well-bred stars or with claiming stables.

When a trainer of high-priced, well-bred horses is in the midst of a streak, he is showered in praise. When the streak is by a claiming trainer, he is showered in suspicion. Any trainer that prepared the stable for a big meet by resting, refreshing and preparing for a number of selected races, should be respected as a trainer trying to make the best of his stable. When the success is mid-meet, with horse after horse experiencing sudden form reversals, then the suspicions are easily understood.

One trainer that always can be counted on to unveil a number of live horses in a short period of time is Richard Matlow. Known as a specialist with debuting horses, Matlow's focus in 2000 favored one track in particular of the three Southern California ovals, Hollywood Park.

Date	Track	Horse Name	Race	Distance	Surface	Jockey	FP
02Feb00	SA	Aclare	Mdnclm	6.5f	D	Gomez G	3
18Mar00	SA	Aclare	cMdnclm	6f	D	Gomez G	8
29Apr00	Hol	Kissesfor	Mdnclm	6.5f	D	Gomez G	7
05May00	*Hol*	*Retired Habit*	*Mdnclm*	*6f*	*D*	*Gomez G*	*1*
05May00	Hol	Baldwin County	MSWT	4.5f	D	Gomez G	2
10May00	*Hol*	*Devine Wind*	*cMdnclm*	*7f*	*D*	*Gomez G*	*1*
12May00	Hol	Fairhope	Alw s(f)	6f	D	Black C	5
26May00	Hol	Kissesforthecook	Mdnclm	7.5f	D	Gomez G	9
28May00	*Hol*	*Retired Habit*	*Alw s*	*7f*	*D*	*Gomez G*	*1*
03Jun00	*Hol*	*Baldwin County*	*MSWT*	*4.5f*	*D*	*Gomez G*	*1*
04Jun00	*Hol*	*Majestic Holiday*	*Mdnclm*	*6f*	*D*	*Gomez G*	*1*
15Jun00	*Hol*	*Wake The Tiger*	*Mdnclm*	*7f*	*D*	*Black C*	*1*
18Jun00	Hol	Red Work	MSWT	5f	D	Gomez G	8
29Jun00	Hol	Retired Habit	Alw48000	6f	D	Flores D	3
06Jul00	*Hol*	*Really A Lush*	*cMdnclm*	*5f*	*D*	*Pedroza*	*1*
23Jul00	*Hol*	*Farah Love*	*cMdnclm(f)*	*6f*	*D*	*Gomez G*	*1*
30Jul00	DMR	He Said Maybe	Mdnclm	6f	D	Gomez G	9
31Jul00	DMR	Timely Silver	cMdnclm	5.5f	D	Gomez G	8
05Aug00	DMR	A Real Knockout	MSWT	5.5f	D	Gomez G	5
05Aug00	DMR	Wake The Tiger	Alw s	1 1/16	D	Black C	2
13Aug00	DMR	He Said Maybe	Mdnclm	6f	D	Pedroza	7
14Aug00	DMR	Majestic Holiday	Clm20g	6f	D	Gomez G	5
17Aug00	DMR	Queen Jimmy	Mdnclm	6f	D	Pedroza	6
19Aug00	DMR	Barkin' Charley	MSWT	6.5f	D	Alvarado	8
20Aug00	DMR	Pelican Point	MSWT	6f	D	Gomez G	5
26Aug00	DMR	Wake The Tiger	Alw s	1 1/16	D	Black C	7
03Sept00	DMR	A Real Knockout	MSWT	5.5f	D	Gomez G	9
08Sept00	DMR	Majestic Holiday	cClm12.5g	6f	D	Gomez G	3
11Oct00	SA	Fancy Contessa	Mdnclm	6f	D	Valdivia	5
14Oct00	*SA*	*Wake The Tiger*	*Alw s*	*1 1/16*	*D*	*Blanc B*	*1*
14Oct00	SA	Barkin' Charley	MSWT	6.5f	D	Blanc B	5
21Oct00	SA	The Griff	MSWT	5.5f	D	Flores D	2
10Nov00	*Hol*	*Wake The Tiger*	*AlwN$Y*	*1m*	*T*	*Gomez G*	*1*
12Nov00	*Hol*	*Western Lonestar*	*MSWT*	*6f*	*D*	*Gomez G*	*1*
22Nov00	Hol	Fancy Contessa	Mdnclm	7f	D	Gomez G	3
23Nov00	Hol	Barkin' Charley	MSWT	1m	T	Blanc B	--
26Nov00	*Hol*	*The Griff*	*MSWT*	*6f*	*D*	*Gomez G*	*1*
02Dec00	*Hol*	*A Real Knockout*	*Mdnclm*	*5.5f*	*D*	*Blanc B*	*1*

Table 2: Racing History for Richard P. Matlow, 2/1/2000 to 12/31/2000

Source: Bloodstock Research Information Services, Inc. (*www.brisnet.com*)

Trainer Richard Matlow clearly had his sights set on Hollywood during the year 2000. He went 0/12 at Del Mar, and 1/4 at Santa Anita's Oak Tree meet, but went 8/14 in the spring/summer meet at Hollywood, and was 4/6 in the winter meet as well. 13/36 is a fine mark for the year, but focusing on Matlow at Hollywood netted a 12/20 score—that's 60% wins!

A trainer can plan for a particular meet by "training up" to the meet's opening. Horses can be rested, then frequently worked, and entered in races that they should contend in. With this pattern showing, it makes sense for the handicapper to anticipate the possible win streak.

A trainer that wins 17% of his starts overall, Nick Zito clearly has had his stable set to roll at the Keeneland Fall meet each of the last two seasons. In the last two fall meets, he has accumulated 22 wins with 58 starts, a 38% win rate. Even comparing that to his Keeneland Spring meet tally of 6 wins in 61 starts (10%) shows a huge difference in performance.

This could be just a short-term anomaly. But it could also be that in the spring, the Zito barn is still in "tune-up" mode, looking to get horses in condition to campaign throughout the year. Horses are entered into races they may "need" to get experience, stamina, practice, etc. Yet in October, each horse is nearing the end of its season and is raced where it can put in the strongest showing. Without trying to speculate too much, the horseplayer should at least recognize the clear pattern and play accordingly.

Date	Track	Horse Name	Race	Distance	Surface	Jockey	FP
05Apr03	KEE	Holiday Lady	Stakes	1 1/16	D	Santos J	3
05Apr03	KEE	Alpine Mountain	MSWT	1 1/16	D	McKee J	5
05Apr03	KEE	Shoo Brush	MSWT	1 1/16	D	McKee J	4
06Apr03	KEE	Gulch Approval	Alwn1x	1 1/16	D	McKee J	5
06Apr03	KEE	American Style	Alwn3m	1 1/16	D	McKee J	4
09Apr03	*KEE*	*Danger Point*	*MSWT*	*7f*	*D*	*McKee J*	*1*
09Apr03	*KEE*	*A. P. Aspen*	*Clm15g*	*1 1/8*	*D*	*McKee J*	*1*
09Apr03	KEE	Quest	Alwn3x	1 1/16	D	Coa E M	3
09Apr03	KEE	Grand Scam	MSWT	7f	D	Coa Dan	2
10Apr03	KEE	Bird Town	Stakes	7f	D	Coa E M	2
10Apr03	KEE	Foreign Authority	Clm25g	1 1/16	D	Farina T	6
11Apr03	KEE	Discover The Glory	MSWT	7f	D	Coa E M	2
12Apr03	KEE	Captain Fantastic	Alwn2L	7f	D	McKee J	7
12Apr03	KEE	Crimson Hero	Alwn1x	1 1/16	D	McKee J	3
12Apr03	KEE	Gold N Silver	Alw s	1 1/8	D	McKee J	4
12Apr03	KEE	Seek Gold	Alwn2x	7f	D	McKee J	5
13Apr03	KEE	Najran	Stakes	7f	D	Coa E M	7
13Apr03	KEE	Three Roses	Alwn2L	7f	D	Coa E M	9
13Apr03	KEE	Devil's Gulch	Alwn3x	1 1/8	T	Coa E M	10
13Apr03	KEE	Governor Hickel	Alwn2x	7f	D	McKee J	6
18Apr03	KEE	Elusive Gentleman	Alwn1x	1 1/16	T	Desormeaux	4
18Apr03	KEE	Hit Record	MSWT	7f	D	McKee J	5
19Apr03	KEE	Alpine Mountain	MSWT	1 1/8	D	Coa Dan	3
19Apr03	KEE	Shoo Brush	MSWT	1 1/8	D	McKee J	3
24Apr03	KEE	Showdown	Alwn2x	1 1/16	D	Desormeaux	--
25Apr03	KEE	American Style	Stakes	1.125	D	Bailey J	2
25Apr03	KEE	Grand Scam	MSWT	7f	D	Coa Dan	2
25Apr03	KEE	Gulch Approval	Alwn1x	7f	D	Desormeaux	4

Table 3: Racing History for Nicholas P. Zito, 2003 Keeneland Spring Meet

2003 Keeneland Spring Meet: 2 wins in 28 starts (7%)

Source: Bloodstock Research Information Services, Inc. (*www.brisnet.com*)

Date	Track	Horse Name	Race	Distance	Surface	Jockey	FP
03Oct03	KEE	Gold N Silver	cClm7.5g	1 1/8	D	Castellano	4
03Oct03	*KEE*	*Najran*	*Stakes*	*6f*	*D*	*Castellano*	*1*
04Oct03	KEE	The Cliff's Edge	Stakes	1 1/16	D	Sellers	6
04Oct03	*KEE*	*Eurosilver*	*Stakes*	*1 1/16*	*D*	*Castellano*	*1*
04Oct03	KEE	Inca Storm	MSWT	1 1/16	D	Castella	7
05Oct03	*KEE*	*Fast Train*	*MSWT*	*6f*	*D*	*Prado E*	*1*
05Oct03	KEE	Crimson Hero	Alwn1x	1 1/8	D	Prado E	4
05Oct03	KEE	Shots	MSWT	1 1/16	D	Day P	3
08Oct03	KEE	Perfect Lady	Alwn1x(f)	1 1/8	D	Sellers	2
08Oct03	KEE	Cherokee Park	Clm10g	7f	D	McKee J	8
09Oct03	KEE	Ballado Chieftan	Stakes	7f	D	McKee J	2
10Oct03	*KEE*	*Bornwithit*	*cMdnclm*	*1 1/16*	*D*	*Sellers*	*1*
11Oct03	*KEE*	*Discover The Glory*	*MSWT*	*1 1/16*	*D*	*SantosJ*	*1*
11Oct03	*KEE*	*Greedy Executive*	*MSWT*	*7f*	*D*	*Sellers*	*1*
11Oct03	KEE	Thunder Force	Alwn1x	1 3/16	T	Prado E	2
12Oct03	*KEE*	*Quick Start*	*MSWT*	*7f*	*D*	*Sellers*	*1*
15Oct03	*KEE*	*Gulch Approval*	*Alwn2L*	*7f*	*D*	*Day P*	*1*
16Oct03	KEE	Holiday Lady	Alwn2x(f)	1 1/16	D	Day P	2
17Oct03	KEE	Father Party	MSWT	6.5f	D	Sellers	3
17Oct03	KEE	Confirmed	MSWT	1 1/16	D	Sellers	2
18Oct03	*KEE*	*El Prado Rob*	*Alwn1x*	*1 1/16*	*D*	*Sellers*	*1*
18Oct03	KEE	Distinguish	Alwn1x	1 1/16	D	McKee J	6
19Oct03	*KEE*	*Crimson Hero*	*Alwn1x*	*1 1/16*	*D*	*Velasquez*	*1*
23Oct03	KEE	Malayeen	Alwn1x	1 1/16	T	McKee J	8
23Oct03	KEE	Shoo Brush	Mdclm	1 1/16	D	Sellers	2
23Oct03	KEE	Cherokee Park	Clm7.5g	7f	D	Velasquez	4
24Oct03	KEE	Wildcard Cat	MSWT	7f	D	Sellers	11
24Oct03	KEE	Island Saga	MSWT	7f	D	Velasquez	4
24Oct03	KEE	Inca Storm	MSWT	7f	D	Sellers	3
25Oct03	KEE	Quest	Stakes	1 1/8	D	Sellers	7
25Oct03	*KEE*	*Ghost Mountain*	*Alwn2L*	*7f*	*D*	*Sellers*	*1*

Table 4: Racing History for Nicholas P. Zito, 2003
Keeneland Fall Meet

2003 Keeneland Fall Meet: 11 wins in 31 starts (35%)

Source: Bloodstock Research Information Services, Inc. (*www.brisnet.com*)

Date	Track	Horse Name	Race	Distance	Surface	Jockey	FP
02Apr04	KEE	Gulch Approval	Alwn3x	6.5f	D	Bailey J	10
02Apr04	KEE	Confirmed	MSWT	1 1/16	D	Prado E	2
02Apr04	KEE	Ghost Mountain	Alwn2x	7f	D	Prado E	2
02Apr04	*KEE*	*Shots*	*MSWT*	*1 1/16*	*D*	*Sellers*	*1*
03Apr04	KEE	Showdown	Alwn2x	1 1/8	T	Blanc B	--
03Apr04	KEE	Emerald Sea	MSWT	1 1/16	D	Sellers	3
03Apr04	KEE	Boot Strap	MSWT	6f	D	Velasquez	3
03Apr04	KEE	Dixie Waltz	Alwn2x	7f	D	Sellers	5
03Apr04	KEE	American Style	AlwC	1 1/16	D	Sellers	2
04Apr04	KEE	Mahzouz	MSWT	7f	D	Day P	2
04Apr04	KEE	Preach It	Alwn2L	6.5f	D	Bailey J	5
04Apr04	KEE	Tell J	Clm10g	6f	D	Martinez	3
04Apr04	KEE	Storm Legacy	MSWT	7f	D	Sellers	7
07Apr04	KEE	Greedy Executive	Alwn2L	6.5f	D	Guidry M	7
07Apr04	KEE	Island Saga	MSWT	7f	D	Sellers	6
08Apr04	KEE	Streamline	MSWT	7f	D	Sellers	4
09Apr04	*KEE*	*Sir Shackleton*	*Alwn1x*	*7f*	*D*	*Bejarano*	*1*
09Apr04	KEE	Inca Storm	MSWT	7f	D	Sellers	--
09Apr04	KEE	French Flag	Alwn1(f)	1 1/16	T	Bailey J	5
10Apr04	*KEE*	*The Cliff's Edge*	*Stakes*	*1.125*	*D*	*Sellers*	*1*
14Apr04	KEE	Boot Strap	MSWT	6f	D	Sellers	4
14Apr04	KEE	Cherokee Lite	Alwn$y(f)	6.5f	D	McKee J	3
14Apr04	*KEE*	*Wildcard Cat*	*MSWT*	*6f*	*D*	*Sellers*	*1*
14Apr04	KEE	Go Now	Alwn1x	1 1/16	D	Sellers	2
15Apr04	KEE	Skydive	Mdnclm	6f	D	Sellers	8
15Apr04	KEE	American Racer	MSWT	6.5f	D	Bejarano	5
16Apr04	KEE	Distinguish	Clm50g	7f	D	Sellers	7
16Apr04	KEE	Gulch Approval	Alwn3x	1 1/16	D	Sellers	2
14Apr04	KEE	El Prado Rob	Stakes	1 1/16	D	Sellers	6
17Apr04	KEE	Confirmed	MSWT	1 1/8	D	Prado E	2
22Apr04	KEE	American Style	Stakes	1 1/8	D	Sellers	5
22Apr04	KEE	Island Saga	Mdnclm	7f	D	Day P	3
23Apr04	KEE	Storm Legacy	MSWT	7f	D	Bejarano	2

Table 5: Racing History for Nicholas P. Zito, 2004 Keeneland Spring Meet

2004 Keeneland Spring Meet: 4 wins in 33 starts (12%)

Source: Bloodstock Research Information Services, Inc. (*www.brisnet.com*)

Date	Track	Horse Name	Race	Distance	Surface	Jockey	FP
08Oct04	KEE	Storm Legacy	Alwn2L	7f	D	Castellano	5
08Oct04	KEE	In The Gold	Stakes	1 1/16	D	Castellano	3
09Oct04	*KEE*	*Burnish*	*Alwn2L*	*6f*	*D*	*Day P*	*1*
09Oct04	KEE	Father Weist	Stakes	1 1/16	D	Martinez	9
10Oct04	*KEE*	*Silent Fred*	*Clm15g*	*1 1/16*	*D*	*Bejarano*	*1*
10Oct04	*KEE*	*Confirmed*	*Alwn1x*	*1 3/16*	*D*	*Day P*	*1*
13Oct04	*KEE*	*Our Friend Timmy*	*MSWT*	*1 1/16*	*D*	*Castellano*	*1*
14Oct04	*KEE*	*Commentator*	*Stakes*	*7f*	*D*	*Bejarano*	*1*
15Oct04	*KEE*	*Chief Commander*	*MSWT*	*7f*	*D*	*Day P*	*1*
15Oct04	KEE	Preach It	Alwn2(f)	6f	D	Bejarano	2
15Oct04	*KEE*	*Highgrove*	*MSWT*	*7f*	*D*	*Day P*	*1*
16Oct04	KEE	Wildcard Cat	Alwn2(f)	6.5f	D	Bejarano	9
16Oct04	KEE	Holiday Lady	Alwn3(f)	1 1/16	D	Bejarano	3
17Oct04	KEE	Andromeda's Hero	MSWT	7f	D	Bejarano	3
21Oct04	*KEE*	*Judgement Maker*	*Mdnclm*	*1 1/16*	*D*	*Bejarano*	*1*
21Oct04	KEE	Electric Light	MSWT	6.5f	D	Day P	3
21Oct04	KEE	Broadway View	Alwn3x	1 1/16	D	Bejarano	4
22Oct04	*KEE*	*Storm Legacy*	*Alwn1x*	*6.5f*	*D*	*Day P*	*1*
22Oct04	KEE	Father Weist	Alwn1x	1 1/16	D	Bejarano	2
22Oct04	*KEE*	*Wanderin Boy*	*MSWT*	*7f*	*D*	*Day P*	*1*
23Oct04	KEE	Preach It	Alwn1(f)	6.5f	D	Perret C	4
23Oct04	KEE	A Real Lady	MSWT(f)	7f	D	Bejarano	6
27Oct04	KEE	Confirmed	Alwn2x	1 1/8	D	Day P	2
28Oct04	*KEE*	*Silent Fred*	*cClm25g*	*1 1/8*	*D*	*Bejarano*	*1*
29Oct04	KEE	J P Jewel	Alwn2L	7f	D	Hernandez	4
30Oct04	KEE	Holy Silver	MSWT	7f	D	Hernandez	2
30Oct04	KEE	Quest	Stakes	1 1/8	D	Hernandez	5

Table 6: Racing History for Nicholas P. Zito, 2004
Keeneland Fall Meet

2004 Keeneland Fall Meet: 11 wins in 27 starts (41%)

Source: Bloodstock Research Information Services, Inc. (*www.brisnet.com*)

Despite being known primarily as a trainer that focuses on 3-year-olds pointing to the Triple Crown, Zito clearly can gear up his stable for this select fall meet.

Similarly, a trainer may start a series of runners that perform poorly or give lackluster efforts, then improve with the second race of a meet, and/or second start off a layoff. Again, the trainer pattern becomes predictable.

When a trainer can perform miraculous form reversals with horses just claimed, or with horses showing a series of recent poor performances, then the chances of predicting the improved performances are small.

The Purse Snatcher

Opening meets are not the only times that trainers can master condition books and prepare their stable to win. On a smaller scale, trainers can also watch condition books throughout a region and find golden opportunities to enter horses.

Look for trainers shipping a horse into a meet for a specific non-stakes race when the trainer otherwise doesn't compete at the track. Opportunities exist for trainers that are willing to take the time to review the condition books at tracks other than their normal venue. A race at the right level and distance may not be offered at their home track for weeks, and they often look around for the right race, usually at a level comparable to what the horse has been facing.

Stakes races will attract shippers of all kinds, pitting them against local specialists for higher purses. With non-stakes races, the lower purse usually means that the horse has to win to make the trip worthwhile. Why else would the trainer bother? Shipping horses is expensive.

A good example would be a competitive allowance runner at Hollywood shipping to an overnight feature race at Bay Meadows. The top Bay Meadows horses may be an easier challenge than the Hollywood allowance ranks. As a result, the horse is in prime position to win against easier foes, perhaps for an equal or better purse.

Avoid "fire sale" horses shipping while plummeting in claiming price. A bad sign would be a competitive $40,000 claimer from Hollywood entering a $15,000 claimer at Bay Meadows, with no indication of why the horse isn't still running at the $40,000 level. The horse will be an odds-on favorite. The trainer must have a reason for offering a $40,000 animal for only $15,000.

Expect heavy betting action. Low prices are offset by a high success rate with this type of move. Some trainers have a real knack for this. If you recall past successes with a given trainer, expect continued success and be on the lookout for such moves in the future.

The Endurance Test

Trainer angles are only as valuable as the information they are based on. Solid meaningful information leads to solid plays.

Coincidences or skewed statistics lead to future disasters. Just because twenty-twenty hindsight shows a profitable angle does not mean that the same circumstances will win often enough, or for high enough mutuel payouts, to be profitable. It doesn't mean the same circumstances will ever produce a winner again. It doesn't even mean the same circumstances will ever happen again!

Understanding what is really going on behind all the statistics is what proves to you that the data is meaningful. If a trainer's rational methodology leads to success over and over, that trainer can be expected to repeat it time and again. Coincidences may lead to wins, but trainers do not stay in this business by relying on coincidences.

Without digging deeper (as we are about to), it is hard to blindly accept, and base future wagers on, an angle such as the following:

— *An average of eight times a year, a trainer starts a turf horse in a marathon (greater than 10f) after a single 8 to 9f turf race following a layoff of at least 60 days. 25% of the time, the horse wins. The average mutuel is $20.* ***The angle: Trainer X's horses stretching out on the turf the second start following a layoff.***

On this information alone, this seems like a great angle to have uncovered, but suppose we break this down further and achieve a better understanding of what has really happened.

The trainer takes horses and gives them vacations for whatever reason (injury, rest). He knows the goal is a turf marathon and probably a $25,000 first-place payday. He gets the horse fit on a training farm and then enters it at a middle distance turf race. His only instructions to the jockey are to keep the horse well-positioned until the far turn, then get clear and take a shot in the home stretch.

Once in a blue moon, the horse fires big and wins. This happens perhaps once in fifteen events and is fine with the trainer but unanticipated. Fourteen out of fifteen times, the horse stays close to the pace, running the first three quarters in 1:11 or so. The horse finds the pace tiring, and makes only a mild move around the far turn before fading.

Unfortunately, once in a while, the horse hurts itself in this prep race. This inevitable setback is accepted by the trainer.

Barring injury, now that a tiring prep race has been run, the trainer gives the horse five days of rest then starts giving the horse daily long, slow gallops. After five or so gallops, the trainer instructs the exercise rider to jog the horse for 2 miles then work it for 4f.

Five days later, the horse is spotted in a 1 1/2 mile race. The past performances show a horse that faded badly following a long layoff. This makes the horse look unbettable to most handicappers. Speed figure players certainly won't be interested.

Now the horse is entered in a race where the pace will be around 1:14. If it ran *that* slowly in its previous start, the horse would have trailed by 20 or more lengths in the early stages. It might have launched a decent rally but probably would have run out of ground before threatening the leaders.

Instead, the horse finds itself midway through a 1 1/2 mile race, is not tired, and the jockey can even let the horse lope along for another quarter mile without any pressure. The jockey sees who is getting exhausted and having trouble keeping up.

There is still 1/2 mile to be run in the race. The jockey lets the horse gear up just a little bit. After a mile and a quarter, most of the field is running on empty. The jock angles clear and asks the horse for its best run. All the other horses are staggering. The question becomes whether or not the horse can sustain this rally all the way to the finish line.

There are other concerns. Whether or not anyone else is rallying too. With tiring horses bearing both in and out, whether or not the horse can run unimpeded all the way to the wire. As the statistics show, 25% of the time, the horse wins. Success is not guaranteed, not at all. But from the trainer's perspective, this is one of his most successful means of getting a good win. 25% is a great hit rate in this game.

A closer look at the average mutuel payoff for this 25% angle is necessary before committing to an automatic bet. Suppose some thorough research reveals the following about this angle:

— Over the past 6 years, the trainer has tried this 48 times.
— There have been 12 wins, at a $20 average mutuel.
— A $2 bet on every instance would cost $96 dollars and net $240 in payoffs, a profit of $144.

It sounds great but . . .

Betting an angle like this for long-term profit is often difficult. Three out of four times, the horse loses. Only eight opportunities have occurred per year, on average. This means you can expect to cash two winning bets per year.

To be able to take advantage of this little nugget of information, you must bet a horse (at an average odds of 9-1 for that $20 average payoff) when it is following a race it may have finished poorly in, knowing that there is only a one in four chance it will win.

There may be a month or more before the opportunity presents itself again.

These facts are not easy to stomach. The person who can set aside $20 for win bets on this angle can expect to enjoy two winners worth $200 each and six losses, for a profit of $240 per year ($1,440 since the angle began 6 years ago).

Two things stand out from this example. First, the $20 average payoff could have come from winners that paid the following: $56, $28, $8, $4, and $4. In this case, the horse was at longshot odds on only two occasions! This would make it very difficult to bet the ones going off at 3-1 or less.

Second, can the 25% statistic be filtered better? Of the 48 runners, what if half were at the odds of 4-1 or less? Suppose the half at 4-1 or less accounted for four of the winners, and the other

24 runners at more than 4-1 accounted for eight of the winners. Now we have a "super" filter because you can throw out the horses going off at 4-1 or less, and what remains is a case with eight winners from 24 starters going off at above 4-1 win—33% win rate. Even without the occasional $56 payoff shown above, this is still a very profitable scenario. Best of all, you are dropping 24 low-priced horses that were included in the original angle but in reality were reducing the profitability.

A Better Way To Bet Trainer Angles

Even an angle that is profitable at first glance deserves personal research. Do this in order to refine the angle and make it more profitable. Confirm there are reasonable explanations behind the numbers. Knowing what is going on and why is the only way to come out ahead in the long run.

Handicapping Humor: Top Ten Heartbreaks of 1998

Each year I put together a personal list of the top ten "tough beats" I experienced along with a top ten "big scores" list. The goal is not only to avoid repeating mistakes and to remember what worked, but to keep a sense of humor about how thoroughly this game can humble you. In 1998, most of my tough beats involved trainer angles.

10. It is announced with 8 minutes to post that Letthegoodtimesroll got permission to wear a muzzle, after two straight DQs for savaging—and wins costing me a Pick 6 with a half million dollar carryover pool.
9. Holding a mere $2 win place ticket on a Nick Zito trainee that I have touted to everyone I know as it wins going away at 19-1.
8. Holding my head between my legs to keep from passing out after hearing over the results hotline that "automatic bet-back" Isaacsmyman just won and paid $44.60 without me getting a bet down.
7. Cashing in on a three horse exacta box that finished 1-2-3 and paid $118, then realizing the same combination paid $2,217 as a trifecta I didn't play.
6. My 24-1 bomb dead heats with the 3/5 favorite, dropping the win payout from $50 to $9.80.
5. Even worse, my daily double with the same 24-1 shot pays a mere $10.40 after showing a will-pay of $288.
4. Cashing four consolation Pick 6 tickets after using four of the five runners in the last leg of the Pick 6, and watching the horse I left out win in a hand ride.
3. Halory Hunter's troubled fourth in the Derby at 9/2 odds (it sounds worse if I mention I was holding a $50 future book ticket at 50-1).

2. A $5,000 claimer from an "0-for1997/1998" trainer wins, paying $208.00 at Gulfstream on the final day of a handicapping tournament, knocking me and anyone else not desperate enough to be picking 99-1 shots out of the standings.
1. Victory Gallop costing *me* a Pick 3 by getting up to win in the final stride of the Belmont Stakes—and, oh yeah, also costing Real Quiet the Triple Crown.

"Human Intelligence": Jockey Stats

The second stop in seeking out inside information through Human Intelligence sources is the jockey. Jockeys can break your heart in more ways than you could ever imagine. Some never seem to get a clean start. Some tend to rush their horse into contention regardless of the pace or their horse's running style. Some seem to overreact when in tight quarters.

How many times have you liked a horse and bet it with a less than successful jockey, watched it get in trouble and lose? You add it to your "trip handicapper" list and wait patiently for it to show up in the entries. The trainer puts the same jockey on it, and amazingly the horse runs up the heels of its competition—again—and loses. Is it unpredictable, is the horse getting itself in trouble (which happens), or is the rider making the same mistake under the same race strategy and conditions as last time?

If the trouble/bad trip is unpredictable, then it's a random fact of racing that cannot be accurately accounted for in your handicapping. If it's the horse, you won't know until it has run a number of races, different conditions, different jockeys, which ends up too little information too late to really help you. But if it's the jockey, you can factor this in and weigh it accordingly.

Here are the basic concepts to factor into your betting decisions:

— Which jockeys win the majority of the races

—On today's racing surface
—Win stats compared to place/show
—Riding styles

— Jock/trainer combos
— Safety rider and check rides
— Overkill—Don't overthink the jockey factor

Which Jockeys Win the Majority Of Races

At nearly every track, the top eight riders will win 80% of the races at a given meet. Dozens of riders will account for the remaining 20%. Aside from the top eight, riders that also deserve your attention are those that either a) ship in for a feature event, or b) don't frequently ride at a meet but maintain a high win percentage. All other things being equal, betting on horses with jockeys outside these categories will seriously deflate your win percentage.

The top six to eight jockeys win the vast majority of races at a meet. At bigger venues like the Southern California and New York circuits, there are plenty of other good riders and many of them do their best work only with certain trainers. (Jockey/trainer combinations are discussed in more detail later in this section.)

Back to the average field size and 12.5% rule of thumb for randomness, if a jockey is winning less than 12% it is safe to say that the jockey is not one of the meet's top riders. Most jockeys actually fall into this category.

Below 8%, a red flag should go up. Try to find out if the rider wins with the trainer listed—maybe it's one of the trainer-jockey niches at the meet. If not, now a ***big*** red flag goes up. Next, see if this rider has won on this horse—a good signal if he has. If not, another red flag. A jockey that wins less than 8%, is not successful with this trainer, and has not won with this horse? Alarms should go off. Why would the trainer ride this jockey if he planned on winning? Trainers stick with what works. Where they deviate, take notice.

Surface Notes

Top riders can win races when riding a contender under any circumstances. However, most jockeys tend to demonstrate strengths and weaknesses that hold up over periods of time. Some jockeys have super dirt percentages but poor turf percentages, or vice versa. This is worth noting, especially for jockeys with win percentages in that 8 to 15% range.

If a jockey has a 12% win average, maybe the 12% comes from 20% dirt sprints, 15% dirt routes, 5% turf. This changes things a little, depending on the race type. The following charts show actual jockey stats for 2002, to illustrate how to identify strengths and weaknesses.

Many jockeys consistently perform over a variety of racing conditions, as this chart demonstrates. Whether or not they are a high percentage winner, their success rate varies little despite changes in distance and surface.

Name	Route	Sprint	Turf	Off Track	Overall
Albarado R	21%	18%	17%	19%	20%
Melancon L	12%	15%	10%	13%	13%
Prado E	20%	17%	20%	19%	19%
Migliore R	16%	15%	12%	14%	15%
Santos J	16%	13%	15%	18%	15%

Table 7: Jockey Win Percentages—Overall 2002

Source: Thoroughbred Sports Network (*www.tsnhorse.com*), *Track Stats 2003*

Not all jockeys are as consistent. In fact, some of the best known and most successful jockeys show clear preferences for certain conditions. The following chart shows that meaningful trends can be found, even in the upper echelons of jockey colonies.

Name	Route	Sprint	Turf	Off Track	Overall
Bailey J	27%	22%	27%	**16%**	25%
Castellano J	16%	15%	7%	21%	16%
Chavez J	19%	18%	14%	**25%**	18%
Coa E	20%	22%	20%	**15%**	21%
D'Amico A	10%	12%	**4%**	13%	11%
Day P	20%	25%	**18%**	24%	22%
Kuntzweiler G	16%	9%	**1%**	11%	12%
Luzzi M	12%	11%	**6%**	15%	11%
Velazquez J	19%	23%	**15%**	**25%**	21%

Table 8: Jockey Win Percentages—Overall 2002

Source: Thoroughbred Sports Network (*www.tsnhorse.com*), *Track Stats 2003*

Points To Remember:

— Few jockeys maintain the same percentage in each category.
— Few jockeys are solid in all categories—surface as well as distance.
— Off tracks are one key situation where some riders clearly excel and others are terrible.
— Generally, turf races have fewer real specialists. Most jocks win 11-14% which means 1 in 8 or so. With an average field of 8 runners, the outcomes of turf events seem more random.

Win Vs. Place/Show

Some jockeys win more than place/show, some win less than place/show. This is self explanatory, but is worth discussing briefly. Some top jocks win at a decent percentage with more wins than seconds/thirds. Likewise, some jocks with a similar number of mounts have far more seconds/thirds than wins.

Both types of riders may have a high in-the-money percentage. This shows both are getting on live contenders. Certain jocks manage week in, week out to get the win, and others seem to pick up the pieces an awful lot.

The figure below shows a sample of what information to look for. Riders A and B have comparable in-the-money stats, but significantly different win percentages.

	Starts	Wins	2nd	3rd	Win %	ITM %
Rider A	200	42	30	23	21%	47%
Rider B	200	28	35	40	14	54

Figure 6: Comparison of Win vs. In-the-Money Stats

Even with a 54% in-the-money showing, Rider B only wins at a 14% clip. This is something that should be factored into your plan. If you planned to bet the horse in a trifecta box, the difference is not significant—in-the-money is good enough. If you planned a heavy win bet, the difference would be important to note. Stats like this exist at real tracks—with substantial differences in win stats vs. place/show stats—and can help complete the race picture.

Riding Styles

Certain jockeys have tendencies that seem to either repeatedly help them win, or cost them a chance at victory. The following are seven profiles worth observing when making rider notes at the meets you play.

1. **Aggressive leaving the gate (positive).**

Gate riders. Jockeys that can beat the gate, get a frontrunner clear of the rest of the field, and give the early leader every possible advantage of early positioning. These riders are a big plus in any race where a well handled frontrunner can lead the field from wire to wire.

2. **Patient (positive).**

Jockeys that don't panic when the frontrunners open daylight on the field. They bide their time and move when their horse is ready to roll. These jockeys can be leading on the far turn, and know not to ask their runner for everything just because an early challenger is ranging up on the outside. Horses that could easily be used too early or too late are most aided by such patient handling.

3. **Easy/Loose leaving the gate (negative).**

These are jockeys that frequently seem unprepared for a start. When the gate opens, their horses tend to drift inward, outward, or get off in a tangle. Horses accelerate from zero to 40 miles per hour in the first moments of the race. Not all horses can accelerate in a straight line. Some jockeys seem ready for some strong handling to keep a line. Others repeatedly seem caught off guard by a bad break, and either collide with other runners or are out of position right from the start.

Head-on instant replays show these tendencies better than the "pan" shots. Such riders should be most worrisome when a runner will need to get good position right from the start. Two-turn races starting very near the clubhouse turn are just one example.

4. Always wide (negative).

Whether it is a fear of getting into tight quarters, or just an inability to control the horse, little good comes from a rider that won't even try to maneuver through the pack or hug the rail. Few tracks in North America favor runners that take an overland route. Riders that make their mounts run extra yards may be keeping the horse out of harm's way, but will also, more times than not, keep it out of the winner's circle as well.

5. Always in a mess (negative).

The classic "wrong place at the wrong time" rider. Sometimes it's a hole that closes before the rider can go through it. Then it's a 99-1 shot stopping cold on the far turn, and this rider is the only one not to notice it backing up through the field until it's too late and his horse must take up to avoid clipping heels. This rider has little chance of winning on a closer.

6. Panicky (negative).

The jockey that takes up when there's only a bit of traffic. The rider that won't fight for the lead if it means skimming the rail. There are Hall of Fame riders that will take big chances on a $12,500 maiden claiming mount in order to win. Then there are journeymen that aren't going to take any chances with their life even for a stakes win. It's a risky profession, and some are more willing (courageous, careless, whatever) than others to do what's necessary to win.

7. **Bias oblivious (negative).**

The rider that pays no attention to the deep, sandy rail and runs through quicksand all afternoon to no avail. The rider that fails to use a frontrunner's natural early speed to take the lead, taking back on a day when no race has been won from off the pace. These riders, perhaps more than any other, can drive a handicapper mad. How can they be blind to what everyone else can so plainly see?

Jock/Trainer Combos

Much has been written about certain trainers using certain jockeys. Knowing a trainer's "go to" guy is valuable stuff, but sometimes it's the other riders that get the live longshots. Such lesser knowns are likely to throw other bettors off the scent of a juicy longshot. So while there is value in studying trainer-jockey combinations, be aware that it is information that tends to be overbet by the public.

Safety Riders or Check Rides

Some high profile trainers are known for giving their horses a "once-over" when returning from sabbatical, injury, or illness. These trainers often put a jockey on the horse that they can trust to take care of the animal. The goal is to check the horse out and make sure it is ready to return to top level competition.

The jock may let the horse run early, then not push too much when sensing that the runner is tiring. Or the jock may take the horse back, allow it to settle into a nice rhythmic stride and make a wide late move, clear of any trouble.

Such high profile connections may attract heavy support at the mutuel windows, but may not be planning to give 100% in that first race back. This can be with a graded stakes runner returning in an allowance tune-up. Or, it could be a maiden returning with Lasix after bleeding in an early race.

The best way to judge check rides is to note trainers that seem to do this and remember to bet against them in similar situations. This can be a great long-term angle. Barring any other evidence, sometimes a runner will show a similar check ride earlier in its career. A layoff, followed by an odds-on loss in an allowance, then a big stakes try. If the horse is once again returning in an allowance following a long rest, it's a good bet that it is another soundness check.

Overkill: You Can't Always Blame Riders

Any time a handicapper makes a losing bet, the natural tendency is to question the ride the jockey gave the unsuccessful runner. Even when horses win, handicappers often breathe a sigh of relief and still feel the ride was only barely competent. Often the criticism is legitimate. However, unlike any other professional sport, horse racing allows rank amateurs (apprentices) to match skills with the all-stars of the sport. Mistakes occur—it is to be expected. Even the best jockeys are bound to make errors when steering a 1,000-pound animal with a mind of its own through traffic at over 40 miles per hour. But handicappers are not rational when their money is on the line.

I have provided more than enough reasons to second guess the jockey, but these warning signs can be noted to avoid losers. Still, don't overthink jockeys too much. Even the best handicappers only win 25 to 30% of their bets, so all of them lose *most* of the time. As a result, you'll always have 20/20 hindsight about riders if you note when they lose and chalk it up to just the rider's deficiencies. Often they simply were not on the fastest horse.

Non-Math Lessons About Jockeys

A bit of a sidetrack, but worth discussing all the same. The following information about apprentices, agents, and jockey changes should help apply logic to situations where many bettors do a lot of second guessing.

Apprentices

In no other sport can players with little or no experience jump right into the major leagues and test their skills against all-stars. Yet in racing a 100 lb. 16-year-old kid can get a leg up and compete with the best jockeys in the business. In auto racing rookies are notorious for making mistakes that lead to problems on the raceway. So too in horse racing, but at least in auto racing the drivers have to first "qualify" before lining up on race day.

There's an old racing adage that apprentices win sprints, but should be played against in route races. In the past several decades various studies have claimed to both confirm and refute this adage. Some apprentices indeed have stats that show they are better in shorter races. On the other hand, the weight break allowed for apprentices should have more of an impact on longer races than on shorter ones. Sprint or route aside, there is an easy way to assess the apprentice dilemma.

Apprentices are the least experienced jockeys on the track. Steering a 1,000 lb. animal and measuring its pace is, obviously, a difficult thing to do. All other things being equal, apprentices will be most effective when faced with the simplest tasks. This means riding horses that can stay clear of trouble and are less dependent on a certain kind of pace. An apprentice rider on a lone frontrunner has the easiest riding assignment imaginable. Break cleanly, take the lead, and try to keep the horse clear.

When apprentices have more decisions to make, the lack of experience is more likely to be a problem. Deciding whether to move inside or outside of horses, deciding to take back or move for the lead, judging the pace to be too fast or too slow—these are decisions that take years of experience to master. As a result the "*apprentice on lone frontrunner*" is the *best apprentice proposition.*

This situation can arise in a sprint or a route. In sprint races, however, there is less effort required to maintain a sustainable pace. In sprints, the race is also over quicker, so there is the added benefit of having less time to screw up.

Apprentices on the turf are often a terrible prospect, again for obvious reasons. Turf races typically are run in a slow herd-like gaggle early, then a dash to the finish once the strongest runners emerge from the pack and get clear sailing. This takes good timing and maneuvering skills. Again, when on a lone frontrunner, the task becomes much simpler and the chances of a rookie's success increase.

Another old adage for apprentices is that the cheaper the animal, the more likely an apprentice will win on it. This is absurd. When you pause to consider that expensive animals are no harder or easier to ride in a race based on their worth, why would apprentices have an easier time on cheaper mounts? If a trainer has concerns about the priciest horses in his barn, he is unlikely to name the least experienced jockeys on the track in the first place. The apprentice may ride more often on the cheaper animals, but a good trainer will put apprentices on the ones in the barn that are easiest to handle.

Agents

A jockey's agent works hard to get good prospects for his client. A good agent can get good horses lined up on the schedule. A recent example is John R. Velasquez' success in New York in the late 1990s. After years of intermittent success, his win percentage increased dramatically when Angel Cordero, Jr. started managing his career.

Sometimes jockeys with excellent riding skills still can't get the mounts. This is not a comment against the jockeys. The jockeys usually ride what their agents can put them on. A rider's win percentage will be determined by both skill on the track and the skill of the jockey's agent.

Jockey Changes

These moves almost always mean less than the public reads into them.

A jockey getting off a horse that he won with recently is generally considered a very negative unknown in the race. Is the jockey switching because the old mount won't win? Does the jockey think the new horse will win? Usually it's interpreted as a negative for the recent winner to lose its rider to another starter, and a positive for the horse gaining that jockey. This is especially true if the jockey is a top jock for the meet.

This is by no means a real sign of anything relating to the horse's form or win chances. The agent may be trying to establish connections, the jockey may have ridden the horse in the mornings, or the trainer may have convinced the agent that another horse is on the way up. There may be a previous commitment to ride someone else's horse.

Scenarios To Drive You Crazy

Provided as food for thought, the following scenarios are likely to occur on any afternoon at any racetrack. These scenarios illustrate the kinds of dilemmas where subjective decisions are required and no one correct way exists to interpret available data prior to the running of the race.

The handicapper must make do with what information is available and decide whether or not the race offers value or is too indecipherable to risk money on. In many cases, even the connections have no idea how their runner will perform. Bettors are advised to pass the majority of these scenarios unless experience and research provide reasons to feel confident wagering in these circumstances.

Scenario #1: A leading claiming trainer has multiple wins using an apprentice and a mediocre journeyman rider. Today, one of the trainer's claimers is entered with a leading, nationally recognized rider. The riders he usually wins with are not on other horses in the race. The horse makes sense, and with the leading connections, the crowd makes it heavily favored.

You interpret this as:

A) The horse is super-well set up and the marquee rider is just added insurance.

B) The trainer would use leading riders all the time if he could, but leading riders rarely take cheap claiming races. He must have talked the rider's agent into it, or maybe the rider/agent knows the horse is set after seeing it in the mornings.

C) If the horse is ready, the top rider may hurt the price, but it won't hurt the chances of winning.

D) If the trainer wins just fine with his eager lesser-known riders, why mess with success? Something seems strange and at short odds, I'm more willing to pass on the race than jump on the bandwagon.

Scenario #2: A top barn ***not*** known for debuting horses ready to win at first asking enters a well-bred sort and names a leading jockey. No other high-profile connections are present. The horse's odds start out at 5-1 but creep down to 3-1 during the post parade, and down to 8/5 as post time nears.

A) This is a "hot" horse from a top outfit. Here's my whole wallet, this horse can't miss!
B) This outfit rarely wins with firsters but the money's pouring in. They must know they've got something good.
C) Any first time starter is a big question mark, especially with connections that do not consistently make winning debuts. I'll save my money for other races.
D) This money is just dumb money spent on name recognition. Any horse showing real ability is now an interesting overlay, and if this one beats me, it beats me.

Scenario #3: A trainer with a decent win percentage enters a horse that looks best on paper in a typical $25,000 1 1/16 claiming race. The rider he names is 0/32 at the meet. The horse has drawn outside, and is not known as a frontrunner. Still, the horse has the best recent speed figures and has been running at this distance.

A) The speed figures tell the story, the trainer's not getting the good win percentage by making bad decisions. That's good enough for me.
B) At this claiming level, the jockey is an important factor. I'll look for another contender with a more successful rider.
C) With an 0/32 jockey, this horse will take some skill to ride if he's breaking from the outside and will not clear the field. I think that a win is possible but unlikely today. Unless the horse goes off at longshot odds, I'll pass.

Scenario #4: A leading rider is known for riding all of a certain barn's runners. Today he is riding for another outfit, but the barn he usually rides for also entered a horse. Both barns have entered legitimate contenders.

A) If the rider doesn't know which animal is better, the agent surely does. Follow the rider.
B) The rider probably wanted to ride for his usual connections but must have promised to ride this other horse and now is obligated.
C) The rider must have his reasons to not ride for his usual outfit. Then again, beating his normal connections might cause problems, so maybe he won't give it 100%.
D) Without being part of the inner circle or a mindreader, it's impossible to know why the rider chose one horse over the other. If both horses are being ridden by capable jocks, it's not the most important factor to consider.

Scenario #5: A trainer with a solid win percentage ships a horse out of town and names a very low percentage rider. The horse is a legitimate contender on paper. As far as you can tell, the rider has not previously won for the trainer in this situation.

A) The horse figures on paper, and the trainer wins his fair share. If he's not worried about the jock, then neither am I.
B) Maybe the trainer couldn't get a top rider. The horse still figures, I'll risk a bet on him.
C) Conflicting info leaves the situation too murky. I'll pass.
D) The trainer is stuck with a lousy rider. Why is not important. The horse will get plenty of action off its good form alone, I'll play against.

Scenario #6: A horse with abysmal form in recent races now gets a leading rider. No other changes in equipment, distance, or class level.

A) Top riders don't become #1 by riding losers. The jock's agent must know something that doesn't show up in the *Daily Racing Form*.

B) I'll bet the trainer wasn't happy with the rides the horse has been getting, and wants no excuses this time.
C) The trainer probably ran out of ideas and wants an expert to ride, like having the mechanic drive your car to identify any problems.
D) Riders lose 80% or more of their starts, which means even the best riders also ride their fair share of stiffs.

Scenario #7: A top ship-in rider is getting on horses on the stakes undercard. The horses are not from ship-in trainers, just run of the mill "locals" with a typical variety of pros and cons going for them.

A) The rider didn't come here to ride stiffs. Even if the horses only look ordinary, the jock's agent probably found out the horses are "ready."
B) The rider didn't come here to ride these, he came here to ride in the feature. These others are just to give him a feel for how the track is playing.
C) A contender's a contender, a pretender's a pretender. A top rider won't make any difference—if the horse is not the best horse, it will probably lose. If it's the best horse, it will probably win.

Scenario #8: A horse with poor recent form is returning to its preferred distance of its last win and switches to a top rider. The horse looks like a non-contender based on recent races at distances that it looks like it did not like.

A) The connections are pulling the trigger and the rider switch is a key indicator.
B) The connections must think that this horse responds well to this jockey. The distance and jockey changes should improve their chances.
C) The connections are desperate and are resorting to the last thing that worked.
D) The connections are playing musical riders so there's no telling what the horse is likely to do today.

Know the Battlefield

In addition to critical information about the "live" participants in today's race (including horse, trainer and jockey), there is critical information you need about the setting for the competition. Every track is unique and different, from the normal wind conditions up the backstretch to the diameter of the turn. First-hand knowledge about the track can help dispel nonsense or find a good opportunity as a new meet opens.

This first-hand knowledge does not have to be obtained by attending the actual track and watching tractor operations every day. The information can also be gathered by studying the results—watching races and being sensitive to pace and pressure. This section discusses a variety of track-related phenomena: running styles, speed and pace, track conditions, and track biases. All combine to accurately describe the setting for the day's races.

Running Style Stats—Don't Be Misled

"Running style" stats are probably the most deceptive stats used today, such as a stat that reads: "50% of 6 furlong dirt races have been wire-to-wire this meet."

All the above statement says is how half the six furlong races were won. It does not imply that the horses that won wire-to-wire had been frontrunners in prior races. **It does not mean that a horse with a lot of front running efforts in its past performances has a 50% chance of winning today.**

It means 50% of the time, the horse leading at the first call went on to win. That alone is valuable information. If you project a horse will make the lead, it will be running in a style that has proven very successful at this track, this distance. Don't read any more into it than that—knowing that is good enough.

It gets even more misleading when people assign percentages to "pace-pressers," "closers," "early speed," "sustained runners," etc. Coming up with these stats requires a definition of each type of running style. For example, how many lengths back is a presser? 2 to 5 lengths? 1 to 6? How far back must a horse lag behind to be a closer? Does this vary with distance? What if a horse is 15 lengths back early, but gains the lead at the 3/8th pole?

Even harder to interpret, what if a slow-paced route leaves the entire field separated by only 4 lengths until mid-stretch? Is the horse running last now considered a closer? With a fast pace, the same field might be strung out over 20 lengths and the horse running second might be 6 lengths off the leader. Would the number crunchers consider this horse in second to be a closer? The stats don't always include this information, and one person's presser stats can be different from another's.

Speed and Pace Figures

Some readers have been wondering since about page 2, "When is he going to talk about speed figures?" The very notion that this book is not all about speed figures will leave some believing that I'm not a "figure handicapper." I am a figure player and prefer to make my own numbers. When I don't have time for that, I rely on Bloodstock Research, or Beyer Speed Figures. But figures are a tool, an indicator of ability and a rating of past effort. They are not an expression of future ability, or a predictor of today's performance.

Speed figures indicate capability. If you are going to develop a winner's profile, a key consideration should be the average winning figure earned in a certain class and distance of race. These figures are referred to as "Par," just like par in golf. You can sometimes find "Par charts" of Beyer Speed Figures in the *Daily Racing Form.* BRIS publishes its own Pars, and other information services also make such figures available.

Accurate speed figures are the clearest expression of what a horse has accomplished that a handicapper can reference. One of my best meets was in the summer of 1992 at Arapahoe Park, in Denver, Colorado. After being closed for years, the track reopened with a modern air-conditioned grandstand, off season simulcasting, and live racing from Memorial Day to Labor Day, Fridays, Saturdays, and Sundays.

Arapahoe Park had two distances: 1 1/6 miles and 6 furlongs. Routes or sprints. The occasional race would be run at an odd distance but most were either 6f or 1 1/16. The track had about 7 class levels in the condition book: Maiden Claiming, MSWT, ALWNX1, Claiming2-L, Allowance (open), Claiming (open), and Handicap. I constructed a big graph paper chart and pasted final times under the appropriate class/distance. It soon became clear what the average time was at each level. The weather rarely changed, so times/track variants were amazingly consistent. Assigning a "figure" of 80 for the 6f and 1/16 average times for open claiming, I assigned values to races based on how much faster or slower than average they ran.

By mid-meet, I knew where each horse belonged on the class ladder. A troubled trip received an asterisk next to the figure, noting it could have been a better effort, but making no effort to quantify the trouble. Few horses shipped in (so no mystery horses) and my numbers held up well. In a way, this was at an end of an era. This was just a year before Beyer Figures began appearing in the *Racing Form*. My crude figures held up so well that I didn't even need past performances, except for results charts so I could add to my data. My win percentage exceeded 40%, even though the horses were generally slow and inconsistent.

Pace Figures

Pace figures are not in the *Daily Racing Form* (yet) but are available through Bloodstock Research (BRIS) and other sources. Generally they are expressions of effort for the first 1/2 mile in sprints, and 3/4 mile in routes. Ever notice that most races are all but over by the time the leaders are entering the stretch? At the very least, the race is usually down to the real contenders at that point. This is why pace figures and pace pars are valuable both for developing a winner's profile and for quantifying what runners have been capable of in the past.

Additional Things To Keep In Mind Regarding Speed and Pace

— *Non-Contenders That Are Pace Factors*

How does one deal with horses that show early speed and tire badly, which are outclassed but will still impact the opening half-mile time? This is frequently a concern but deciding how much it affects the classier frontrunners remains ambiguous.

— *Tracks That Compromise Stretch Runners*

Is there consistently a limit to the number of lengths a horse can be from the leaders and still have any chance to win? Certain tracks put late-runners at a natural disadvantage. Also, late-runners almost always have to contend with traffic, guaranteeing they will rarely enjoy a career of clean trips on the best part of the racing surface. This is especially a hindrance when contending with large fields and/or small ovals with tight turns.

— *The "Average Speed" Myth*

A horse that can run a three quarter mile race in fractions of :22, :45, 1:12, will get the same speed figure as one that runs the same distance race in :24, :48, 1:12. Both "average" 24 seconds per quarter mile, but the one capable of setting the faster early splits will almost always be able to rate comfortably and conserve energy if his only competition is 10 lengths slower in the opening quarter, and 15 lengths slower through a half mile. Unless the speedier horse is forced by another speedball to crank out the blistering early fractions, it should control the match up comfortably.

— *Dawdling Early Fractions*

At times entire marathon fields, particularly on turf, will saunter along at a pace that ensures a slow final time. For example, suppose a typical 1 1/4 turf race has a 3/4 mile fraction of 1:14 at a given track. Whether an event is run in 1:16 or 1:18, if the entire field is running as a herd, none of them are likely to record a fast final time. Final closing fractions will not make up for the time that lapsed during the early going.

It will also be difficult to judge who benefitted the most from the same slow pace. Horses that unleash a powerful closing kick will be credited with a lackluster figure, even though they may be capable of delivering a similar boost when a race has a faster early pace.

— *Stretch Runners*

This refers to instances when horses aren't exerting themselves in a race until the stretch. Certain out-of-the-clouds types choose to take themselves back 15, 20 or more lengths regardless of the pace the frontrunners set. For reasons only the horse knows, the horse lets the others in the race get away, and then tries to reel them in. Thus the final time and chances of winning are at the mercy of the pacesetters.

Note that this does not refer to horses that maintain their own consistent pace. Those animals may run an opening half mile in :48 and be right up with the pace setters if the opening 1/2 mile goes in :47 3/5, or they may be far back if the opening is in :45. Other animals will not necessarily affect the speed figures of this runner.

— *Notice Inaccuracies In Fractional Times*

Inaccuracies in fractional times render all quantitative analysis such as speed figures useless. By rounding to the nearest fifth of a second, actual times vary by 3 lengths (6 points) in sprints, and 2 lengths (4 points) in routes. In most races, the main contenders will consistently show past performances within 4 or 6 points of each other. Thus the race SHOULD be judged a toss-up by a speed handicapper.

Amazingly, a 1- or 2-point advantage will often make one horse the overwhelming favorite. In races where a contender does have more than a 4- or 6-point advantage, it will almost certainly be an odds-on favorite! The built-in inaccuracy of fractional timing guarantees that speed figures are a reliable reference only for general ability.

— *Ignore Turf Times*

In turf races, especially at "about" distances, temporary rails are used which make the distances of the races (and thus the final times) inexact. Even at venues where many turf races are run, many turf races are still hand-timed for the fractions. Add to that the repositioning of the rail by up to 30 feet on any given day—to preserve the lawn—and 92 feet can be added or subtracted from a 1 mile race.

The exact time of past races becomes meaningless. Typically the real question isn't how fast the frontrunner or field is going, it's how fast a certain horse is going relative to the field, which the time won't show anyway.

— *Changing Weather Conditions*

When weather and track conditions wildly vary, the final times of races vary as well. For example, a midafternoon thunderstorm may leave the track sloppy and cause times to either speed up or slow down depending on the racing surface. Variables such as horses remaining at least 10 feet off the rail to avoid puddles cannot be easily accommodated. Despite the best efforts to adjust track variants midway through the day's races, the true impact of such condition changes is not easily expressed in a number.

Track Biases

Running style stats can be affected by long term as well as short term track biases. There are certainly handicappers who do not believe in track biases. There are definitely *track superintendents* who do not believe in biases. However, track biases are not mystical—like believing or not believing in leprechauns.

A long-term track bias can lead to the same running style statistics for an entire meet, or for the same meet from year to year. If you watch every day's races at your preferred track, you will undoubtedly observe long periods of time where a particular style seems to dominate.

Just like a trainer's overall 12% win percentage can be broken down into more significant trends, overall running style statistics might be the sum of short-term track biases.

Not all tracks have recurring biases, and not all races are affected by the same bias. One-turn sprints may have a bias that does not affect two-turn routes. Turf races are run on a different track and would have a different bias.

What does a bias look like? Suspect a bias when consistently a horse's performance is better than you would expect, based on what path the horse took around the track. For example, if a 12-1 shot that you thought little of runs on the lead and on the rail, then wins while contenders just can't get by on the outside, by itself that is not significant. But it becomes significant when the same thing happens in six races on the card, where the horse seems to expend less energy running in one path on the track compared to another.

The most common long-term biases are speed and rail biases. For example, tracks become compacted at the rail due to constant training and grooming, with less attention paid to the middle paths on the track. The first illustration below is for the speed bias, where the three horses on the lead up the backstretch remain on the lead and finish first, second, and third.

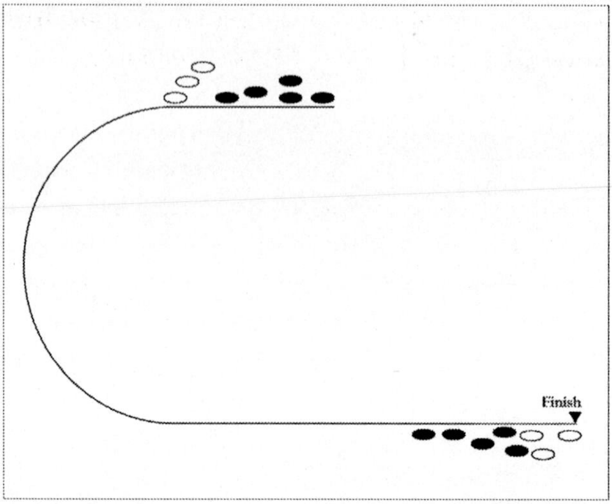

Figure 7: Speed Bias—Frontrunners Dominate

Another common bias is the rail bias, favoring horses that run along the inside throughout the race. Key signs are when horses running on the inside noticeably lose momentum when they move to a more outside path to pass, or when stretch duels are *always* won by the inside horse by a nose or a head.

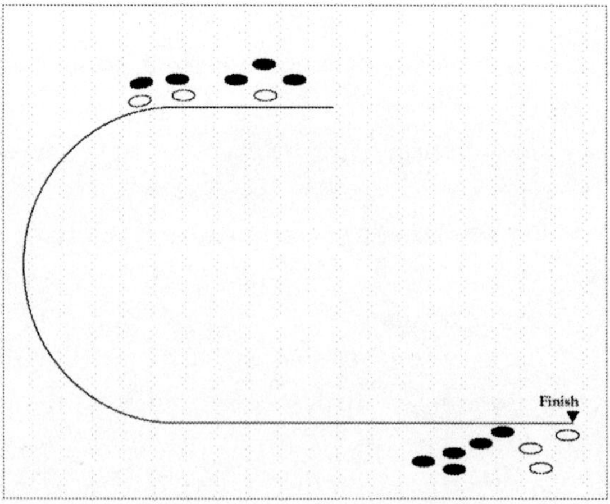

Figure 8: Rail Bias—Inside Runners Dominate

A closer bias would be evident when horses in the back of the pack early swallow up the entire field as a group:

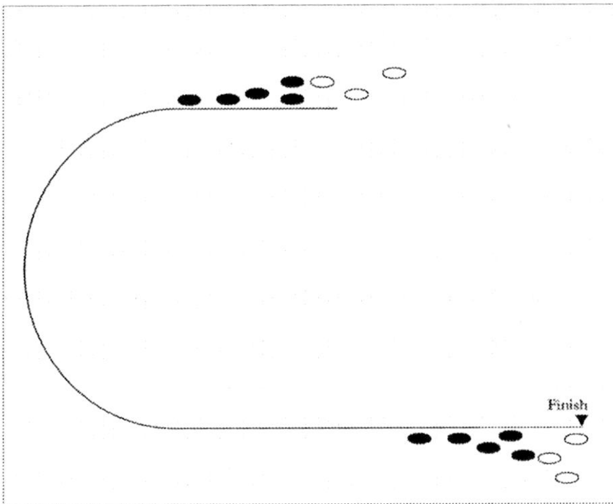

Figure 9: Closer Bias—Late Runners Dominate

The fourth bias worth illustrating is a "dead" rail, where the horses on the rail seem to inexplicably fade in the stretch:

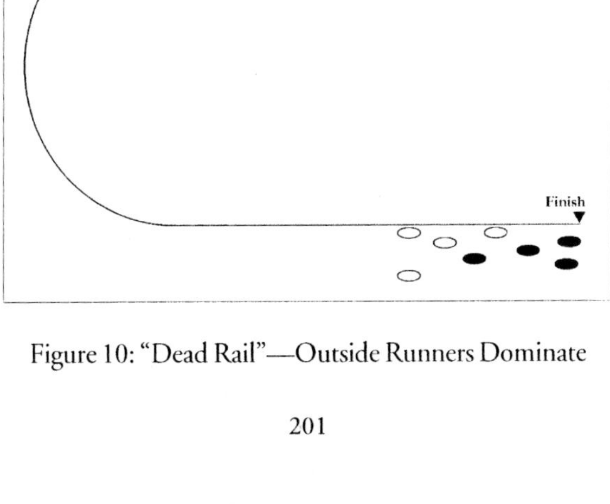

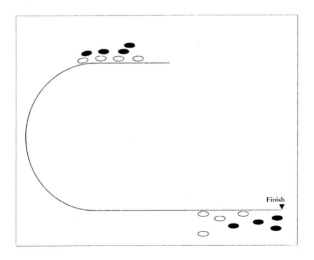

Figure 10: "Dead Rail"—Outside Runners Dominate

Some tracks have a dead rail in sloppy conditions, where closers down the middle of the track have better footing than in the drainage path by the rail. Short-term "dead rail" biases sometimes happen if a track has been speed-favoring, then is heavily dug up and watered along the rail, resulting in a running surface like wet beach sand at the rail.

Biases are one thing better seen than heard. If you hear from the track commentator that speed has been winning, or read it in a newspaper column, you have less knowledge about the bias than if you watch the races. You may know the bias is there, but you won't know what it looks like, or why frontrunners are winning over and over again.

This is especially important so you can recognize when the reign of a bias is over. The only way to recognize a changed bias is to watch the races and know slow vs. fast vs. normal fractions. If a horse runs on the lead today and loses, did it perform worse than the horse that ran on the lead yesterday and won? Or did the track actually behave differently? This will always be a judgment call.

Keep in mind that track conditions can change drastically from one day to the next. Track maintenance may use 1" harrows one day, 6" harrows the next. A radical change like this in how the track was prepared can affect the outcome of the races.

On track, you may have seen what the track looked like yesterday and can adapt the next day if it looks different. The off-track bettor generally does not have this information available. Some tracks such as California tracks provide information as part of their telecast regarding how deeply the track was furrowed for the day's races. However, most tracks do not provide details either on—or off-track.

Track conditions can and will change during the day.

If it rains and the posted track condition goes from fast to sloppy, everyone knows that the track changed. But what about regular track maintenance between races? This can change how the track plays mid-day. A single track variant doesn't cover two distinct samples, so this may be difficult to pick up on.

Be prepared to adapt if you think that a bias has changed.

If you think that you have identified a bias, don't be afraid to take advantage of it. If you are right, you can make an early profit before others catch on. If you are wrong, at least this aspect is only one factor in your handicapping—if you accurately identify the best horse in the race, it can win regardless.

How Do Biases Relate To Running Style Stats?

— Stay aware of the running style statistics in general terms at your track.
— Be aware of any long-term bias.
— Take advantage of any short-term bias that you have identified, especially if it's not widely recognized. There are two ways to do this:

1. The short-term bias may mean that for the later races in a card you completely change your wagering strategy.
2. You may want to note horses especially hurt or helped by the bias, and watch for them next time they run. Today's effort will show up next time in the past performances, but you won't see comments like "aided by extreme speed bias" or "had no chance due to bias."

A bias is only one of many handicapping factors. The best horse on a given day usually wins—after all, favorites win 33% of the time no matter what their running style is.

A Better Way To Quantify Track Stats

Trends such as "speed is holding up well" are best left as general tendencies, not numbers. Therefore I try to keep track of these trends by noting the daily trend.

I describe speed/positional biases like this:

— Frontrunners are tiring quickly.
— Frontrunners are holding on well.

— Frontrunners are holding on very well.
— Frontrunners are drawing off with ease, regardless of early pace!
— Closers aren't getting anywhere.
— Closers are catching the leaders only when the pace is solid.
— Closers are catching the leaders before they are even asked to run!

As for the inside/outside track biases:

— The rail is the only place to be.
— Sweeping wide is the only way to win. Sometimes this is very easy to notice—even jockeys on the lead stay 10 feet or more off the rail.

In summary, I love stats, but not for running style and/or bias profiles. I ***don't*** like stats that say things like:

For the week of May 11 through May 18,
Dirt sprints were won as follows:
40% frontrunners
25% early pressers
20% pressers
15% closers

Whatever the actual percentages, the stats all depend on the exact definition for each running style. Each style is defined based on rigid beaten lengths criteria without considering pace and field size, both of which spread out or condense the field. Besides, all are based on small samples. One win here or there can drive a 10% or more change.

Here is the bottom line: No matter how strongly a surface seems to favor a certain path or running style, don't "invent" or rely on numbers when it is more appropriate to be aware of the trend in a general way. Watch each day's races for changing conditions. Start each meet with a knowledge of what worked in what kinds of races at the most recent meeting.

For example, the spring meet at Keeneland is different from the fall meet, although at the same venue. Aqueduct's outer dirt is significantly different from the inner track, and the winner's profile should be adjusted as soon as racing moves from outer to inner dirt.

Keep in mind that running style is at most only half the horse's doing. The other half is the jockey's game plan. The jockey that fails to recognize a bias will not adapt his game plan to the track conditions. Sometimes horse and rider fight each other all the way around the oval! Many a "bias handicapper" has been ruined by a failure to recognize that the rider must steer to the good part of the track, or must know to make the lead or take back, in order to win.

Short-term jockey records are available in addition to overall meet records. The *Daily Racing Form* sometimes includes figures for the last 30 days. Some information services provide more data, such as Bloodstock Research providing records for the last 7 days. Short-term jockey records along with short-term bias knowledge can show opportunities on a daily basis. If a jockey is 7/10 in dirt sprints in the last 4 days and you recall him winning wire-to-wire on a speed-favoring track, you have a jockey with an improved chance to win under the bias conditions. If this jockey is then on one of three equal sprint contenders at roughly equal odds, you can factor this jockey's recent success into your race assessment.

Overall, when watching races, pay attention to track conditions, and how the winners got across the wire first. If you see trends, take advantage of them before everyone notices. Expect certain jockeys to know where the "good" part of the track is, and give their contenders preference under the same track conditions.

The best horse should win every race. On a speed-favoring track, a closer is not the best horse that day, under those conditions. On a "dead rail" track, a frontrunner will tire and not be the best on that day. If you know what conditions are prevailing, you can more accurately select the best horse.

SECTION 4

Special Situations

Dealing With Special Situations

The following chapters deal with a variety of situations and race classifications that cannot be dealt with in an ordinary fashion. Traditional handicapping analysis remains important. However, special attention must be paid to certain facts and realities that produce situations that should be zeroed in on whenever they occur.

The following topics will be discussed:

— In Pursuit of Front Runners: Taking Advantage of Late Scratches and Speed Duels
— All-Stars: Build Your Own Fantasy Stable
— Maiden Races (Baby Races, For Older Horses, etc.)
— Starter Allowances
— Marathons
— Steeplechases
— Handicapping the Handicaps

Outside of daily racing, there are other general trends that seem to be the result of a wide variety of operations planning effective campaigns for their racehorses:

— Summer Favorite-itis
— Fall Campaigns
— Winter Racing

Finally, a brief discussion of one area where the handicapping required to win is among the most specialized in the sport:

— Handicapping Contests

These chapters will discuss unique aspects of each special situation that the astute handicapper can take advantage of.

In Pursuit of Front Runners

Although betting frontrunners is rarely a bad idea, there are two specific scenarios where frontrunners are temptingly overlooked. The first situation is when late scratches produce a lone frontrunner from a previously speed-saturated race. The second situation occurs if one speedster can outrun the other speed horses significantly during the first quarter of the race.

Late Scratches

Late scratches can significantly change a race profile and its likely pace scenario. It is well established that the "lone frontrunner" is one of the most reliable plays in racing. If a frontrunner can seize the early lead unchallenged and settle into stride, it can often coast at a comfortable pace and reserve energy to fight off late challengers. In contrast, when two or more horses battle for the lead, none of the leaders get to relax, the pacesetters will weaken, and the race becomes a free-for-all.

Ordinarily, if a lone frontrunner can be identified, its chances of winning are good but chance of profit is poor. Many handicappers will notice and the horse will be heavily bet.

If, however, a race at first appears to have an excess of early speed and subsequent scratches remove all but one speed horse from the race, a lucrative betting opportunity is immediately created. The late scratches will lower odds on all remaining contenders, but not everyone will notice the resulting "lone speed" horse. Enough bettors will abide by their original handicapping.

Even a horse that was considered a longshot as one of several frontrunners may now be a legitimate contender. Better still, it will probably offer generous value compared to the odds it would be if it seemed destined to be a lone frontrunner from the moment entries were drawn.

Speed Duels

When a race projects to have a speed duel develop, most handicappers will either pass the race or look for closers to bet. On occasion, though, one horse will show significantly faster early fractions than the other frontrunners. When this occurs, this fastest speed horse will often prevail and usually eliminate the other speed horses in the process. It takes only fractions of a second to give one speedster a definite edge, since 1/5 second equates to more than one length.

The sharpest frontrunner often wins through a combination of factors. In the opening stages, horses that break cleanly and get up to top speed quickest seize the lead. Other riders must decide either to ask their runners to go faster and challenge the lead, or to concede the early lead. For many speed horses, being asked to rate and settle off the lead is discouraging and keeps it from delivering a top performance. For pacesetters, being anything other than the fastest frontrunner is usually a lose / lose situation.

By the end of the first quarter mile, the early pace may set up as anything from merely brisk to downright suicidal. But again one horse may be comfortable going :22 while another is accustomed to :22 and 2/5. That extra 2/5 faster time can be comfortable for one and meltdown pace for the other.

For runners that conceded the lead early in the race, it is rarely an easy task to catch the frontrunners. If a horse breaks first, opens a 2-length lead, and maintains it for a 1/4 mile in :22 flat, the chasers have run the opening fraction in about :22 and 2/5. If they want to draw even with the leader, they must make up that 2/5 second advantage. If the leader is on its way to a :44 flat half-mile time (another :22 flat quarter), the pursuer would have to accelerate to a sub-22 second second quarter—just to catch up. Such a taxing effort often leaves the closest pursuers exhausted before the stretch drive and closers with a lot of traffic to work through. The tiring frontrunner races weakened challengers and, with the entire field tired, the horse still on the lead in the stretch has an advantage.

Pico Central, for example, was capable of leading a race in fractions of :22 and :44. He won 5 of 7 races during 2004, and was only beaten by deep closers reserving energy by trailing far back early, then running the entire field down in the stretch. No runner that followed closely behind Pico Central had enough oomph left in the end to catch him.

Pico Central (Brz)
Own: Tanaka Gary A

Dk. b or b. h. 6 (Oct)
Sire: Spend a Buck (Buckaroo)
Dam: Sheila Purple*Brz (Purple Mountain)
Br: Haras Fronteira P.A.P. (Brz)
Tr: Lobo Paulo H

Life	15	9	0	3	$1,183,145	116
2004	7	5	0	2	$1,139,000	116
2003	3	1	0	0	$13,874	-
D.Fst	7	5	0	2	$1,139,000	116
Wet(314)	1	1	0	0	$1,692	-
Turf(268)	7	3	0	1	$42,453	-

27Nov04-9Aqu	fst	1	:22^{2} :44^{1} 1:08^{1} 1:33^{2}	3↑CigarMiH-G1	108	1	1^{hd}	1½	1^{hd}	2^{hd}	3^{1¼}	Espinoza V	L123	*.95	97-07	LionTamer115^{1¼} BadgeofSilver115^{no} PicoCentrl123^{4¾}	Set pace, weakened	8
2Oct04-8Bel	fst	6f	:22^{3} :45^{3} :57^{1} 1:09^{3}	3↑Vosburgh-G1	114	5	4	2½	1^{hd}	1½	1^{4}	Espinoza V	L124	2.20	91-22	Pico Central124^{4} Voodoo124½ Speightstown124^{hd}	Speed 3 wide, clear	5
15Aug04-8Dmr	fst	7f	:21^{4} :43^{4} 1:08^{1} 1:21	3↑OBrinBCH-G2	103	3	1	1^{hd}	1^{hd}	2^{2}	3^{5¾}	Flores D R	LB122	*.40	91-10	Kela116^{4½} Domestic Dispute116^{1¼} Pico Central122^{4}	Inside duel,held 3rd	5
31May04-9Bel	fst	1	:23^{2} :46 1:10 1:35^{2}	3↑MtropltH-G1	116	8	2½	2½	2^{hd}	1^{hd}	1¾	Solis A	L119	3.45	84-34	PicoCentrl119¾ BowmnsBnd114^{2¼} StrongHop119^{1½}	Bobbled start, gamely	9
10Apr04-9Aqu	fst	7f	:21^{3} :43^{2} 1:07^{2} 1:20^{1}	3↑CarterH-G1	116	3	5	2^{hd}	1½	2^{hd}	1^{1¼}	Solis A	L117	4.30	104-04	Pico Central117^{1¼} Strong Hope119^{2} EyeoftheTiger114¾	Came again on rail	9
7Mar04-8SA	fst	7f	:22^{1} :44 1:08^{2} 1:21	4↑SnCrlosH-G2	113	5	2	1½	1½	1^{2½}	1^{2}	Flores D R	LB116	43.20	100-11	Pico Central116^{2} Publication116^{2} Pohave112^{1}	Bit off rail,held gam	10
25Jan04-7SA	fst	6½f	:21^{1} :43^{3} 1:08^{3} 1:15^{1}	4↑OC 100k/n3x-N	95	8	2	1^{hd}	1^{hd}	1½	2¾	Espinoza V	LB119	37.50	95-08	[D]Ride andShine119¾ PicoCentral119½ Arsen119^{no}	Dueled,game,edged late	9

Placed first through disqualification Previously trained by R Morgado Jr

18May03♦Ciudad Jardim (Brz)	fm	*1	ⓣLH 1:32^{3}	3↑Grnde Premio Pres da Republica-G1 Stk 15300	6^{9}	Santos R L	128	*1.30	Autoridade Maxima132^{4¼} Super Atleta128^{3¼} Pronasteron128^{1} 17
9Mar03♦Gavea (Brz)	gd	*1⅛	ⓣLH 2:08^{4}	GP Jockey Club Brasileiro-G1 Stk 24600	11^{15½}	Guimaraes G	123	*.40	Jockey's Dream123^{1¾} Great Communicator123^{nk} Britanic123^{nk} 14
9Feb03♦Gavea (Brz)	fm	*1	ⓣLH 1:33^{3}	GP Estado do Rio de Janeiro-G1 Stk 24500	1^{5½}	Guimaraes G	123	4.40	Pico Central123^{5½} Hard Buck123^{1} Naguchi123¾ 16
29Dec02♦Gavea (Brz)	gd	*6f	LH 1:11^{1}	Pr Drtr Stud Book Brasileiro Alw 2800	1^{6¾}	Guimaraes G	123	*.30	Pico Central123^{6¾} Cigar of Cord123^{2¼} Modella112^{8¾} 6
31Aug02♦Gavea (Brz)	gf	*5f	ⓣLH :56	3↑GP A de Faria & R G de Faria-G3 Stk 9800	4^{6½}	Guimaraes G	117	*.70	Major Dodge117^{2¾} Eleicao Direta128^{1¼} Harponneur132^{2½} 12
3Aug02♦Gavea (Brz)	gf	*5f	ⓣLH :56^{1}	3↑Grande Premio Major Suckow-G1 Stk 38600	1^{1½}	Guimaraes G	117	*2.50	Pico Central117^{1½} Eleicao Direta128^{4¾} Nortek130^{nk} 15
6Jly02♦Gavea (Brz)	gf	*5f	ⓣLH :55^{4}	3↑Grnde Premio Cordeiro da Graca-G2 Stk 13600	3^{3¾}	Guimaraes G	117	7.90	Major Dodge121^{nk} Eleicao Direta128^{3½} Pico Central117¾ 12
Previously trained by B Rocha									
30Mar02♦Gavea (Brz)	gf	*5f	ⓣLH :56^{4}	Premio Fort Dodge Maiden 4800	1^{5}	Santos R L	121	*1.40	Pico Central121^{5} King Pad121^{1¼} Proximo Milenio121^{nk} 12

WORKS: Jan14 Hol 3f fst :38^{4} B *43/44* Nov20 Hol 5f fst 1:01^{2} B *25/60* Nov14 Hol 6f fst 1:14^{1} H *9/21* Nov7 Hol 6f fst 1:14^{1} H *11/15* Oct31 Hol 5f fst 1:02^{1} B *26/47* Oct24 Hol 4f fst :48^{4} B *11/37*

Horses rarely go head-to-head for very long before one gives up the fight. If a frontrunner duels other speed horses into defeat early in the race, it can often relax and coast before closers pose a late challenge. Runners near the leader tire around the turn and the accelerating closers have to work through the resulting traffic.

Some final words of caution: Pass on races where no individual speedster holds an edge. Do not bet "the speed of the speed" if it has led and faded every time it has tried today's distance. And, last but not least, pass on horses that have forfeited uncontested leads in the past. A horse that has had this opportunity and failed will fail again.

All-Stars: Build Your Own Fantasy Stable

Every handicapper follows favorite horses throughout their careers. Perhaps it's a superstar that is vying for Horse of the Year. Maybe it's a well-bred juvenile that will hopefully bloom into the next Kentucky Derby winner. Maybe it's a $15,000 claimer that repeatedly wins at huge odds. Only the coldest cynics fail to become a fan of a horse from time to time.

When these personal racetrack heroes are entered, it can be almost impossible to resist betting them. As previously stated, although it's important to distinguish "rooting" from handicapping, there are indeed horses worth following and betting throughout their career—horses that are proven over-achievers, win at least 20% of their starts, and rarely go off the favorite. These All-Stars exist and a handful of such horses can make up a successful All-Star Betting Fund—racing's do-it-yourself version of fantasy sports leagues.

The premise of this approach is simple: Identifying a good horse to follow throughout its racing career can help lead to a number of lucrative betting opportunities. Loyalty to these overachievers will pay off! Here are some key ideas to consider in pursuing an All-Star Betting Fund:

— Horses have short careers compared to other athletes, resulting in high turnover in any stable.

— Include a variety of horses competing in different conditions to avoid competing against yourself and to have an opportunity to play multiple races per week. (In other words, don't pick only 2-year-old colts or handicap/stakes horses.)

— Be prepared for a negative factor: The trainer decides when and where to run, and the bettor following a particular animal is at the trainer's mercy. (Continuing the fantasy sports league analogy, in other sports, the schedule is published before the season starts. The coaches don't pick the games or the venues.)

- Be sure to use horses from winning connections. A 5% win trainer is not the best place to make long-term investments.
- Use a service like StableMail at DRF.com or Stable Alert at Brisnet.com to track an All-Star's activity. These tools will communicate not only when the horse will run, but also when it works out and the workout results.
- The horse must have won at least once. Wait for a horse to win its maiden race before adding it to your All-Star list. Too many talented runners fail to ever win.
- As a bettor, the ideal kind of horse to follow is one that wins periodically and runs uninspiring races between wins. A horse that can repeatedly jump up and win after races in which they were badly beaten becomes a longshot machine.
- As long as the horse stays under the care of competent connections and gives no indication of infirmity, trust your All-Star selections and resist the temptation to bet the horse only a finite number of times before giving up. If a horse loses 4 in a row, it becomes more and more testing to bet the 5th, 6th, and 7th start since the last win. The bettor becomes afraid to stop betting out of fear that the next race will be the one that the horse returns to the winner's circle. If the reason behind an All-Star selection remains valid, its losses simply increase its odds and therefore future payoffs.

Runners that compete at a consistent level of conditions are usually the best candidates for an All-Star list. Only a rare animal like Furlough can climb up the ladder from maiden to Grade I winner in an orderly fashion:

Furlough
Own: Phipps Ogden

B. m. 11 (May)
Sire: Easy Goer (Alydar)
Dam: Blitey (Riva Ridge)
Br: Phipps Stable (Ky)
Tr: McGaughey III Claude R

Life	33	8	9	2	$671,844	107	
1999	10	2	2	0	$331,406	104	
1998	12	3	3	0	$242,958	107	
D.Fst	27	6	7	2	$569,844	107	
Wet(306)	5	2	2	0	$102,000	95	
Turf(270)	1	0	0	0	$0	64	

28Nov99-9Aqu	fst	1	:231 :46 1:103 1:352	3↑ⒻDALTpFlH-G2	90	1 79 66 63¼ 46 27¼	Smith M E	L118	*.80e	84-20	Belle Cherie1137¼ DH Furlough118 DH Harpia1173¼	Broke slowly, wide trn	7
6Nov99-6GP	fst	6f	:22 :44 :554 1:074	3↑BCSprint-G1	94	1 14 1411 149½ 1112 1011¼	Smith M E	L123	53.10	92 -	Artax126½ Kona Gold1262¾ Big Jag126½	Bumped start,outrun	14
18Sep99-8Bel	fst	1 1/16	:231 :454 1:101 1:414	3↑ⒻRuffianH-G1	102	1 55¾ 56½ 41¾ 2hd 2nk	Smith M E	L116	8.80	88-14	Catinca119nk Furlough1162½ Keeper Hill118nk	Inside move turn, game	5
22Aug99-8Sar	fst	7f	:22 :443 1:092 1:23	3↑ⒻBalrinaH-G1	103	6 5 1015 109¾ 22½ 1no	Smith M E	L114	7.20	90-16	Furlough114no Bourbon Belle1171½ DH Catinca121	Angled out, up on wire	10
4Aug99-9Sar	fst	6f	:214 :444 :564 1:092	3↑ⒻHnrblMsH-G3	96	2 8 1012 97 67 43¾	Smith M E	L115	4.90	90-11	BourbonBelle1163½ GoldPrincess116nd LicenseFee114½	Good finish inside	10
19Jun99-8Bel	fst	1 1/16	:231 :461 1:094 1:403	3↑ⒻHmpstedH-G1	85	6 57½ 58 55 59 515	Castillo H Jr	L114	6.90	79-06	SisterAct117½ BeautifulPleasure1129¼ Catinca1224¾	Hustled inside,empty	6
15May99-8Bel	fst	6f	:213 :45 :572 1:102	3↑ⒻGnunRskH-G2	93	5 9 914 96¼ 75½ 43¼	Castillo H Jr	L116	4.30	86-12	Foil1141¼ Harpia1181 Gold Princess1151	Inside,going well late	9
17Apr99-8Aqu	fst	1	:23 :452 1:094 1:344	3↑ⒻBdORsBCH-G3	78	3 54 44½ 52¼ 65¾ 611¼	Smith M E	L116	3.25	83-18	Catinca1202¼ Foil113no License Fee1132¾	Rail, no response	6
13Mar99-8Aqu	fst	7f	:23 :461 1:104 1:231	3↑ⒻDistfBCH-G2	104	8 5 99¼ 96½ 2½ 1hd	Castillo H Jr	L115	14.10	86-20	Furlough115hd Catinca1211 Tomorrows Sunshine1131¾	Clear trip on rail	9
21Feb99-3GP	fst	7f	:23 :464 1:112 1:241	4↑ⒻAlw 43560N$Y	80	2 4 42 42½ 44 46¼	Smith M E	L116	3.30	73-20	Gold Princess121hd Colonial Minstrel1161¼ U Can Do It1165	Faltered	4
27Nov98-8Aqu	wf	1	:233 :461 1:103 1:354	3↑ⒻDALTpFlH-G2	95	4 43 45½ 44½ 47 26¾	Davis R G	L115	5.40	83-24	Catinca1196¾ Furlough115½ Glitter Woman120¾	Split rivals, got 2nd	5
7Nov98-6CD	fst	6f	:21 :441 :561 1:09	3↑BCSprnt-G1	94	13 2 1311 139¾ 127 106¾	McCarron C J	L123	86.60	91-03	Reraise1242 Grand Slam124hd Kona Gold1261	Failed to menace	14
10Oct98-7Bel	sly	1⅛	:45 1:084 1:332 1:461	3↑ⒻBeldame-G1	84	6 58 512 410 411 420¼	Velazquez J R	L123	8.10	78-14	ShrpCt12311 TomisusDlight1232½ PochosDrmGirl1237	Inside, no response	7
19Sep98-8Bel	fst	1 1/16	:223 :454 1:10 1:422	3↑ⒻRuffianH-G1	107	6 65 54½ 43 34½ 23	McCarron C J	L115	18.00e	84-18	Sharp Cat1243 Furlough115½ Stop Traffic1197	4 wide move, gamely	8
23Aug98-8Sar	fst	7f	:213 :442 1:091 1:221	3↑ⒻBalrinaH-G1	80	5 3 517 515 69¼ 412	Smith M E	L115	6.30	82-16	StopTrffc1187 RunpthColors1161½ UCnDoIt1153½	Came wide, no response	6
5Aug98-9Sar	fst	6f	:213 :451 :581 1:111	3↑ⒻHnrblMsH-G3	90	5 4 614 65 2hd 12	Smith M E	L113	6.20	85-15	Furlough1132 AngelsTearlet1145½ DixieFlag1192	Swung wide, going away	6
27Jun98-7Bel	fst	6½f	:23 :453 1:091 1:153	3↑ⒻVagrncyH-G3	92	2 3 55½ 45 34 22	Smith M E	L114	4.80	92-14	Chip1152 Furlough114¾ Parlay1152	Inside move,game	6
6Jun98-2Bel	fst	7f	:222 :461 1:112 1:241	4↑ⒻAlw 50000c	90	5 8 79½ 63 2½ 12	Smith M E	L114	7.20	81-11	Furlough1142 Parlay1221 Surina Star1153½	Taken to inside,clear	8
16May98-8Bel	fst	6f	:222 :451 :572 1:101	3↑ⒻGnunRskH-G2	80	6 6 78 65¾ 52½ 65	Bridgmohan S X	109	25.75	85-14	J J'sdream1182½ Tate1121¾ Capote Belle118no	Inside trip,good fin	8
18Apr98-8Aqu	fst	1	:223 :451 1:091 1:333	3↑ⒻBdORsBCH-G3	92	9 66 66½ 32½ 46 48¾	Bridgmohan S X	110	2.60e	92-05	DixieFlag1174 HiddenReserve1134 UCanDoIt118¾	Wide move,nothing left	9
2Apr98-6Aqu	fst	1	:234 :47 1:111 1:363	4↑ⒻAlw 37000N3X	89	5 41 3½ 1hd 1½ 12	Bridgmohan S X5	109	*.75	86-18	Furlough1092 Real Merry1122½ Vivacious Suzi122¾	4 wide turn,ridden out	5
14Mar98-8Aqu	fst	7f	:223 :454 1:11 1:24	3↑ⒻDistaffH-G2	80	6 7 75¼ 83¾ 63¼ 74¼	Bridgmohan S X	110	12.70	80-20	Parlay114nk Lucky Marty113hd Green Light114nk	6w move 1/4 pole	9
27Nov97-9Lrl	fst	1⅛	:473 1:121 1:381 1:511	ⒻAnnArndl-G3	84	5 77½ 79 68 56½ 58	Cordova D W	115	8.70	74-25	G. O'Keefe115hd Snit122½ Cotton Carnival1224	Wide 2nd turn, empty	9
9Nov97-8Aqu	sly	1	:221 :452 1:111 1:372	3↑ⒻAlw 35000N2X	84	3 612 58 1½ 15 1¾	Davis R G	116	*1.45	83-20	Furlough116¾ Your Gorgeous1216½ Hail116½	Clear,driving	6
30Oct97-9Aqu	fst	1	:223 :451 1:094 1:36	3↑ⒻAlw 33000N1X	89	5 68 610 46½ 2½ 13	Smith M E	113	*1.70	90-17	Furlough1133 Quiet Trail1126 Golden Fortune1127	Inside move,clr late	8
20Sep97-4Bel	fst	7f	:223 :461 1:112 1:24	3↑ⒻAlw 37000N1X	82	2 9 910 85½ 3nk 22	Smith M E	118	8.00	79-21	Nimble Tread1132 Furlough1183 All the Moves1132	Wide move,game	9
29Aug97-9Sar	sf	1 Ⓣ	:23 :46 1:11 1:382	3↑ⒻAlw 39000N1X	64	5 713 712 63¾ 63¾ 711¾	Smith M E	113 b	12.70	67-24	MinglingGlnces1094 OrngJsmin112nk MsClbsh1121½	Wide 2nd trn,no rally	9
13Aug97-4Sar	sly	6½f	:214 :451 1:122 1:193	3↑ⒻMd Sp Wt 34k	73	7 6 78¼ 38½ 21½ 13	Smith M E	118 b	2.15	79-19	Furlough1183 Right Chanel1182 Miss Du Bois1132	Wide move,going away	7
23Jly97-6Sar	fst	7f	:224 :461 1:112 1:24	3↑ⒻMd Sp Wt 34k	56	7 3 64¾ 54 27 214½	Smith M E	116 b	2.60	70-13	A. B. Prospect11614½ Furlough1163 Tasha1161½	Rallied for place	7
28Jun97-4Bel	fst	1 1/16	:23 :462 1:12 1:441	3↑ⒻMd Sp Wt 36k	59	2 13½ 14 2½ 38 315½	Smith M E	114 b	*.65	62-13	Panama Canal1143½ Ruby Crescent11412 Furlough1141¾	Spd for 3/4's,quit	7
13Apr97-2Aqu	sly	1	:224 :46 1:104 1:362	ⒻMd Sp Wt 33k	78	1 22½ 21 1hd 2hd 2¾	Velazquez J R	119	*1.25	87-12	PnyWoods119¾ Furlogh1197½ EndrngChng119nk	Spd bwtn,stayed gamely	7
16Mar97-1GP	fst	6f	:223 :46 :584 1:12	ⒻMd Sp Wt 29k	64	7 5 4¾ 33½ 35 37¼	Balley J D	120	*.40	73-16	Green Light1205 Fusaichi Grace1202¼ Furlough1201	Close up, gave way	9
23Feb97-4GP	fst	7f	:223 :454 1:103 1:233	ⒻMd Sp Wt 28k	68	5 7 72¼ 52¼ 22 22¼	Smith M E	120	*.70	84-11	Hasta1202¼ Furlough1201¾ Mint Leaf120nk	Poor start, rallied	11

Furlough (although not consecutively) rattled off wins in the MSWT, ALWN1X, ALWN2X, ALWN3X, ALWN$Y, Grade III, Grade II, and Grade I class levels in order! Note that any bettors who waited for her to win her maiden race avoided six losing starts at favored odds. After clearing preliminary "non-winners-of" allowance levels, she continued to improve and climb the class ladder, and each win rewarded her followers with scores at 6-1 or better!

Another All-Star example is Newfoundland. Bred to be royalty, Newfoundland brought $3.3 million at auction. He was trained by Aidan O'Brien, one of Europe's most recognized trainers, yet was unable to hit the board following his maiden win. He was shipped to North America and was stabled with another top outfit, Todd Pletcher.

Newfoundland proceeded to win 6 of 18 North American starts, and never went off as a post time favorite! Never! Back to back allowance wins didn't sway the public. Neither did back to back Grade 3 wins.

Newfoundland
Own: Sumaya Us Stables

Ch. h. 5 (Feb)
Sire: Storm Cat (Storm Bird) $500,000
Dam: Clear Mandate (Deputy Minister)
Br: G. Watts Humphrey (Ky)
Tr: Pletcher Todd A

Life	22	7	3	2	$677,534	111	D.Fst	14	4	3	2	$569,670 111
2004	9	2	3	1	$523,750	111	Wet(429)	3	2	0	0	$90,954 100
2003	9	4	0	1	$137,234	98	Turf(346)	5	1	0	0	$16,910 73

30Oct04-9LS	fst 1¼	:47 1:111 1:351 1:59	3↑BCClasic-G1	98	10 41½ 31½ 117 1212 1217½	Coa E M	L126b	38.80	- -	Ghostzapper1263 RosesinMay1264 PleasantlyPerfect126¾	Wide trip, tired	13
2Oct04-10Bel	fst 1¼	:473 1:113 1:362 2:022	3↑JkyClbGC-G1	111	6 3½ 2hd 1½ 1½ 2¾	Prado E S	L126fb	20.30	84-13	FunnyCide126¾ Nwfoundlnd1261 ThCliffsEdg1223¾	Drifted stretch, game	7
11Sep04-10Bel	fst 1⅛	:453 1:083 1:331 1:461	3↑Woodward-G1	83	4 53½ 52½ 59½ 514 518¼	Velazquez J R	L126b	6.10	82-15	Ghostzapper126nk Saint Liam1269¼ Bowman's Band1267¼	Wide trip, tired	7
7Aug04-9Sar	fst 1⅛	:451 1:084 1:344 1:482	3↑WhitneyH-G1	98	9 75½ 63 99 89¾ 79¾	Velazquez J R	L114b	5.60	83-14	RosesinMy114no PrfctDrift1172¼ BowmnsBnd114no	Wide both turns, tired	9
3Jly04-7Bel	fst 1¼	:461 1:091 1:334 1:592	3↑SuburbnH-G1	111	2 21 3½ 31 3½ 2nk	Velazquez J R	L114b	8.40	100 -	PeceRules120nk Newfoundlnd114no FunnyCide117¾	Speed 3 wide, gamely	8
12Jun04-7Bel	fst 1⅛	:451 1:082 1:332 1:461	3↑BroklynH-G2	107	2 4¾ 2hd 2½ 33 33¼	Velazquez J R	L115b	3.25	97-03	Seattle Fitz116½ Dynever1172¾ Newfoundland1155¾	Vied inside, tired	6
3Apr04-9GP	fst 1¼	:472 1:112 1:362 2:024	3↑GPH-G2	104	3 22 22½ 21½ 32½ 22	Chavez J F	L116b	1.90	98-15	Jackpot1132 Newfoundland1161 TheLdysGroom1131¾	Stalked, outfinished	6
13Mar04-13GP	fst 1 1/16	:24 :481 1:12 1:431	3↑SkipAwyH-G3	105	6 42 31½ 3½ 11 1½	Velazquez J R	L116b	6.00	93-15	Newfoundland116½ SupahBlitz1142¼ BowmansBnd1174¼	3 wide, prevailed	10
31Jan04-8GP	sly 1 1/16 ⊗	:233 :471 1:114 1:444	3↑CanTurfH-G3	100	4 52¾ 41½ 2½ 21 1nk	Velazquez J R	L115b	2.70	85-29	Nwfondlnd115nk MllnnmDrgon1188½ EvrythngtoGn1135¼	Hit gate, just up	6
29Oct03-8Aqu	my 1⅛	:47 1:112 1:372 1:51	DiscvryH-G3	96	4 65½ 64 75¼ 69 56¼	Velazquez J R	L117b	3.75	75-27	During120no UnforgettableMax1141¾ Inamorato1144¼	Inside, no response	8
9Oct03-6Bel	fst 1	:243 :464 1:103 1:36	[R]CornadoQst65k	98	4 3½ 3nk 2hd 1½ 11¼	Velazquez J R	L122b	3.10	86-12	Newfoundland1221¼ Conservation119½ Qais1191¼	Between rivals, clear	5
12Sep03-8Bel	fst 1 1/16	:232 :462 1:101 1:413	3↑Alw 52000n3x	98	3 2hd 2½ 2hd 11½ 12¾	Bailey J D	L120b	4.70	92-21	Newfoundland1202¾ Private City1162¼ Blue Boat1235¼	Pressed pace, clear	5
9Aug03-8Sar	fst 1⅛	:481 1:122 1:37 1:492	3↑Alw 50000n2x	95	8 41 31½ 3½ 2½ 2nk	Velazquez J R	L115b	8.00	88-12	[D]ThompsonRog119nk Nwfondlnd1151½ Anshd1194	Game outside, brushed	8
Placed first through disqualification												
12Jly03-9Mth	fst 1 1/16	:234 :48 1:113 1:432	LBrnchBC-G3	78	1 53 51¾ 51¾ 66¾ 612	Lopez C C	L112b	3.20	82-11	MxForvr113hd ChrstnsOtlw1152¼ ChllyRoostr112hd	Out in strip, flattened	6
14Jun03-5Bel	gd 1 1/16 ⊗	:24 :473 1:114 1:431	3↑Alw 46000n1x	92	7 3½ 3½ 2hd 2hd 1nk	Velazquez J R	L114b	5.10	84-19	Nwfoundlnd114nk Snortr1165¼ MllnnumGhost1146¼	Determinedly outside	7
29May03-6Bel	fst 1 1/16	:221 :443 1:091 1:423	3↑Alw 46000n1x	79	4 62½ 41 75½ 513 35	Velazquez J R	L115b	8.80	82-20	ChillyRooster1052½ Prhelion1152½ Nwfoundlnd1153¼	Bumped backstretch	8
9Mar03-11GP	fm 1 1/16 ①	:234 :474 1:114 1:414	+ Alw 36000n1x	73	10 83 87¼ 85½ 77¼ 55¾	Velazquez J R	L118	2.60	80-10	Remind1222¾ Coalition1181¼ Regal Bear118½	Failed to menace	10
15Feb03-5GP	fst 6f	:22 :45 :572 1:101	Alw 36000n1x	68	5 8 86 54¾ 68½ 69½	Velazquez J R	L118	3.10	83-08	Massive1181 Letters1181¾ Tactical Delight1224	Poor start, 4 wide	8
Previously trained by Aidan O'Brien												
28Sep02♦Ascot (GB) Timeform rating: 89	gf 1 ①RH	1:421	Royal Lodge Stakes-G2 Stk 187000		89¼	Smullen P J	123	16.00		Al Jadeed123hd Bahamian Dancer1231½ Van Nistelrooy1262½	*Slowly away, towards rear throughout. Puma 7th*	9
31Jly02♦Goodwood (GB) Timeform rating: 100	gd 7f ①RH	1:272	Vintage Stakes-G3 Stk 78200		53	Kinane M J	123	12.00		Dublin1231¼ Bourbonnais123½ Sarayat123½	*Rank, bumped wide after 1f, finished well without threatening*	10
30Jun02♦Curragh (Ire) Timeform rating: 100	yl 6f ①Str	1:17	Railway Stakes-G3 Stk 99000		43¼	Scallan P J	122	10.00		Hold That Tiger122nk Pakhoes1221 Luminata1192	*Led to 1-1/2f out, weakened*	4
29May02♦Fairyhouse (Ire) Timeform rating: 78+	sf 6f ①RH	1:183	Ratoath EBF Maiden Maiden 16800		1hd	Kinane M J	128	*.40		Newfoundland128hd Penalty Clause1281½ Mejhar128nk	*Tracked in 5th, dueled 1f out, led near line*	12

WORKS: Oct24 Bel tr.t 5f fst 1:004 B *3/30* Oct17 Bel 5f fst 1:022 B *14/20*

Despite losing his final 7 starts, he delivered a healthy profit to anyone faithful enough to follow him. Did the $3.3 million price tag label him as an underachiever for failing to win championship events? Perhaps, but it's hard to believe a well-bred successful campaigner could be ignored at the window 18 times in a row!

Claiming horses are good All-Stars when they remain at or around a given price for multiple seasons. A horse that can win 12 of 40 starts at non-favored odds can consistently yield profitable wins. Some horses can even manage to do much more than that, like Onnagata.

Onnagata raced from 1985 through 1994. By the end of his 4-year-old season, Onnagata had raced 40 times with 8 victories. Most horses would be done with their careers at that point, but Onnagata was just getting started.

At age 6, he returned from an 18-month layoff to resume his career. Onnagata would go on to make 135 more starts and win 19 more times. His 1991 record as an 8-year-old is shown below. He made 30 starts and amassed 7 wins, never as the favorite. That's a lot of running, and a lot of cashed tickets.

Onnagata
Own: Miller James A

Ch. g. 22 (Mar)
Sire: Wajima (Bold Ruler)
Dam: Saturday Matinee (Silent Screen)
Br: Stephen A. DiMauro (Ky)
Tr: McMichael Nancy C

Life	175	27	28	22	$465,624	107	D.Fst	54	10	7	7	$117,631 107
1994	11	1	2	2	$2,735	58	Wet(285)	19	1	2	2	$3,268 60
1993	19	2	2	4	$6,897	79	Turf(244)	1	0	0	0	$25 19

Date/Race	Cond	Dist	Fractions	Race	Spd	PP	Running line	Jockey	Wt	Odds	Pace	Top finishers	Comment/Field
27Dec91-3Aqu	fst	1⅛ ⊡	:474 1:134 1:404 1:543	3↑ Clm 15500	–	1	68 56½ 44 33½ 21¼	Madrid A Jr	115 b	6.40	- -	Space Above1171¼ Onnagata1151¾ Dressed Shipper114no	Gamely 8
18Dec91-6Aqu	fst	1⅛ ⊡	:471 1:123 1:392 1:522	3↑ Clm 20000	–	5	94¾ 810 77½ 77½ 720¼	Madrid A Jr	113 b	*1.00e	- -	Beyond Tomorrow1134 Roman Cat1175¼ Iroquois Drive1173	no rally 9
11Dec91-2Aqu	fst	1 1/16 ⊡	:234 :474 1:114 1:44	3↑ Clm 15500	–	4	53 53 41 3½ 1nk	Madrid A Jr	113 b	6.70	- -	Onnagata113nk Space Above119nk Charming Buck110hd	up in final strides 7
5Dec91-3Aqu	fst	1 1/16 ⊡	:24 :482 1:133 1:464	3↑ Clm 14000	–	6	53½ 55½ 44 47 25¾	Madrid A Jr	117 b	4.30	- -	Matt's Schtick1175¾ Onnagata117½ Irish Diplomacy1152½	Rallied 8
22Nov91-1Aqu	sly	1⅛	:471 1:12 1:374 1:513	3↑ Clm 17500	–	6	811 812 78 710 713¾	Chavez J F	117 b	9.20	- -	A. M. Swinger1177 Willy Day117¾ Matt's Schtick1171½	failed to menace 8
7Nov91-9Aqu	fst	1	:23 :463 1:114 1:372	3↑ Clm 17500	–	2	62¼ 51¾ 42½ 55½ 610¾	Pezua J M	117 b	5.30	- -	Iroquois Drive117hd Space Above1172 Arctic Beat1174	no rally 10
Previously trained by Monaci David													
31Oct91 2Aqu	fst	1⅛	:483 1:144 1:41 1:542	3↑ Clm 14000	–	1	52¾ 52¼ 1hd 2hd 33¾	Mojica R Jr	117 b	3.10	- -	SaucyTemper1102¾ RooneysChamp1151 Onnagat117no	Dueled, weakened 9
14Oct91-3Bel	fst	1 1/16	:231 :464 1:12 1:44	3↑ Clm 22500	–	8	85¾ 74¾ 85¼ 86¼ 812¼	Bailey J D	115 b	3.10	- -	Roman Cat1191 Gallant Hitter110hd Space Above115nk	Outrun, five-wide 8
Previously trained by Garren Murray M													
28Sep91-1Bel	fst	1 1/16	:24 :474 1:121 1:431	3↑ Clm 17500	–	8	41 42 43 45½ 48	Mojica R Jr5	114 b	*1.50	- -	FlwlessStone1154 DressdShippr1151¼ IrishDiplomcy1152¾	Four-wide, tired 8
14Sep91-2Bel	my	1⅛	:463 1:111 1:36 1:491	3↑ Clm 25000	–	9	65 76½ 78½ 912 719	Mojica R Jr5	117 b	6.60	- -	NotableTsar1102½ HwkingSW1153 PocketStreker11711	Outrun, four-wide 9
2Sep91-3Bel	fst	1 1/16	:234 :471 1:114 1:432	3↑ Clm 20000	–	4	74 83½ 94 2½ 11¾	Mojica R Jr5	110 b	5.80	- -	Onnagata1101¾ Battle Fox117nk Space Above114½	Angled 5w, driving 9
24Aug91-9Sar	fst	1⅛	:47 1:121 1:381 1:512	3↑ Clm 20000	–	11	86¾ 66¼ 32½ 12½ 14	Mojica R Jr5	108 b	6.00	- -	Onnagata1084 Dancing Tricks115½ Scavenger Hunt1172	Rated 5w, driving 11
14Aug91-1Sar	fst	1 3/16	:473 1:114 1:371 1:57	3↑ Clm 22500	–	3	2hd 1hd 13 23 36½	Vasquez M O	115 b	5.80	- -	Hawking S. W.1176½ Sayaret117no Onnagata115¾	Inside speed, wknd 8
21Jly91-2Bel	fst	1⅛	:472 1:112 1:371 1:504	4↑ Clm 17500	–	4	21 1hd 13 14 12	Vasquez M O5	112 b	3.90	- -	Onnagata1122 Shooting Up1172¼ Lusty Leader1126	Rail, drew off, drvng 8
10Jly91-1Bel	fst	1 1/16	:232 :464 1:113 1:444	4↑ Clm 16500	–	6	53½ 64 51¾ 51¼ 2no	Vasquez M O5	110 b	5.40	- -	Bowdoin Street117no Onnagata1101¾ Hawking S. W.1173¼	4w, lost head bob 8
4Jly91-2Bel	fst	1 1/16	:232 :463 1:103 1:432	4↑ Clm 14000	–	5	53¾ 1hd 12 13½ 13	Vasquez M O5	114 b	4.10	- -	Onnagata1143 Dancing Tricks1172 Freezer Burn113nk	Rail, clear ld, drvng 11
19Jun91-1Bel	wf	1⅛	:462 1:104 1:351 1:474	4↑ Clm 17500	–	5	810 812 716 717 731	Smith M E	119 b	5.20	- -	Notable Tsar1133 Bowdoin Street117½ Shooting Up117½	Always far back 8
7Jun91-1Bel	fst	1 1/16	:232 :462 1:11 1:43	4↑ Clm 17500	–	3	31 41½ 11 12½ 1½	Smith M E	117 b	9.60	- -	Onnagata117½ Lusty Leader1172¼ Shooting Up1171¾	Circled, driving 9
31May91-2Bel	fst	1 1/16	:23 :453 1:10 1:42	4↑ Clm 22500	–	4	75¾ 77¾ 76½ 1011 1017½	Velazquez J R	115 b	16.30	- -	Space Above115nk Proud Cat1173 Sayaret1171½	Saved ground, no bid 10
18Apr91-5Aqu	gd	1	:224 :462 1:121 1:382	4↑ Clm 22500	–	4	710 711 77½ 714 717½	Madrid A Jr	115 b	7.60	- -	MountinGhost112¾ ThreeChoptRod117¾ BowdoinStret117¾	Always far back 7
4Apr91-5Aqu	fst	1⅛	:472 1:112 1:38 1:513	4↑ Clm 45000	–	1	67½ 711 710 610 614¼	Krone J A	113 b	10.50	- -	Advancing Ensign1176 Golden Vigor113hd A. M.Swinger1133	Wide, outrun 7
22Mar91-5Aqu	fst	1	:233 :463 1:111 1:363	4↑ Clm 35000	–	2	52½ 42½ 41½ 53¾ 66½	Madrid A Jr	113 b	14.50	- -	A. M. Swinger1172½ Wind Chill1172 DH Johnny Ross115	Well placed, no bid 8
13Mar91-6Aqu	fst	1	:223 :451 1:094 1:363	4↑ Clm 45000	–	6	912 916 714 612 69¾	Madrid A Jr	113 b	15.90	- -	Greek God1152 Mottly Moseley1104½ Roman Cat113nk	No factor 9
1Mar91-6Aqu	fst	1 1/16	:233 :464 1:104 1:434	4↑ Clm 30000(35-30)	–	6	67¼ 65¼ 45½ 43 35½	Chavez J F	115 b	5.50	- -	Johnny Ross1151 A. M. Swinger1174½ Onnagata115nk	Five wide bid, hung 6
18Feb91-3Aqu	fst	1⅛	:473 1:13 1:401 1:53	4↑ Clm 30000(35-30)	–	2	67¾ 69½ 62¾ 2hd 11½	Madrid A Jr	113 b	9.30	- -	Onnagata1131½ Turning ForHome1083 Banker'sJet1081	Inside, angled out 7
8Feb91-5Aqu	fst	170	:234 :474 1:123 1:414	4↑ Clm 30000(35-30)	–	2	68 52½ 31½ 47½ 414¼	Cordero A Jr	113 b	6.80	- -	Calhoun1155 Carotic108nk Banker's Jet1089	Rushed up, no rally 6
3Feb91-1Aqu	fst	6f	:223 :461 1:111	4↑ Clm 30000(35-30)	–	7	3 75 76¾ 77 75½	Samyn J L	113 b	15.40	- -	Night Thunder1172 Postal Strike115¾ Rodeo Spurs1171	Outrun 7
23Jan91-3Aqu	fst	6f	:212 :44 1:084	4↑ Clm 30000	–	10	1 107¾ 911 811 69½	Sellers S J	113 b	17.90	- -	Dandy Cut1193¼ Night Thunder1143½ Postal Strike115no	Outrun 10
13Jan91-5Aqu	my	1⅛	:471 1:124 1:524	4↑ Alw 33000NC	–	2	53¾ 67½ 66½ 510 514¾	Krone J A	117 fb	7.80	- -	Speedy Gussini119¾ Island Music114no Wild Away1177½	Checked; no rally 6
5Jan91-2Aqu	fst	1⅛ ⊡	:48 1:13 1:524	4↑ Clm 30000	–	9	45½ 42½ 3½ 4nk 51¾	Smith M E	113 b	9.30	- -	Panganur117½ Im New115nk Scavenger Hunt117no	4-wide; bid, hung 9

Another example of consistency in the claiming ranks is the California fan favorite Palmdale. The following excerpt from his long career are his final 30 starts before being retired following an injury:

Palmdale
Own: Anderson R G Jr

B. g. 17 (Apr)
Sire: Dance Bid (Northern Dancer)
Dam: Cuvee (Buckpasser)
Br: Crook Investment Co. (Ky)
Tr: Cerin Vladimir

Life	87	17	16	12	$487,510	100	D.Fst	51	9	11	9	$213,663 100
1996	9	1	2	1	$69,612	96	Wet(255)	4	0	2	0	$10,725 81
1995	16	5	2	0	$149,625	100	Turf(312)	24	6	3	1	$207,087 100

Date/Race	Cond	Dist	Fractions	Race	Spd	PP	Running line	Jockey	Wt	Odds	Pace	Top finishers	Comment/Field
14Sep96-11Fpx	fst	1 1/16	:231 :47 1:12 1:44	3↑ PDShepherd72k	93	1	54½ 53 44 42½ 43	Hunter M T	LB115f	5.50	- -	Oncefortherod1171½ ShrKing117¾ ColerMeSped117¾	No speed, mild rally 5
21Jly96-8Hol	fm	1 1/16 ⓣ	:24 :474 1:11 1:41	4↑ Clm 50000(50-45)	89	5	64½ 63½ 53½ 56 53¼	Almeida G F	LB116f	7.40	- -	Bal Eclat119½ Roo Tale116½ Nucay1162	Finished well inside 8
2Jun96-5Hol	fm	1½ ⓣ	:474 1:123 2:021 2:27	4↑ Alw 62500s	94	8	34½ 32½ 32 53¾ 53¾	Douglas R R	LB114f	12.50	- -	Big Sky Jim1161 Complot114½ Busy Banana1161¾	Contended, weakened 9
11May96-4Hol	fm	1¼ ⓣ	:493 1:132 1:373 2:014	4↑ Alw 62500s	86	7	67½ 69 78 75¾ 64½	Douglas R R	LB115f	9.70	- -	Auvergne115nk Vagamo122no Siebe1153	Showed little 8
27Apr96-5Hol	fm	1⅛ ⓣ	:48 1:12 1:351 1:47	4↑ Clm 80000(80-75)	88	5	42½ 43½ 41½ 33½ 44¾	Stevens G L	LB116f	3.40	- -	Skylaunch1151 Younqui1161 Concordial1112¾	Middle of pack, evenly 7
4Apr96-2SA	fm	1⅛ ⓣ	:49 1:123 1:373 1:502	4↑ Clm 90000(100-85)	94	1	54½ 42 52¼ 52¼ 23½	Stevens G L	LB114f	2.90	- -	AwesomeThought1213½ Plmdl114nk Signortto116¾	Long rally wide for 2d 5
10Mar96-8SA	fm	1⅛ ⓣ	:48 1:122 1:372 1:493	4↑ Clm 62500(62.5-55)	96	5	41½ 23 41½ 11½ 1hd	Stevens G L	LB116f	*2.20	- -	Palmdale116hd L'Hermine1162¼ Auvergne1135	Lead inside,just lastd 9
11Feb96-4SA	fm	1⅛ ⓣ	:474 1:113 1:361 1:483	4↑ Clm 75000(80-70)	94	2	42¼ 41¾ 33 32 31¾	Stevens G L	LB115f	*2.50	- -	Skylaunch1171½ Storiths117nk Palmdale1151¼	Closed willingly wide 8
12Jan96-6SA	fm	1¼ ⓣ	:472 1:123 1:381 2:03	4↑ Clm 62500(62.5-55)	94	10	74½ 72¾ 53¼ 3½ 21¼	Stevens G L	L117f	5.40	- -	Swiss Mirage1171¼ Palmdale1171¼ Dourbadakan1143½	Bid 1/8, 2nd best 10
20Dec95-6Hol	fst	1 1/16	:223 :454 1:093 1:411	3↑ Alw 32000s	77	3	45 33 34½ 48½ 411¾	Almeida G F	L119f	2.50	- -	Geenger Man117hd R Friar Tuck110¾ La Taj11511	Middle move, gave way 5
3Dec95-5Hol	fm	1 1/16 ⓣ	:224 :46 1:094 1:403	3↑ Alw 40000s	86	1	54 54 42¼ 61½ 73½	Almeida G F	L119f	3.20	- -	Fawlty Towers116½ Semi Maar1162 Pricelessly116no	Blocked str 11
9Nov95-8SA	fm	1 ⓣ	:23 :471 1:12 1:361	3↑ Alw 49000c	92	5	53½ 54 63¼ 54½ 22½	Almeida G F	L116f	10.30	- -	Lynton1162½ Palmdale116nk Swank116nk	Dropped back,rallied 9
1Oct95-7Fpx	fst	1⅜	:493 1:152 1:41 2:181	3↑ Hcp 25000s	93	5	52 51¾ 41 2hd 1nk	Almeida G F	LB120f	*.80	- -	Palmdale120nk Welcome Day1162 JudgementMaker1193	Rallied 3-w,all out 6
14Sep95-8Fpx	fst	*1⅛	:472 1:123 1:374 1:504	3↑ Alw 12500s	98	5	51¼ 41¼ 3½ 16 17½	Almeida G F	L113f	*2.10	- -	Palmdale1137½ Truly a Pleasure1211½ Jaltipan1082	Quick gain,much best 8
13Aug95-5Dmr	fm	1 1/16 ⓣ	:242 :48 1:113 1:414	3↑ Clm 70000	74	6	64 57 67½ 610 612¼	McCarron C J	L114f	7.70	- -	Tychonic1174½ Dourbadakan1171½ Turkish Blazor117½	Showed little 8
21Jly95-8Hol	fm	1⅛ ⓣ	:473 1:112 1:361 1:49	3↑ Alw 16000s	84	4	41½ 62¼ 63¼ 63 53	Valenzuela F H	LB119f	*.50	- -	Ofuscador119nk Moondust1191 Known Lover1151¼	Settled, empty 8
9Jly95-1Hol	fm	1 ⓣ	:224 :451 1:09 1:342	4↑ Clm 80000	93	4	46½ 59 611 65½ 33	Valenzuela F H	LB119f	4.10	- -	Duplicity1162 Kingdom of Spain1161 DQ Palmdale119½	Late rally wide 6
Disqualified and placed 6th													
21Jun95-3Hol	fm	1⅛ ⓣ	:472 1:112 1:354 1:483	4↑ Clm 80000	100	4	53½ 53 52¾ 42½ 1¾	Valenzuela F H	L116f	6.30	- -	DQ Palmdale116¾ Duplicity1152¾ Campanology116nk	Strong rally wide 5
Disqualified and placed 5th													
29May95-7Hol	fm	1 1/16 ⓣ	:23 :463 1:102 1:404	4↑ Clm 80000	89	3	31½ 42 52 63½ 74½	Valenzuela F H	L116f	4.70	- -	Turkish Blazor1162 Ocean Orbit116hd Siebe116½	Contended, faded 11
10May95-8Hol	fm	1 ⓣ	:231 :46 1:094 1:334	4↑ Alw 54000c	88	8	22 24 42½ 63 85½	Valenzuela F H	L117f	4.40	- -	Sharman1152 Geenger Man116½ Saltgrass1151	Contended, faded 8
22Apr95-3SA	fst	1	:24 :48 1:12 1:36	4↑ Alw 57000c	95	3	32 31½ 31 21 21	Valenzuela P A	L117f	2.60	- -	Straight to Bed1151 Palmdale1172½ Duc d'Sligovil115¾	Bid 1/8, 2nd best 5
23Mar95-2SA	fst	1⅛	:481 1:124 1:37 1:493	4↑ Alw 48750c	88	1	2hd 2½ 1hd 11 12¾	Valenzuela F H	L116f	*.40	- -	Palmdale1162¾ Garrick1163½ Hot Number116nk	Dueled in hand,driving 4
2Mar95-1SA	gd	1⅛ ⓣ	:49 1:141 1:40 1:531	4↑ Clm 90000	100	4	33½ 31½ 31½ 2hd 12	Valenzuela F H	L117f	2.70	- -	Palmdale1172 DQ Cocooning1131 Service Ace1152¾	Drew clear, driving 6
11Feb95-2SA	fm	1 ⓣ	:233 :471 1:112 1:364	4↑ Clm 75000	100	1	44 54½ 44 3½ 11¾	Nakatani C S	L115f	*1.90	- -	Plmdle1151¾ ShrpWords114½ Plesedontexplin1173½	Strong finish,rddn out 8
26Jan95-6SA	gd	1⅛	:451 1:101 1:361 1:491	4↑ Clm 80000	81	3	44¾ 45½ 46 46 49¾	Nakatani C S	LB116f	3.20	- -	Bucking Bird1162 Cocooning1121¾ River Rhythm1166	No rally 7
21Dec94-8Hol	fm	1 1/16 ⓣ	:233 :472 1:12 1:431	3↑ Clm 75000	99	9	42 43½ 41½ 2hd 1hd	Valenzuela F H	L117f	3.70	- -	Palmdale117hd Fanatic Boy116hd Varadavour117¾	Wore down rivals 10
1Dec94-8Hol	fm	1 1/16 ⓣ	:231 :464 1:111 1:414	3↑ Clm 75000	94	10	63 73½ 64½ 53 41½	Valenzuela F H	L117f	3.70	- -	Service Ace114½ The Informer119nk Tychonic116½	Strong rally inside 10
11Nov94-8Hol	gd	1 1/16 ⓣ	:24 :483 1:133 1:454	3↑ Clm 75000	99	1	1½ 21 32 1hd 12	Valenzuela F H	L114f	12.70	- -	Palmdale1142 Sorrienkal115hd Fernandazo117¾	Drew clear, gamely 8
10Oct94-9SA	fst	1 1/16	:231 :464 1:11 1:421	3↑ Clm 35000	94	10	52½ 52¼ 3½ 2½ 1no	Valenzuela F H	LB114f	13.70	- -	Palmdale114no Miniffirm116hd Goldgusher1172	Wore down rivals 11
15Sep94-7Fpx	fst	1 1/16	:232 :472 1:121 1:441	3↑ Clm c-25000	89	1	1½ 1hd 2hd 2½ 2½	Flores D R	LB116f	*.80	- -	ImperilRidge116½ Plmdle1152½ MgnificentRd1161½	Outfinished,long drive 6

Claimed from Pacifica West for $25,000, Spawr Bill Trainer 1994(as of 9/15): (-)

Palmdale raced in class levels as high as graded stakes, and as low as $10,000 Claiming. When claimed for $25,000 by Vladimir Cerin, the 6-year-old rattled off 9 wins in 30 starts as he climbed back up the class ladder, even winning at the $100,000 level.

Likewise, a stakes horse that maintains form like North East Bound can yield numerous winning bets. I was hooked as a North East Bound fan when he dead-heated for a win at 49-1. Sharing the purse with a co-winner kept it from being the score of a lifetime, but *that* score came just two starts later as he rocked the tote board again at over 40-1! Despite all his success, his most recent three graded stakes wins all paid double digits.

North East Bound
Own: Demarco Julian and Disano, Richard J

Dk. b or b. g. 9 (Apr)
Sire: D'Accord (Secretariat)
Dam: North East Dancer (Far North)
Br: Scott E. Ricker, Julian Demarco, & Richard J. Disano (Ky)
Tr: Perry William W

Life	50	12	7	3	$1,363,228	108	
2004	5	0	0	1	$6,080	91	
2003	6	0	1	0	$10,440	95	
D.Fst	9	2	1	0	$279,165	106	
Wet(315)	5	2	0	0	$151,320	102	
Turf(255)	36	8	6	3	$932,743	108	

5Sep04-10Mth fm	1	Ⓣ:241 :474 1:114 1:364	3↑BobHarding60k	91	1	42½	42½	73½	61½	63¾	VelezJAJr	L115b	18.70	84-17	Stormy Roman115¾ Green Line115¾ Burning Roma1191	No clear path lane	8
22Aug04-6Mth fst	1 1/16	⊗:232 :463 1:113 1:434	3↑OC 65k/n4x	71	3	45½	45½	54½	58½	516¼	Elliott S	L118b	3.90	78-20	GlintSr1209¼ RocknOnRdy1184¾ BruckrsBrothr1172	Outside,gave way turn	5
22Jly04-7Bel fm	1 1/16	Ⓣ:231 :46 1:10 1:411	4↑Clm 50000(50-40)	90	6	2½	1hd	1½	2½	3¾	↓Nigliore R	L120b	15.50	90-11	Morning Watch121¾ To Go120hd [DH]Cap116	Vied outside, stubborn	9
27Jun04-8Mth fm	1 1/16	Ⓣ:223 :452 1:081 1:394	+3↑Alw 53000c	58	2	33	35	37½	69½	717½	VelezJAJr	L117b	13.40	83-05	Kathir1172¾ Spruce Run117nk Stormy Roman1171½	3p,gave way 1/4	7
5Jun04-10Mth gd	5f	Ⓣ:211 :44 :56	3↑WolfHill60k	64	9	4	106½	109¾	109½	1010	King E L Jr	L115fb	15.30	85-05	Rudirudy1151½ Manofglory115hd Blakelock1171	Outside, never factor	10
4Oct03-8Bel fm	1	Ⓣ:24 :471 1:103 1:343	3↑KelsoBCH-G2	95	4	1½	1½	3½	5½	84½	VelezJAJr	L115b	39.25	83-15	Freefourinternet113no ProudMn1141 Rouvres1151½	Vied inside, gave way	10
31Aug03-10Mth fm	1	Ⓣ:233 :464 1:103 1:351	3↑BobHarding50k	95	6	41½	32½	2hd	2hd	2½	Beckner D V	L113b	12.10	92-11	SprucRun113½ NorthEstBound113nk AmrcnFrdom119½	Game bid,held 2nd	10
10Aug03-8Sar sly	1 1/8	⊗:462 1:111 1:364 1:502	4↑Alw 58000c	–	4	2½	33½	727	-	-	VelezJAJr	L118fb	16.90	- 22	Even the Score118no Crafty Shaw1189 Free of Love1181½	Eased stretch	7
22Mar03-3GP fst	7f	:214 :434 1:071 1:202	4↑OC 150k/n$Y-N	39	5	3	32½	45	514	533	VelezJAJr	L116b	20.20	73-02	Lord Abounding1165½ Medal Play1162½ Keats122½	3 wide, faded, eased	5
29Jan03-9GP fm	*1 1/16	Ⓣ:23 :474 1:114 1:43	+4↑Alw 46000c	82	5	3nk	3½	3½	61¾	87¾	Day P	L116b	5.90	81-12	Statement116½ SirBriansSword1162¾ WaltzinStorm116hd	3 wide, gave way	9
4Jan03-10GP gd	1	Ⓣ:232 :472 1:121 1:374	3↑AppletnH-G2	72	7	21½	21½	22	89½	913	VelezJAJr	L116	8.00	64-29	Point Prince1151½ Krieger115nk Red Seal1141¾	Prompted pace, tired	9
2Nov02-9Aqu yl	1 1/8	Ⓣ:504 1:154 1:402 1:522	3↑KnkrbkrH-G2	91	3	12	11	1½	2hd	63	VelezJAJr	L117	*2.85	73-23	DwnoftheCondor1142 SerilBride114nk PolishMiner114½	Set pace, faltered	9
6Oct02-6Kee fm	1	Ⓣ:233 :463 1:111 1:352	3↑KeeTurfM-G1	88	6	21	2½	42	54½	67¼	VelezJAJr	L126	25.00	83-13	Lndseer123nk TouchofthBlus126½ BtHollow1263¼	Forwardly between,tire	8
25Sep02-8Med sly	5f	⊗:213 :44 :56	3↑TomEdison100k	72	7	7	76½	77¾	77¾	710	VelezJAJr	L119f	3.80	91-10	Bop121nk Rudirudy1213 Texas Glitter1192½	Mostly widest	7
24Mar02-8FG fm	*1 1/8	Ⓣ:481 1:114 1:361 1:484	4↑ExploBdH-G2	97	10	32	31½	31½	22	63¾	Nigliore R	L117	17.40	96 -	Sarafan116nk Beat Hollow1152¼ Even the Score116nk	Forward 3w, faded	14
23Feb02-11GP gd	1 1/16	⊗:24 :474 1:114 1:44	3↑CanTurfH-G3	102	2	11½	1½	11	12	14¾	VelezJAJr	L116	*1.20	88-17	NorthEastBound1164¾ Capsized1143½ FlyingAvie1121½	Off rail, drew away	4
26Jan02-10GP fm	1 1/16	Ⓣ:24 :484 1:121 1:412	+3↑FtLdrdlH-G3	102	1	21½	21	21	1hd	2nk	VelezJAJr	L117b	3.80	88-14	DlMrShow119nk NrthEstBnd117½ TvSprtsDrctr1124¾	Slim lead, just failed	7
5Jan02-11GP gd	1	Ⓣ:243 :491 1:14 1:392	3↑AppletnH-G2	103	6	2hd	1hd	1hd	1hd	2hd	Day P	L117b	5.40	69-35	Pisces113hd North East Bound1172½ Capsized114½	Vied, clear, failed	10
28Oct01-8Bel fm	1	Ⓣ:241 :47 1:103 1:333	3↑NassauH131k	87	3	2½	3½	2½	42	58	VelezJAJr	L119b	4.60	82-13	Aldebaran1133½ Capsized114nk Tubrok1144½	Between rivals, tired	7
7Oct01-6Kee fm	1	Ⓣ:234 :472 1:12 1:354	3↑KeeTurfM-G2	79	6	1hd	1hd	32½	89½	813¾	VelezJAJr	L126b	7.10	75-15	Hap1261½ Where's Taylor126hd Aly's Alley126¾	Pace,faded,far turn	9
26Aug01-10Mth fst	1 1/8	:473 1:11 1:362 1:492	3↑PlselinH-G2	92	4	1½	1hd	2hd	35	49¾	VelezJAJr	L118b	5.20	79-19	Broken Vow1192 First Lieutenant1157 Sir Bear117¾	Steadied briefly 3/16	5
5Aug01-10Mth fm	1 1/16	Ⓣ:23 :463 1:10 1:401	+3↑OcenprtH-G3	100	5	4¾	42½	41½	21	2½	VelezJAJr	L121b	*1.00	95-07	Key Lory111½ North East Bound121½ Crash Course115¾	Couldn't get past	13
1Jly01-10Mth fm	1 3/8	Ⓣ:481 1:14 1:374 2:132	3↑UntdNtnH-G1	97	1	1½	11	1½	2hd	44¼	VelezJAJr	L117b	3.80	96-09	[D]With Anticipation113hd Senure1163 Gritty Sandie1121½	Pace,game to 1/8	8
19May01-9Pim fm	1 1/8	Ⓣ:482 1:124 1:37 1:482	3↑Dixie-G2	92	3	1hd	11½	11	21	64	VelezJAJr	L124b	2.40	92-11	Hap1191½ MakeNoMistake1191½ CynicsBeware119hd	Rail, pace,surrendered	8
13Apr01-8Kee fm	1	Ⓣ:232 :462 1:102 1:342	4↑MakrsMrk-G2	108	4	21½	21½	2½	1hd	1nk	VelezJAJr	L120b	5.90	96-03	NorthEstBound120nk Brhms1231½ StrtegicMission116no	Drift out late,drvg	8
3Feb01-11GP fst	1 1/8	:464 1:11 1:36 1:484	3↑DonnH-G1	44	7	1hd	1hd	21½	614	743¾	VelezJAJr	L116b	6.90	49-13	Captain Steve1201½ Albert the Great11910½ Gander1151½	Outside, faded	7
4Nov00-5CD fm	1	Ⓣ:234 :474 1:112 1:343	3↑BCMile-G1	107	14	11½	11	11	1hd	2nk	VelezJAJr	L126b	42.30	102 -	War Chant123nk North East Bound126no Dansili126no	Yielded grudgingly	14
7Oct00-9Med fst	1 1/8	:452 1:092 1:351 1:484	3↑MedCupH-G2	106	9	31½	3nk	1hd	13	13½	VelezJAJr	L116b	10.40	83-12	NorthEastBound1163½ LordSterling115nk WheresTylor113¾	Steady urging	10
22Sep00-9Med fm	1 1/16	Ⓣ:233 :474 1:112 1:413	3↑ClfHngrH-G3	104	2	2½	2½	2½	1½	12¾	VelezJAJr	L118b	4.90	89-16	NorthEastBound1182¾ JohnnyDollar114¾ Swmp120½	Clear,steady pressure	11
26Aug00-7Sar fm	1 1/16	Ⓣ:24 :472 1:103 1:401	3↑4strdavH-G2	98	5	1½	1½	1hd	2½	44¾	VelezJAJr	L116b	34.75	90-08	Hap118¾ Altibr1152¾ Weatherbird1121½	Vied inside, tired	11
6Aug00-8Mth gd	1 1/8	Ⓣ:513 1:153 1:393 1:52	3↑BatUfield70k	98	2	11½	12½	11	11½	11½	VelezJAJr	L119b	*2.00	74-27	NorthEstBound1191½ ElMrsol119¾ ColonlBrdly115hd	Kept clear & to task	10
15Jly00-9Mth sly	1 1/16	⊗:234 :471 1:112 1:443	3↑OcenprtH-G3	98	4	1hd	1½	12	13	13½	VelezJAJr	L114b	4.20	78-21	North East Bound1143½ Rize1125¾ Selective114nk	Set pace, driving	6
29May00-9Mth fm	1	Ⓣ:232 :463 1:10 1:344	3↑RedBankH-G3	95	1	42½	31½	21½	42	74½	VelezJAJr	L116b	6.00	91-09	Mi Narrow1141½ Deep Gold114no Inkatha117no	In close inside 1/8	9
7May00-9Pim fm	1	Ⓣ:223 :451 1:084 1:332	3↑CEckmnMile40k	98	9	57	54	44½	31	1nk	VelezJAJr	L115b	3.30	104-01	NorthEstBnd115nk ByngRn1151¾ DylghtSvngs115no	Swung out 1/4,drivng	12
7Nov99-9GP fm	1	Ⓣ:224 :463 1:101 1:34	Steinlen200k	84	1	21½	21	21	72	87	VelezJAJr	L119b	4.00	- -	Beckon the King1121½ Hap1141 Super Red1161½	Stalked, tired	11
2Oct99-8Cnl fm	1 1/4	Ⓣ:484 1:112 1:351 1:594	VrgniaDrby200k	97	3	1hd	1hd	1hd	1hd	32	VelezJAJr	L119b	4.40	100 -	PhiBetDoc1171½ Pssinetti115½ NorthEstBound1193¾	Pace 2w, grudgingly	13
29Aug99-10Mth gd	1 1/8	Ⓣ:484 1:131 1:381 1:51	Choice60k	99	6	21	22	1½	13½	13¾	VelezJAJr	L122b	*1.90	81-22	NorthEastBound1223½ ImaginrySword1222½ CndysDevil115¾	In hand late	11
25Jly99-6Del fm	1 1/8	Ⓣ:492 1:124 1:382 1:514	KentBC-G3	96	2	11	1½	1hd	1½	1nk	VelezJAJr	L114b	22.50	81-18	North East Bound114nk Courtside113no Swamp1191	Came out all out	8
3Jly99-9Mth sf	1 1/16	Ⓣ:243 :482 1:123 1:45	LamplghtrH75k	86	1	2½	1½	1½	1hd	35	VelezJAJr	L116b	6.60	71-24	Phi Beta Doc1164½ Green Fee111½ North East Bound116hd	Led, tired	7
13Jun99-8Mth fm	1	Ⓣ:222 :451 1:092 1:344	SpendABuck45k	87	4	21½	21½	21	1½	22¼	VelezJAJr	L119b	3.60	98-02	Crash Course1172¼ North EastBound119hd Draupner1142¼	Led, held place	6
2Apr99-6Kee fm	1	Ⓣ:22 :452 1:102 1:35	Transylvna113k	63	1	11½	11½	21	86	814½	VelezJAJr	L114b	6.00	82-03	Good Night1141½ Air Rocket114½ Make Your Mark1142	Pace, tired	10
5Mar99-10GP fm	*1	Ⓣ:232 :471 1:104 1:352	TheVid54k	93	4	12	11½	1hd	11½	12¾	VelezJAJr	L115b	41.80	92-08	North East Bound1152¾ Wertz1221½ Belasco115½	Inside, proved best	10
15Feb99-10GP fm	1 1/8	Ⓣ:464 1:111 1:36 1:481	PalmBch-G3	76	10	33½	33	32	34	99½	VelezJAJr	L114b	94.50	82-14	Swamp1142 Marquette1141½ Valid Reprized115½	Chased pace, faded	12
23Jan99-3GP fm	1 1/16	Ⓣ:24 :481 1:121 1:424	+ Alw 32000n2L	87	10	11½	13	12	1hd	11½	↓VelezJAJr	L120b	49.50	85-11	[DH]North East Bound120 [DH]Monkey Puzzle1201½ PressType1172½	Gamely	12
3Jan99-3GP sly	1 1/16	⊗:231 :47 1:124 1:473	Alw 32000n1x	5	8	42	43½	99¾	924	1044	VelezJAJr	L117fb	44.50	23-27	Gorjeador1173½ Poirot1172½ Savoy1172¾	Bmpd st, thru early	10
20Dec98-8Crc fm	1 1/16	Ⓣ:23 :49 1:13 1:44	Alw 18500n1x	72	3	1½	1hd	1hd	2hd	44	VelezJAJr	L117	11.70	75-21	Tornadic117¾ Mr Major1202 Country Joe1201½	Weakened late	10
21Nov98-4Crc fst	7f	:222 :452 1:103 1:25	Alw 18500n1x	43	3	5	32	65	614	618¾	Boulanger G	L120f	17.20	65-16	Deputy Mac1101½ Kelski1201¾ Gorjeador1207¾	No factor, wide	7
27Oct98-6Del fst	1	:244 :50 1:15 1:41	Alw 25600n1x	55	1	11½	11	21	23	29¾	Elliott S	L119	4.50	65-27	Flask1169¾ North EastBound119nk [DH]YaTaHay116	No match, saved place	7
25Sep98-3Med fst	1	:23 :464 1:123 1:391	Md Sp Wt 18k	56	4	1hd	11	1hd	12½	13¾	Elliott S	L118	13.10	84-09	North EastBound1183¾ DoublePunch1182¾ ConnecticutRiver118¾	Driving	9
6Sep98-1Mth fst	5½f	:222 :463 :59 1:062	Md 35000(35-30)	21	5	7	77½	77¾	713	512½	Elliott S	118f	11.10	80-09	Peter Joseph1181 Native Pappa1145½ Sugar Boy1162½	Passed tiring rivals	7

More difficult to gauge are conditioned runners trying to climb through allowance ranks, such as Black Blade.

Black Blade
Own:

Dk. b or b. g. 10 (May)
Sire: Saint Ballado (Halo) $125,000
Dam: Native Nita (Native Charger)
Br: Edward Wiest (Fla)
Tr:

Life	20	8	1	5	$239,819	107	D.Fst	14	7	1	4	$223,409	107
2000	3	0	0	2	$4,319	–	Wet(343)	3	1	0	0	$13,640	76
1998	15	7	1	3	$226,900	107	Turf(279)	3	0	0	1	$2,770	85

28Nov98-9Lrl	fst	$1\frac{1}{8}$	:47 1:11^{1} 1:35^{4} 1:48^{1}	Annapolis100k	103	2	2^{1}	2^{hd}	2^{hd}	1^{5}	$1^{8\frac{3}{4}}$	Winnett B G Jr	L117 fb	2.50	97-10	Black Blade117$^{8\frac{3}{4}}$ P Day122$\frac{1}{2}$ Scatmandu122^{5}	3wd bkstr,drw off,drvg	6
31Oct98-7Del	fst	$1\frac{3}{16}$	:50 1:15 1:40 1:57^{4} 3↑	Kelso50k	107	6	1^{1}	1^{3}	$1^{1\frac{1}{2}}$	1^{4}	1^{6}	Winnett B G Jr	L113 fb	*1.10	104-11	BlackBlde113^{6} [DH]Testing115 [DH]TrickyMister115$^{14\frac{3}{4}}$	Slow pace, ridden out	6
17Oct98-9Pha	fst	$1\frac{1}{16}$	:23^{2} :46^{3} 1:10^{3} 1:42^{1} 3↑	[R]RHANixonMH43k	104	5	$2^{1\frac{1}{2}}$	2^{1}	1^{hd}	1^{3}	$1^{9\frac{3}{4}}$	Winnett B G Jr	L117 fb	*.60	102-16	Black Blade117$^{9\frac{3}{4}}$ Swiss Asset114$\frac{1}{2}$ Leave It to Beezer114$\frac{1}{2}$	Rated, driving	7
3Oct98-11Cnl	fm	$1\frac{1}{4}$ (T)	:49 1:13^{4} 1:36^{4} 2:00^{1}	VrgniaDrby250k	79	10	3^{1}	$3^{\frac{1}{2}}$	$4^{\frac{3}{4}}$	$7^{6\frac{1}{4}}$	$8^{8\frac{3}{4}}$	Winnett B G Jr	L115 fb	10.50	- -	CrowdPleser117^{3} DistntMirg115^{2} ErrntEscort115^{hd}	5wd 1st,prmptd 3w,tir	10
7Sep98-11Pha	fst	$1\frac{1}{8}$	:47 1:10^{3} 1:35 1:47^{3}	PaDerby-G3	106	8	$11^{5\frac{3}{4}}$	$11^{6\frac{1}{2}}$	6^{5}	4^{4}	$3^{2\frac{1}{2}}$	Winnett B G Jr	L119 fb	10.40	99-08	Rock and Roll114$^{1\frac{1}{4}}$ Tomorrows Cat114$^{1\frac{1}{4}}$ Black Blade119$^{2\frac{1}{4}}$	Off a step slow	11
22Aug98-9Pha	fst	$1\frac{1}{16}$	:23^{2} :46^{4} 1:10^{4} 1:41^{2}	Warminster42k	101	4	$3^{1\frac{1}{2}}$	$2^{1\frac{1}{2}}$	2^{hd}	1^{1}	$1^{3\frac{1}{2}}$	Winnett B G Jr	L116 fb	*1.40	106-09	Black Blade116$^{3\frac{1}{2}}$ Eastern Daydream113^{3} Gulliver119^{4}	Rated, bid, driving	6
26Jly98-9Del	fst	1	:23^{2} :46^{2} 1:11^{1} 1:37 3↑	OC 40k/n4x-N	97	3	$2^{1\frac{1}{2}}$	$2^{1\frac{1}{2}}$	$1^{\frac{1}{2}}$	$1^{1\frac{1}{2}}$	$2^{\frac{3}{4}}$	Winnett B G Jr	L110 fb	6.00	94-07	FentonLane116$^{\frac{3}{4}}$ BlackBlade110^{2} KeytoMnhttn116$^{4\frac{1}{4}}$	Drew clear, hung late	7
13Jly98-8Del	fst	$1\frac{1}{16}$	:23^{1} :46^{2} 1:10^{4} 1:42^{3} 3↑	Alw 31500n3x	100	5	$4^{4\frac{1}{2}}$	4^{8}	$3^{4\frac{1}{2}}$	2^{3}	$1^{1\frac{1}{4}}$	Winnett B G Jr	L110 fb	27.30	100 -	Black Blade110$^{1\frac{1}{4}}$ Forest Lover122$^{7\frac{1}{2}}$ Dance Hall Fred110^{1}	Roused, driving	10
28Jun98-8Del	fm	*$1\frac{1}{16}$ (T)	:24^{1} :47^{4} 1:12^{3} 1:44^{2} 3↑	Alw 31200n3x	81	7	3^{2}	4^{4}	$4^{3\frac{1}{2}}$	$5^{3\frac{1}{2}}$	$5^{4\frac{1}{2}}$	Winnett B G Jr	L111 fb	5.60	81-15	Western Nobility116$^{2\frac{1}{2}}$ Cyber Chat116^{hd} Salt Lake116^{hd}	4 wide, outfinished	9
25May98-8Pha	sly	$1\frac{1}{16}$ ⊗	:22^{4} :46^{2} 1:11^{3} 1:44^{3}	LibrtyBell44k	69	3	3^{2}	3^{3}	$3^{1\frac{1}{2}}$	$2^{\frac{1}{2}}$	5^{3}	Winnett B G Jr	L117 fb	*1.00	87-14	[D]Documento117$\frac{1}{2}$ Sabovee117^{nk} Bushs Boy117^{2}	In tight briefly	8
Placed 4th through disqualification																		
17May98-7Pha	sly	1	:23^{1} :46 1:11 1:37^{3} 3↑	Alw 19800n3L	76	2	$3^{3\frac{1}{2}}$	$3^{2\frac{1}{2}}$	2^{hd}	1^{1}	$1^{2\frac{1}{4}}$	Winnett B G Jr	L110 fb	*2.20	90-17	Black Blade110$^{2\frac{1}{4}}$ Documento109$^{5\frac{1}{4}}$ Largo115$^{1\frac{1}{4}}$	3 wide, drew clear	8
24Apr98-10Hia	fm	*$1\frac{1}{16}$ (T)	1:41^{3} 3↑	Alw 17000n2x	85	10	5^{6}	5^{3}	$3^{2\frac{1}{2}}$	2^{hd}	3^{nk}	Winnett B G Jr	L111 fb	15.90	87-17	Archange120^{nk} Warwhatisitgoodfor120^{hd} BlackBlde111^{nk}	Rallied, gamely	10
3Apr98-9Hia	fst	$1\frac{1}{16}$	:23^{4} :47^{2} 1:13 1:48^{2}	Alw 19900n1x	63	7	$7^{6\frac{3}{4}}$	4^{5}	$3^{1\frac{1}{2}}$	2^{hd}	1^{nk}	Winnett B G Jr	L116 fb	3.40	69-30	BlackBlade116^{nk} TwicesBig116$^{1\frac{1}{2}}$ IrishTerror109$^{9\frac{3}{4}}$	Bump stretch,just last	7
14Mar98-9GP	fst	7f	:22^{2} :45^{2} 1:11^{3} 1:24^{3}	Alw 33000n2L	64	2	11	10^{4}	$6^{4\frac{1}{2}}$	$5^{4\frac{1}{2}}$	$6^{8\frac{3}{4}}$	Bravo J	L120 fb	39.50	68-18	RubyLover120^{1} ArmenianSheikh117$\frac{1}{2}$ Ucnclmel117$^{4\frac{3}{4}}$	Pinched back start	11
28Feb98-4GP	fst	7f	:22^{3} :45^{2} 1:11 1:24^{3}	Alw 31000n2L	64	7	5	$6^{4\frac{1}{4}}$	$6^{6\frac{1}{4}}$	$5^{5\frac{1}{2}}$	$3^{7\frac{1}{2}}$	Bravo J	L120 fb	16.10	69-21	He's Unreal117^{3} Gallapiat's Aussie120$^{4\frac{1}{2}}$ Black Blade120^{nk}	Belatedly	7
Previously trained by Goodman Mary M																		
7Oct97-5Pha	fst	$5\frac{1}{2}$f	:22 :46^{1} :59^{2} 1:06	Md Sp Wt 14k	57	6	8	$6^{7\frac{1}{2}}$	$4^{5\frac{1}{2}}$	$2^{\frac{1}{2}}$	1^{1}	Capanas S	L120 fb	11.60	84-17	Black Blade120^{1} Smiling Dancer120$^{2\frac{1}{2}}$ Pal Joey120^{nk}	Split horses, clear	11
29Sep97-1Del	sly	5f	:22 :46^{3} :59^{4}	Md Sp Wt 24k	40	5	8	$9^{8\frac{1}{4}}$	9^{13}	8^{10}	$6^{9\frac{3}{4}}$	Capanas S	119 fb	8.60	75-15	Write Home119$^{2\frac{1}{2}}$ SpintheStars119$\frac{3}{4}$ SmilingDancer119$\frac{1}{2}$	Failed to menace	12

In his brief career, Black Blade won 8 of 17 starts, but was a longshot only twice. He was a stakes quality runner that plowed his way up the ladder before proving his stakes ability. Each step up the class ladder raises a question of whether or not the winning ways will continue against better and better stock. However, with connections happy to beat lesser runners while grabbing allowance purses, Black Blade was seldom a longshot. Why he ever paid $56.60 following two short-odds attempts will never be understood!

Summary For All-Stars

When making an All-Stars watch list, remember that the ideal kind of horse to follow is one that wins periodically, is badly beaten between wins, and in most cases, consistently competes at the same class level. Latching on to a runner with multiple seasons of frequent winner's circle trips can make for lots of "instant wagers." This practice is not only profitable, but time saving as well.

When It All Goes Right

As 1999 was coming to a close, a year of handicapping had left me slightly in the red. Hundreds of hours of work and nothing to show for it. But in the winter cold, I still had horses I waited to see in the entries. On a sub-zero Saturday afternoon, two of my All-Stars made their way on to the track. With $40 in my pocket I began a final push to salvage 1999.

A 2-year-old MSWT 6f field at Aqueduct with two horses I had been waiting to see appear in the entries . . .

Both horses had a debut race. One, Nostalgic, ran third but with a plus-par pace/par speed debut. The other, Bullfrog, was left at the start, was 20 lengths behind the leader after a 1/4 mile, rushed to within 1 length of the lead at the 3/16 pole, then ran out of juice and tired to last.

A third entrant had run second in the race Nostalgic debuted in. It was that horse's fifth start and the horse ran a belated second. This horse became the crowd's 4/5 favorite. Nostalgic ended up a 5/2 second choice, and Bullfrog left the gate at 35-1! If only this race had a trifecta.

I was live in the daily double with both Bullfrog and Nostalgic, with payoffs of $370.50 and $39.00 respectively. I still preferred Nostalgic, and decided that a win bet on him was in order at 5/2. I would already make a score if Bullfrog won. To try and really take advantage of the situation, I bet $9 more: a $5 quinella Bullfrog/Nostalgic, a $2 exacta Bullfrog over Nostalgic, and a $2 quinella of Bullfrog with the other contender.

Nostalgic broke first, Bullfrog last. Around the far turn, Nostalgic dueled with the 4/5 favorite. Bullfrog regained contact with the field, stayed on the rail, and was making up noticeable ground. In the stretch, Nostalgic drew off from the now weakening favorite, so I knew my win bet and modest double were assured. Bullfrog kept closing, and switching to the outside, he got past the tiring favorite just strides before the wire. The rest of the field was far back.

The payoffs? Win: $7.20. Fair for a plus-par maiden runner. Daily double—$39.00. The quinella paid $140.70, so the $5 quinella returned $351.50. (Note that the $2 exacta paid $176 so the quinella returned well over half the exacta.)

Total wagered: $8 in doubles, $20 win, $7 quinellas, $2 exacta, so a total of $37. Profit $425.50, with a $40 bankroll on me.

I profited another $75 on a few spot plays later in the day, making for a $500 day.

Thursday night, I dropped in to bet a Hollywood 2-year-old MSWT race on the turf. My horse went off at 5-1 and ran a dull fourth behind an impressive debuting offspring of Grade I turf mare Possibly Perfect. Salvaging the day was a silly $4 win/place bet at Turfway on a 2-year-old MSWT going 1 1/16 miles in the slop. The only horse with mud caulks was adding blinkers and Lasix while trying a route for the first time, after showing speed at 6f. Lots of good reasons to bet and odds of 11-1. The horse won by 10 lengths and paid $25.80/$12.80 so $4 win/place paid $77.20 in 5 minutes of work.

Friday and two more horses I have been waiting to see in the entries. Waiting for this key race, I played an exacta box of two 6-1 shots that hits, a $1 tri key in a Calder turf race that turns a 6/5 favorite into a $219 trifecta, a $1 tri box at Laurel that keys a 5/2, 5/2, and 3-1 shot. I bet the eventual winner to win when it was 9/2, the late drop to 5/2 would have been disappointing except for the $59.80 payoff for the $1 trifecta. More profit.

Saturday, I stopped by to bet my "watch" horses Granting, High Yield, Our Fair Lady, Psychic Bid, and Brushed Halory. First up was Granting, $40 win, two $2 exactas, $1 tri key. He romps and pays $14.60. The exactas pay another $48.60. The trifecta finished 1st-2nd-4th—too bad because that fourth place finisher was in my tri bet at odds of 11-1. Another few horses hit, but High Yield, Our Fair Lady, Psychic Bid and Brushed Halory didn't: ran second (9/2), second by a nose (6-1), out (27-1), and out (5-1). Still $243 profit.

Sunday, my luck finally ran out. *Two real near-misses but cashed only $197.20 for $200 bet and a loss of $2.80.*

When the dust cleared, $40 became a run for profitability for the season. Not including the expenses of the hobby, this was a moral victory to be sure. So ended 1999. And thanks to my All-Stars, it wasn't such a bad year after all.

Maiden Races

Just about any race card is likely to contain at least one race for non-winners. Many bettors shun these races due to the lack of past performance information on inexperienced entrants as well as the lack of winning efforts by which experienced runners can be judged. Yet these races offer the astute handicapper an opportunity to play horses when the competition includes fields of runners destined to never find the winner's circle. If a talented runner can be identified, it is facing the weakest field it is likely to ever compete against.

The following information looks at the critical factors necessary to understand maiden races. This information can be used for 2-year-old races in the summer and fall. Also included are special considerations for early 2-year-old races, maiden races for older horses, maiden claiming races, and maiden races at route distances. When faced with these situations, the general principles of betting maiden races still apply. However, there are additional factors the handicapper must keep in mind.

Two-Year-Olds

In maiden races full of first time starters, information is limited to:

— Breeding
— Trainer
— Jockey
— Workouts
— Post position
— Appearance and behavior

The first three subjects (breeding, trainer and jockey) require research as previously discussed. Knowing breeding, trainer, and jockey stats allows handicappers to eliminate entrants with low percentage genes or connections, and focus on those runners with significant stats in their favor.

Workouts can be another subjective study. Some trainers seldom give a runner quick works, others show speed unless the horse is incapable of giving it. The only reliable guideline is that any maiden that is working every 5 to 10 days is healthy. Conversely, any horse with big gaps between works (without racing) should be viewed as suspect. If a trainer has a young horse with sufficient problems to keep it from regularly working, it is unlikely that the trainer would push it enough to win first time out. Healthy horses work or run to stay in shape, just like any other athlete.

Post position stats apply just as discussed earlier in the Data Management section. Debuting horses especially tend to struggle when breaking from the rail or from the far outside of the field. The rest of the runners have a horse flanking both sides and should run from the gate and "follow the herd." This by no means promises that they will run straight, or avoid getting squeezed, pinched, boxed, bumped, etc. Debut horses breaking from the far outside often bear out toward the open space, and lose position while being steered back to the inside. Breaking from the rail, debut horses need to break cleanly or else will not hold their inside positions. This is worse for debut horses than other runners because if position is lost, the horse must maneuver—tough in a rookie effort.

Finally, appearance and behavior can be evaluated. Good looking, well behaved horses will not always run well, but awful looking and/or awful behaving youngsters will rarely find the winner's circle. A horse experiencing the excitement and noise of race day for the first time cannot afford to waste energy, but it may not realize that yet. If you take note of these occasions, watch for horses that behaved monstrously last time and are now behaving normally or well, and expect them to have more energy and perform better in the race.

With maiden races filled with first time starters, there are no pace or speed figures, no past performances, no indication of running style. Bettors look to the toteboard for answers. ***Bettors***

will be looking at connections in these races, so the more well known the names, the more money you can expect. Even if the high profile connections are not known for winning with first time starters. Case in point: Bill Mott/Jerry Bailey. Mott is a 21% winner overall, and that number often exceeds 30% with Bailey aboard. But with firsters, he is a 8% trainer and has been for years. Even though he wins with less than 1 in every 12 debuts, you will not see a Mott/ Bailey firster at 12-1 or up.

D. Wayne Lukas is another crowd favorite. A 12% winner with firsters, his bevy of million dollar juveniles often leave the gates odds-on. ***Again, in an 8 horse field the random chances of winning are about 12%!*** You would need to average 8-1 to break even on Lukas firsters, but you'll rarely see one above 4-1. Long term, the crowd gets killed with these.

It's a different story when connections do hit with a high rate of firsters. If a trainer hits 30% of the time with debuts, the crowd will notice and money will pour in. With the high hit rate, the crowd will be vindicated often. So the best scenario for the handicapper is when multiple high percentage trainers enter debut horses in the same race. All will take some action, but the crowd will tend to lean towards one or two as post time approaches. Three entries with equal chance can easily end up 6/5, 5/2, and 5-1. In such situations, it makes more sense to stick with the opinion that all have an equal chance and bet the one offering the best odds, rather than to assume the disparity is rooted in some insider trading.

The scenario that is most difficult to assess is when the first time starter taking all the money is neither from high profile connections nor from high percentage breeding or debut connections. If the horse is not precociously bred, is not showing fast works, and is from a trainer that is not well known and has a low debut percentage, then the money is not coming from the crowd reading the *Racing Form*.

In such situations, it is logical to assume that either someone is exuberantly betting without any regard for the runner's real chances (for example, a very enthusiastic owner), or someone has reason to believe that this particular horse will defy the low percentage of his sire and trainer. You have three choices:

1. Pass the race,
2. Trust your own judgment and enjoy overlay odds on the other contenders, or
3. Trust the inside money and bet a horse at low odds that you otherwise would not even have bet as a longshot.

If you pass the race, there is no reason to regret that choice even if the late money horse wins. You felt you lacked the data necessary to make an informed decision, and saved your money for a better opportunity.

Purchase Price As an Indication of Ability

The amount of money paid for young horses is often highlighted in past performances, but there are important distinctions between money paid when a horse is very young versus once it is in training.

Weanlings

Money spent on weanlings is not a reflection of ability. It's very speculative.

Yearlings

Money spent on yearlings is most important when the horse is exceptionally expensive or surprisingly cheap when compared with the other offspring of that sire that have been sold. If a sire's stud fee is $50,000 but his average sales price is $200,000, one of his horses that sold for anything around $50,000 or less has to be considered suspect.

2-year-olds in Training

Money spent on horses in training is often very important. The prices of 2-year-old in training sales are based on a combination of appearance, ability, and bloodlines. Yearling and weanling sales do not allow for the ability aspect of that equation. A 2-year-old in training sold for a very high price is among the best bets to win one of the first starts of its career. Something can go awry in the horse's debut. The owners, however, probably paid for a known commodity with some demonstrated ability. Barring injury, they will most likely get at least a MSWT win out of their purchase.

Insider Trading On Debut Horses

In maiden special weight races, nothing is harder to interpret than heavy betting on a first time starter. In a race full of debuting horses, big action on the tote board will always get a player's attention. How to deal with this money is worth discussing, because heavy betting action can radically change any preconceived notion of fair wagering value.

Heavy action early in the betting will always get the public's attention. This is especially true when the big money is going on a first time starter. The lack of past performance data leads to the assumption that insiders know a horse has ability. What people assume and what is really known are two completely different things.

The public assumes: Early, heavy tote action on a first time starter is from well-informed insiders that are confident a horse has genuine talent and is also ready to win. The insiders are so sure of their knowledge that they don't care if they tip their hand to the public—the horse is a soon-to-be-winner anyway.

What you really know: A large amount of money in comparison to the small amount of advance wagering money in the pool was bet on a particular runner for reasons unknown.

If the money is on a horse from high-profile connections or an outfit known for having debut firsters ready, the action probably has little to do with today's entrant. The early money is bet on the general knowledge of the connections, and there's absolutely nothing insightful about that.

If the debut horse is from low profile connections, then the assumption commonly held is that the outfit "bet their rent" on their best shot to grab a win with an unknown commodity. Again, it's an assumption and not a true read on the situation.

For every heavily bet debut runner that lives up to its heavy support, many more come up short. If the horse wins, those assuming the smart money shows the way will pick up a mutuel payoff at depressed odds. The heavily bet debut runner that loses can get beat for any of the following reasons:

— The horse looked great in workouts, but didn't deliver when faced with real competition.
— The horse indeed has talent, but was unprepared to put it all together in an initial outing.
— The horse was the victim of circumstances, bad racing luck, or other misfortune that is even more commonplace in races full of inexperienced horses.
— The horse was as good as "they" thought, but another runner was even better.
— The horse was not as good as they thought.
— Or, alas, someone with a lot of money made a big foolish wager without any good inside scoop at all.

Where does this leave the handicapper? Don't ever let heavy money on another runner talk you out of playing your top selection. If the "smart" money is on your top pick, consider exotic pools instead of betting to win.

"Inside" money that shows up in the win pool may not be reflected in the exotics. This can lead to minimal effort bonanzas for the bettor. This action is often narrowly focused on the win pool, leaving exotic wagers as the best hunting ground for value. Without overthinking this disparity, the best explanation is the debuting phenom's connections expect their horse to win and are betting their horse to win. They are not looking to complicate things by guessing who will run second, third, et cetera.

If your personal selection method chooses the same horse as the betting public, expect to be right a high percentage of the time, but look for better value in exotic pools than in the win pools. If your selection differs from the betting favorite, combine both in the exotics. Even if you decide to bet your selection to win, consider boxing your selection with the heavily bet insider in exactas as a sensible saver or supplement to your wagering strategy.

The Baby Race Guide

Baby races include all of the following, as well as similar events from April through July each year at smaller venues:

1. Keeneland Spring: 4 1/2f races
2. Aqueduct: 4 1/2f races
3. Belmont Spring: 5f and 5 1/2f races
4. Churchill Downs: 5f and 5 1/2f races
5. Hollywood Park: 4 1/2f, 5f, and 5 1/2f races

Earlier 2-year-old races include Santa Anita's 2f races and Hialeah's 3f races. These are straight-race dashes down the homestretch and the outcomes seem fairly random. Heavy betting often leads to wins, but also seems directly related to "2-year-olds in training" sale prices, training races, or exhibition workouts. Study Quarter horse betting if you want to bet these races. The distance, strategy, and running of these races is more like Quarter horse racing than thoroughbreds.

For the five categories of baby races above, here are some key considerations:

— Up to 55% of these baby races are won by the favorites at some meets. Small fields contain limited numbers of runners that are truly up to the competition, leading to many lopsided victories by clear standouts.

- In any given event, at least half the field can be expected to have no talent and/or will never win a race.
- Horses purchased as "2-year-olds in training" in Jan/Feb/ Mar often have a big edge in experience based on exhibition workouts:

  - Big money paid for a 2-year-old in training with less-than-magnificent breeding is a very good indicator of talent.
  - A 2-year-old that brought the highest sales price from an iffy stallion often means ability has shown itself. For example, Is It True is a $5,000 sire and rarely does one of his offspring sell for over $100,000. When Yes It's True was bought for $800,000 in March 1998, it was no surprise that he had early ability, winning his first five starts.

- Breeding controls growth and development—the raw talent. Training controls performance—the use of talent. The two are very closely connected. Precocious breeding equals early growth. Good handlers nurture that early advantage into readiness to win. Late bloomers may grow to be superior racehorses, but it is detrimental to try to force great early performance out of an under-developed animal.
- **Experience is valuable.** A horse with race experience has a much better chance of beating maidens than even a well-handled animal making its debut. This applies to early 2-year-old stakes races as well, where posting the fastest previous time is the overwhelming success factor. More information on 2-year-old stakes can be found under Handicapping Stakes Races.

Conclusions:

- In these races, the favorite is automatically a contender, the more positives the better.

— The favorite with high percentage debut percentage sire and/or a dam with past 2-year-old winners is the best bet at the track.
— The favorite without exceptional breeding, nothing special in workouts or sales but high-profile connections is vulnerable to others with precocious breeding or other strong positives.
— Horses with starts that showed early speed, a late run, a middle move, and/or trouble at the start should be favored over debuting horses. Whether the horse showed talent early, middle, or late is less important than the fact it showed some ability.
— When the favorite loses, the "upset" winner usually has noticeable positives labeling it a legitimate contender.
— 15 to 20% of the time, the results are chaotic. Randomness can prevail when a group with so little experience leaves the starting gate.

2-year-old MSWT Races At 2f—March/April

Introduced in 1999, this relatively new race condition is, in my opinion, not a step in the right direction for California racing. I recently read that a study done by the California racing establishment claims that horses who run in the 2f races have careers just as long as horses that do not debut until later in the racing season. Career length in this case was defined based on number of starts and not number of months/years that the horse remained in competition. This is justification enough for them to continue with these "infant" races.

These races are all about leaving the gate like a rocket. The average field size is eight horses, and the average winning odds has been something like 11-1. The median odds have been around 9-1, so the odds are paying better than the random odds of the horses winning. The trainers may know that they have live ones, but the jockey still has to break the horse well and avoid crashing into the horses to left and right if they don't come out straight. To say these races are chaotic is an understatement. Even precocious breeding won't help much in a quarter mile race.

If a horse shows brilliant 2f works or a training race win is noted, the public will hammer the horse at the windows. Again, talent is not enough to overcome the first moments at the start. These are not bettable races unless a trainer known for winning such starts enters a horse at generous odds.

Maiden Rules For Older Horses

Maiden Rules (3-and-up) 1 Jan-30 Apr

Maiden races for horses that are no longer juveniles must be examined differently. In the first 4 months of each year, there are usually two types of maiden races: Races for 3-year-olds, and races for 4-year-olds and older. The 3-year-olds are often still developing young prospects that may have a bright future. Four-and-up races are made up of horses with question marks next to their names. *Something* has kept them out of the winner's circle in their 2—and 3-year-old years.

With 3-year-olds, it is often a test between speedy types that haven't held a lead to the finish yet in their career, and horses bred to be "late bloomers" that should (in theory) be getting better with every start. In races restricted to 3-year-olds, always prefer runners with potential to improve over repeat losers that are a proven commodity.

A runner that has had eight starts and failed to win despite these repeated efforts has already proven its ability, even if those efforts included near misses. Often such runners have finished in the money and posted "competitive" figures. Numbers aside, they have proven that they cannot outfinish a field of horses that have never won. Because the public strongly bets proven losers that placed second in their most recent race, this often creates a great betting opportunity for a less-proven horse that looks to improve.

Maiden Rules (3-and-up) 1 May-30 Nov

By the end of April, maiden races rarely distinguish between 3-year-olds and older. All "non-juveniles" that have yet to win must compete against each other. This far into the season, maiden claimers almost never move up to MSWT and win, so horses that have failed to win MdnClm can be eliminated from non-claiming maiden events. Also, debuting horses must be viewed with skepticism. Most horses that fail to debut until midway through their 3-year-old year or later have had some sort of setback in their career.

Even top outfits are unlikely to have a debuting horse ready to roll. They waited long enough to get the horse to the track that there is no reason to push all-out right away.

Here are some guidelines for handling these older maiden affairs:

— Eliminate horses that last raced in a maiden claiming race.
— Eliminate first time starters without a 20% or higher debut sire.
— Eliminate horses with two or more starts that have yet to finish in the money, unless they are bred for distance and have only raced in sprints until today's route race.
— Eliminate horses that have not raced in the last 22 days and have not worked out since their last start.
— Of any remaining horses, favor contenders in the following order:

    — Finished second in last start, which was over today's distance or longer.
    — Finished second in last race at a shorter distance.
    — Finished third or worse in last start, but finished within 5 lengths of the winner.
    — Regardless of last finish, has run second or third in the past at this exact distance and surface, and has an excuse in most recent start.
    — First time starters with at least a 20% debut sire.

Maiden Claiming (3-and-up)

The horses that find their way into these races are the least talented runners on track. These races are the least predictable because the entrants are inconsistent and incapable of maintaining good form. The winners of these heats will probably not win again until dropped to a claiming price well below the maiden claiming price.

The below guidelines will help avoid pitfalls in these races, and frequently eliminate *all* horses in this kind of race:

— Eliminate any loser at the maiden claiming level.
— Eliminate any debuting horse unless maiden claiming level is $50,000 or higher.
— Horses last raced in MSWT are all that remains.

  — Contenders must have raced within last 22 days and have worked out since.
  — Contenders that last raced within 15 days need no workout.
  — Contenders that last raced more than 30 days ago must have had three or more workouts within last 30 days.

— Bet the horses that meet all of the above criteria. Horses that meet all of the above criteria and finished within 5 lengths of the winner last time are outstanding contenders.

Horses that meet all of the above criteria and finished second in their previous start (in a MSWT) are the very best contenders. This type of horse can be overlooked by the betting public in favor of proven maiden claiming losers that repeatedly hit the board. While longshot odds are unlikely, the odds may still present value compared to the horse's actual chance to win.

Pace Based Plays For Maiden Route Races

Maiden Route Races—3-year-old MSWT Routes

Fields tend to be strung out at the finish of maiden route races. Few non-winners can remain on-the-throttle for a route distance. Horses that give up after 1/2 or 3/4 mile will finish well back. As a result, horses unable to remain in contention at least until nearing the stretch can be left out of any exotic wagering strategies. The key to identifying horses that will be in touch with the leaders at the stretch is ***pace.***

In all of the day's maiden route races (beyond 1 mile), examine each race in terms of pace.

The object is to identify which horse is likely to lead at the pace call (after the first 3/4 mile). This is either the horse with the best pace figures or with the best fractional times. This can be done several ways: with a comparison of pace figures, the final times of 6f sprints, or with the 6f fractional times of previous route attempts. Even with races at 6 1/2f or 7f, use the 6f fraction to compare apples to apples.

— If a horse has been a frontrunner in the past at shorter distances, it should also be on the lead in route races, and probably easily on the lead.

— If a horse has been a frontrunner in sprints but has been tiring badly, compare the horse's final times to the 6f times of the horses that have been attempting routes. When the horse's times are better or comparable to the routers, then the horse is a contender. When the times are much slower, the horse is in trouble.

Some of the best plays are horses with only a few races, that consistently blaze away for very quick opening half miles—under 46 seconds at most tracks—then tire. Even if the final times are not very good, such runners are likely to last longer when allowed to lope along in 48 seconds or so.

The worst plays are horses that have been frontrunners in sprints but in agonizingly slow fractional times. When the horse's final times for sprint races have been slower than the expected pace of the route race, the horse is not a contender.

The betting public will often favor closers that previously gained ground in sprint races. ***These horses, however, often disappoint*** and seldom can make big moves to catch the leaders in the stretch. Lack of ability, competitive spirit, call it what you want—the fact is most of these winless runners are unlikely to make much of a move.

The hotter the pace, the more likely the frontrunners will collapse (no great revelation). Nevertheless, in these races there isn't always a closer willing and able to run down the leaders. Making up a lot of ground in the stretch requires effort at a point when the horses are already tired.

More Points to Remember:

— First time starters are rarely a factor in route races. Only 4% of route maiden races are won by debuting horses. In most races, this helps eliminate a number of horses.

— Looking for the pace horse does not mean looking for the runners that will lead from the start throughout the opening 6f. It means looking for the runners that will be on the lead after 6f, getting there by leading all the way, moving to the lead down the backstretch, or by making a powerful run entering the far turn.

Most route races are 1 mile, 1 1/16 miles, or 1 1/8 miles. At most tracks this means that after 6f have been run, the horses will be either at the top of the stretch, or 1/16 mile from the stretch.

Visualize that you are looking for horses that will be on or very near the lead as they complete their run around the far turn and straighten away into the stretch. At this point in these maiden races, the first four runners probably include the final first three finishers. Even closers need to be close to the leaders at this point to have a chance, barring a total meltdown of the runners on the lead.

Starter Allowances

Starter allowances are allowances or restricted handicaps for horses that have raced for a certain claiming price within a certain amount of time. Certain tracks offer these races as a series, other tracks rarely offer them at all.

Tracks that traditionally offer starters include Churchill Downs, Turfway Park, Keeneland, River Downs, Oaklawn, Philadelphia Park, Southern California, Aqueduct (during the winter months), and Fairgrounds. Canterbury's "Claiming Crown" races are all starter allowances.

Some tracks offer the occasional 6f or 1 mile starter at the $5,000, $8,000, or $10,000 level. Kentucky offers a series of marathon events that usually increase in distance during the duration of each meet, such as: 1 1/4, 1 1/2, 1 3/4, and 2 miles. Certain horses make a career of these events. These are not distances typically run by horses, especially cheap ones. A horse that can compete in these races need only run in the occasional claiming event to remain eligible.

Occasionally a high-class $25,000 claiming level starter allowance is offered, during a stakes undercard or on a big day or weekend. This kind of event usually attracts a tough field of high-class allowance horses, because many good horses will dip into the $25,000 claiming level at some point in their careers.

Tricks Of the Trade

To compete in a route marathon starter series, trainers must find a horse that can run all day. It either needs to have started for a low claiming price, or will have to be run in a low claiming race without getting claimed. It then gets entered in a starter race, and if it wins, it will get additional weight for the next race in the series. Winning the first two events in a series is likely to mean a heavy weight assignment (at an even longer distance) in the next race, maybe 126 to 130 lbs. So trainers either find the rare animal that can take the distances and the pounds, or else they plan on one race in the series to be their best shot and try to get the horse entered with as little weight as possible (by having a string of lackluster efforts leading up to the race).

Horses that have won these races before will win again and again. Horses that do not frequent these races rarely drop in and win. Traditional handicapping fundamentals rarely apply. Horses that fail to contend in a $5,000 claimer miraculously pull themselves together to win a series of $5000s starter handicaps. Having an otherwise losing rider doesn't matter. Neither do the increasing weights nor increasing distances.

Best of all, the horse with multiple starter allowance wins will often go off at odds that are generous. Each event includes horses entering from higher priced claimers or off a commanding non-starter win. The crowd will decide that the starter allowance hero has finally met a field that will outclass him. And he'll prevail again—bet on it.

The Starter Hero

Isaacsmyman is the model for what a starter handicap horse should be. From his 2-year-old year until midway through his 5-year-old season, this gelding worked his way through maiden ranks and two levels of conditioned allowances primarily in sprints. He hit his ceiling at the ALWN3X level, and slid down the claiming ladder until reaching the $5,000 ranks. At this point he had 34 starts, 5 career victories, and was in the barn of his fourth trainer. This trainer stopped entering Isaac in sprints, and began running him long.

Isaac's $5,000 claiming effort qualified him for the Kentucky circuit starter races. Over his next 35 starts, he competed almost exclusively on that circuit, winning 13 races from those 35 starts. During this prolonged campaign he only ran second twice, and third twice, meaning his efforts were usually all-or-nothing. Isaac rarely exerted himself for near-misses. More amazing is that despite winning better than one in three starts, Isaac's wins include hits at 18-1 and 21-1, both without any move up in class!

Isaacsmyman's partial race history is below. The starter allowance is traditionally noted with an "s." Clm8000 is Claiming for $8,000 claiming price. A starter allowance at the same "level" would show as Alw8000s. Horses are eligible if they entered at a claiming price of $8,000 or lower.

Isaacsmyman
Own: Degrella Michael A

B. g. 14 (May)
Sire: Afleet (Mr. Prospector) $50,520
Dam: Mainbocher (Linkage)
Br: Richard L. G. Jones (Ky)
Tr: Lotze Larry E

Life	95	22	13	5	$230,743	93
2001	9	0	3	0	$10,022	75
2000	13	4	4	0	$36,042	83
D.Fst	71	18	10	5	$190,682	92
Wet(365)	18	3	2	0	$34,319	93
Turf(230)	6	1	1	0	$13,742	75

28Nov98-2CD	fst	2	1:402 2:08 3:221	3+ Alw 8000s	65	1	713	714	616	619	627¼	Morgan M R	L121	9.30	104-05	Libertarian1136¾ Private Bet1186¾ Juliannus1182¾	No factor	8
13Nov98-4CD	fst	1½	:483 1:143 2:064 2:332	3+ Alw 8000s	74	4	43	31½	42	44	48¾	Morgan M R	L122	*2.90	91-14	Runaway Affair1131¼ Libertarian1133¾ With Hope1163¾	No late response	9
1Nov98-3CD	fst	1¼	:482 1:141 1:401 2:061	3+ Alw 8000s	85	5	35	32	2hd	11½	11½	Morgan M R	L119	5.00	74-20	Isaacsmyman1191½ RunawayAffair1135 Libertarin1135¾	Drew clear driving	10
21Oct98-3Kee	fst	1⅝	1:143 1:411 2:47	3+ Alw 10000s	77	2	32	42½	33	2hd	13	Morgan M R	L113	21.30	101-20	Isaacsmymn1133 Libertrin1132 APointWellMde1133½	Stalked, hand urging	6
23Aug98-12RD	fst	170	:242 :491 1:14 1:453	3+ Clm 10000	50	6	1hd	2½	53¾	58½	515¼	Neagle J	L116	*1.80	75-23	EskimosKettle116hd Fivfiftn1164 FstivlChirmn116no	Early speed, stopped	6
3Aug98-5EIP	fm	1⅛	Ⓣ :482 1:123 1:382 1:584	3+ Alw 10000s	25	3	32	22	67	717	727¼	Morgan M R	L117	16.90	42-32	Aces Beau1173 Groovy AddVice122¾ LoveHasNoPride1193	3 wide 3/8's pole	7
28Jun98-3CD	fst	1⅜	1:151 1:422 3:004	4+ Alw 8000s	77	7	1½	1hd	2hd	45½	46¾	Morgan M R	L112	7.70	87-03	Private Bet121no This Blade's Sharp1186½ Need a Stack107nk	Pace, tired	7
7Jun98-10CD	fst	1½	:501 1:161 2:09 2:342	4+ Alw 8000s	62	7	63½	93	89	99½	1019	Moss R W	L112	5.10	76-13	This Blade's Sharp1123¾ Tow Zone1121½ Private Bet1212½	4 wide, gave way	12
17May98-4CD	fst	1¼	:484 1:134 1:40 2:071	4+ Alw 8000s	77	1	21½	22½	21½	2½	2no	Moss R W	L113	18.90	69-16	ChckrBoyCoy112no Iscsmymn113nk ElxrSprngs1182½	Gamely, outfinished	10
30Apr98-9CD	my	1⅛	:49 1:142 1:41 1:543	4+ Alw 8000s	50	5	43	42½	43½	815	718	Flores D R	L115	19.20	53-20	ElixirSprings112nk EsternDngr1132 ThisBldsShrp1121¼	Stalked pace, tired	10
12Mar98-10TP	fst	1⅛	:481 1:14 1:413 1:554	4+ Clm c-(10-8)	74	4	1hd	1½	11½	13	13½	Torres F C	L113	3.70	58-40	Isaacsmyman1133½ Turker1132 Need a Stack1153	Dueled, drew clear	10
Claimed from Greenhill Sherri L. for $8,000, Kirby Ronald Trainer 1997: (-) Previously trained by Greenhill Jeff																		
19Feb98-4TP	my	1 1/16	:224 :464 1:13 1:462	4+ Clm 10000(10-8)	56	3	45½	48	33	35	411	D'Amico A J	L115	3.00	60-28	ColonySound1153 Chichswhtchi1157 FinlCll1111	Stalked pace, weakened	7
16Jan98-7TP	my	1 1/16	:223 :461 1:113 1:45	4+ Clm 13500(13.5-11.5)	65	1	55½	55½	65	46	48	D'Amico A J	L115	7.30	70-21	Iron Run1214 Thats Life113hd Quixote's Act1154	Well placed, evenly	8
7Jan98-8TP	sly	1 1/16	:232 :473 1:124 1:46	4+ Clm 17500(17.5-15)	64	2	65¾	65½	47	57½	512	D'Amico A J	L115	4.00	61-30	Golf Ball Hill1154 Open Space1154 Bar Mac1181½	Lacked late response	6
14Dec97-4TP	fst	1 1/16	:233 :473 1:121 1:441	3+ Clm 17500(17.5-15)	73	2	1hd	41½	58	58½	38½	D'Amico A J	L116	8.90	76-25	Blazing Basque1168 Strike Again116nk Isaacsmyman1164	Dueled, gave way	[illegible]
21Nov97-7Hoo	sly	1⅝	:502 2:494	3+ Hcp 5000s	19	8	47	617	742	746	789¼	Thompson T J	LB117	2.00	- 44	ConcordesRevng1151 RcordLvl12232¼ RunningTru1138½	Failed to menace	8
7Nov97-10Hoo	fst	1 9/16	:474 2:391	3+ Hcp 5000s	70	2	48	31	2½	31½	35½	Thompson T J	LB119	*1.60	- -	OurForbes119½ ConcordesReveng1135 Iscsmymn1198	Failed to sustain bid	7
26Sep97-9Hoo	fst	1	:231 :461 1:111 1:362	3+ Hcp ---s	45	7	74½	78½	68½	69	617	Court J K	LB119	2.30	71-18	Irish Bacon1122¾ K. T. Twenty Two115¾ Erudite Leader1161½	No rally	7
1Sep97-12EIP	fst	2	⊗ 3:282	3+ Alw 5000s	78	8	21	2hd	2½	1½	1nk	Martinez W	L113	*1.70	- -	Isaacsmyman113nk Tow Zone113½ Housty Boy1123	Stumbled, prevailed	10
5Aug97-10EIP	fm	1¼	Ⓣ :492 1:141 1:382 2:021	3+ Alw 5000s	59	3	22	3nk	61¾	78	88½	Valdivia J Jr	L114	4.00	81-08	RoringGp108¾ SeminoleSlew1142¼ GrittiMrco113¾	Pressed pace, used up	10
29Mar97-13TP	fst	2	1:414 2:092 3:292	4+ Hcp 6250s	60	4	33	32	2hd	35½	521	Martinez W	L127	*1.00	72-07	PrivateBet1084 BluegrssWrrior1165 RunningTrue1122	Pressed pace, tired	8
22Feb97-7TP	fst	1⅝	:48 1:131 2:34 2:471	4+ Alw 6250s	78	11	38	28	1hd	12	1½	Martinez W	L121	*.80	97-21	Iscsmymn121½ BluegrssWrrior115½ ColonilWinter1156	Drew clear, lasted	11
25Jan97-6TP	fr	1¼	:472 1:14 1:421 2:084	4+ Alw 6250s	79	7	42½	51¾	51¾	11½	12	Martinez W	L121	*1.30	76-34	Isaacsmymn1212 PstTimePlesure112hd AcesBeu1182	Drew clear, ridden out	12
27Dec96-10TP	fst	1½	:491 1:143 2:062 2:34	3+ Alw 6250s	81	5	61¾	33½	23	22	1½	D'Amico A J	L122	*1.30	- -	Isaacsmyman122½ Counsel of Kings1222½ Tow Zone1134	Wore down rivals	11
13Dec96-3TP	gd	1¼	:481 1:13 1:391 2:044	3+ Alw 6250s	83	3	52½	42	41½	1½	12	Martinez W	L122	*1.00	- -	Isaacsmyman1222 Tow Zone113½ Sundarijal1223	Drew clear, ridden out	9
30Nov96-12CD	sly	2	1:444 2:141 3:10 3:353	3+ Alw 8000s	93	2	34	31½	2hd	12	16	Martinez W	L115	*1.70	- -	Isacsmymn1156 Unedited1217 BluegrssWrrior118nk	Drew clear, ridden out	10
25Oct96-7Hoo	fst	1	:231 :462 1:112 1:37	3+ Alw 19400n$y	53	2	1hd	1hd	3nk	54¾	512¾	Zuniga J E	LB114	1.80	- -	PocketOSilver117no CrimsonRef114nk PrincofGllpit1198½	Dueled, faltered	7
13Oct96-10Kee	fst	1⅝	1:161 1:442 2:493	3+ Alw 10000s	92	5	22½	21	1hd	18	114	Martinez W	L113	3.80	- -	Isaacsmyman11314 Royal Title1132½ PrinceCapote1132	Drew clear, handily	10
4Oct96-5TP	fst	1 1/16	:231 :463 1:114 1:444	3+ Clm c-(10-8)	80	5	1hd	1hd	11	11½	1¾	Zuniga J E	L122	*2.10	- -	Isaacsmyman122¾ Every Move U Make1161 Lexnun118hd	Dueled, driving	11
Claimed from Bukowiecki Chris for $10,000, Bukowiecki Chris Trainer 1996(as of 10/4): (-)																		
27Sep96-5TP	sly	1	:222 :46 1:112 1:373	3+ Clm 17500(17.5-15)	80	10	89	98¼	811	67½	43¼	Zuniga J E	L116	16.80	- -	Thats Life114¾ Maxxed116½ Colony Sound1162	Late bid finished well	11
13Sep96-10TP	fst	1 1/16	:233 :472 1:122 1:444	3+ Clm 8000(10-8)	87	5	11	11	1hd	11	13	Zuniga J E	L112	18.30	- -	Iscsmymn1123 DivdndOpton1166 TwoofDmonds1222	Set pace, ridden out	12
1Sep96-1AP	fst	6f	:224 :454 :574 1:094	3+ Clm 14000(14-12)	62	2	1	2hd	3½	43½	411¾	Velasquez J	L117	3.70	- -	Koennecker1195¾ CureThyself1173 GreenAppel1172½	Failed to sustain bid	5
21Aug96-2AP	fst	1	:233 :463 1:112 1:363	3+ Clm 6500(7.5-6.5)	84	5	1½	11	1½	1½	1hd	Velasquez J	L113	7.50	- -	Isaacsmyman113hd Duke of Windsor1175 Riverinn1172½	Held off rivals	7
Previously trained by Martinek Danny L																		
3Aug96-2AP	fst	6f	:223 :464 :593 1:121	3+ Clm 5000	63	4	5	32	2½	1hd	47¼	Meier R	L117b	4.90	- -	DlCorondo1173 OlGrumby1192½ KnollwoodRod1171¾	Hard used weakened	8
25Jly96-4AP	fst	6f	:221 :453 :582 1:12	3+ Clm 5000	64	11	1	11½	1hd	34½	35¾	Meier R	L117b	4.50	- -	Real Alert117¾ Pro Irish1125 Isaacsmyman117nk	Speed held show	12
10Jly96-9AP	fst	6f	:223 :462 :592 1:13	3+ Clm 10000(10-9)	50	8	8	63	65½	69¾	914¼	Meier R	L117fb	20.50	- -	Vnloconqstdr114no Hrrygtsthgld1194 ShpnSlp1172	Swerved start, bumped	11
8Jun96-3AP	gd	6½f	:22 :461 1:123 1:192	3+ Clm c-(7.5-6.5)	54	6	2	23½	31½	89¾	89½	Baird E T	L119fb	5.70	- -	Chace's Story110¾ Sandtucker117no Delicatessen119no	Empty	9
Claimed from Miller Racing Stable, Ltd. for $7,500, Miller Danny L Trainer 1996(as of 6/8): (-)																		
17May96-6AP	fst	6f	:22 :46 :583 1:12	3+ Clm 5000	77	7	1	1½	11	12	11½	Baird E T	L119b	10.20	- -	Isacsmymn1191½ WithWhiteGloves117¾ VerstileTp117¾	Prevailed, driving	12
5May96-4Spt	fst	6f	:223 :463 :583 1:111	3+ Clm 7500n4L	73	9	1	12	11	13	13	Baird E T	L117b	11.70e	- -	Isaacsmyman1173 Pip Style1191 Classic Cobra122¾	Led throughout	9
21Apr96-4Spt	fst	6f	:23 :472 1:00 1:123	3+ Clm 7500n4L	36	4	3	44½	54	68½	719¼	Silva C H	L117b	11.20	- -	Bucorama1171¼ DQPip Style1222¾ Decorated Picture1171¼	Faded stretch	7
6Apr96-7Spt	fst	6f	:224 :464 :591 1:124	3+ Clm 7500n4L	32	6	3	28	35	711	915	Baird E T	L119b	28.20	- -	Ghostbucker1191½ Livelyship1193¾ Coach Mac1221	Dropped back stretch	10

Even at age 9, Isaac found continued success on the Ohio circuit, winning 4 of 13 starts at odds of 9/2, 15-1, 8-1, and 16-1. At age 10, Isaac returned to Kentucky starters, getting four 2nds in races between 1 1/4 and 2 miles! He is among the most durable (and well managed) claimers in recent history, and a great example of how following even a 22-time winner can return big mutuels.

A starter hero for the 21st century is Fan the Flame. Once a Grade 3 winner in 2000, he was dropped into a $5,000 claiming race following two poor races and a short layoff in the spring of 2003. Winning the $5,000 race, he went unclaimed. That entry in a $5,000 claimer qualified him for starter allowances for the next two seasons.

Fan the Flame proceeded to win 8 of his 16 starter allowances, racking up win after win without being risked in the claiming ranks. Not a marathon runner like Isaac, Fan the Flame's wins range from 3/4 mile to 1 1/4 miles. He won stretching out and turning back in distance, showing a unique versatility.

Fan the Flame
Own: Langford Michael

Dk. b or b. h. 8 (Apr)
Sire: Island Whirl (Pago Pago) $1,900
Dam: Horsafire (Hold Your Peace)
Br: Lois C. Harder (Fla)
Tr: Morse Randy L

Life	48	16	5	8	$386,923	105	
2004	11	5	2	2	$48,283	86	
2003	12	6	1	2	$66,850	95	
D.Fst	38	15	5	4	$356,438	105	
Wet(334)	7	1	0	3	$27,110	93	
Turf(245)	3	0	0	1	$3,375	83	

18Nov04-5CD	fst	7f	:233 :463 1:111 1:241	3+ Alw 5000s	70 5 4 63¾ 43½ 37 38½	Melancon L	L123 fb	5.00	72-21	Song Dancer1182¾ Rough Draft1196½ Fan the Flame1231¼	5-6w,no late gain	8
24Sep04-3TP	fst	1¼	:482 1:131 1:384 2:054	3+ Alw 5000s	86 3 12½ 17 112 112 113¾	Hernandez B J Jr5	L117 fb	*.40	111-18	FantheFlme11713¾ AnthemHill1162¾ Thelightsreon1181	Off inside, driving	8
10Sep04-10TP	fst	1	:232 :47 1:114 1:372	3+ Alw 5000s	84 9 21 2hd 2hd 21 22¾	Borel C H	L122 fb	2.80	84-18	SongDancer1162¾ FantheFlame1221¼ GoldCommnderOne1165	Held gamely	9
31Jly04-10EIP	fst	1⅛	:481 1:124 1:39 1:522	3+ Alw 5000s	80 5 21 2½ 1½ 11 14¼	Borel C H	L121 fb	*1.70	86-23	FantheFlame1214¼ ElNinoCliente121½ TrgetWest117no	Off inside, driving	12
10Jly04-8EIP	fst	1	:234 :472 1:124 1:391	3+ Alw 5000s	78 6 3½ 21 2hd 1hd 1nk	Borel C H	L117 fb	2.20	84-13	FntheFlme117nk CptinWllstrt1192¾ RobrtoRoyl121hd	Tracked,gamely,drvg	8
28May04-9CD	fst	1 1/16	:241 :48 1:123 1:452	4+ Alw 5000s	64 6 1hd 1hd 2hd 24½ 310	Borel C H	L119 fb	*1.70	71-19	Rough Draft1199¾ Book Seven121nk Fan the Flame1193¼	Weaken after 3/4s	7
20May04-2CD	fst	6f	:212 :45 :573 1:102	4+ Alw 5000s	81 1 7 57 43½ 1hd 12¼	Borel C H	L119 fb	4.20	89-11	FantheFlme1192¼ ElliesChoice1232¼ ConnorsGlory1195	Split foes,4w,drvg	7
31Mar04-4OP	fst	1 1/16	:231 :47 1:121 1:443	4+ Alw 10000s	83 2 1hd 12 12½ 1½ 2nk	McKee J	L119 fb	3.20	87-15	StrikeRelity123nk FnthFlm1192¾ FrgisShowtim1231¾	Pick pace, grudgingly	6
12Mar04-7OP	fst	1 1/16	:241 :492 1:141 1:453	4+ Alw 7500s	71 1 54½ 31 21½ 43½ 44¼	Marquez C H Jr	L122 fb	*1.30	78-18	FrgsShowtm115¾ RodEsprnz1222½ RngdRog1151	Advanced outside, even	7
22Feb04-6OP	fst	1 1/16	:24 :481 1:134 1:461	4+ Alw 10000s	76 1 21½ 2hd 1½ 11½ 12¾	Marquez C H Jr	L122 fb	*1.40e	79-14	FntheFlme1222¾ CookyJoFltchr122¾ BuzzlWys1185¼	Drove steadily clear	8
1Feb04-6OP	fst	1	:234 :474 1:124 1:384	4+ Alw 7500s	78 1 42 42 51¼ 45½ 45	Doocy T T	L122 fb	*.80	85-13	PlomPrill1183½ FergiesShowtime118hd StrikeRlity1221½	Inside, got out 1/8	9
29Nov03-12CD	fst	1¼	:48 1:123 1:391 2:07	3+ Alw 8000s	87 6 12½ 13½ 13½ 16 14	Borel C H	L121 b	4.10	64-24	FantheFlme1214 LindsLd1174½ AStormIsBrewing1173¾	3-4w,steady drive	11
26Oct03-2CD	sly	1 1/16	:244 :491 1:15 1:49	3+ Alw 8000s	45 2 42 21½ 33 710 718	Bejarano R	L123 fb	*1.70	45-32	Muted1173¼ Contested117¾ Book Seven1174¼	Hop start,tired inside	7
11Oct03-2Kee	fst	1¼	:482 1:13 1:391 2:054	3+ Alw 5000s	82 3 1½ 11½ 13 13 11¾	Bejarano R	L119 fb	*1.70	87-15	FantheFlame1191¾ LindasLad1196½ Intertwining1192¾	Vied inside,driving	9
25Sep03-3TP	fst	1⅛	:482 1:14 1:404 1:541	3+ Alw 5000s	85 1 2hd 2hd 1½ 12 12¾	Bejarano R	L116 fb	*1.80	65-29	Fan the Flame1162¾ Rose Creek116¾ Linda's Lad1163	Inside, driving	10
30Aug03-8EIP	sly	7f	:214 :443 1:10 1:24	3+ Alw 5000s	67 4 9 67¾ 48½ 57 34¾	Shepherd J7	L111 fb	3.80	87-11	Unpeteable1221¾ Code One1223 Fan the Flame111¾	Bmp start,minor gain	9
30Jly03-7EIP	fst	7f	:221 :453 1:122 1:261	3+ Clm 5000	72 10 2 45 46½ 1½ 13	Shepherd J7	L111 fb	2.60	81-21	Fan the Flame1113 Goost118nk DHShip's Silver118	Carried 10w lane,driv	11
30May03-2CD	fst	1 1/16	:24 :471 1:114 1:434	3+ Clm 20000(20-18)	70 5 11 14 31½ 69½ 612¾	Stortz M7	L112 fb	*2.90	76-17	HailtoWildAgain1121¼ RideEmRags1173¾ PapMndM1173¾	Tired after 3/4s	7
26Apr03-7PrM	fst	1	:232 :464 1:114 1:382	4+ OC 40k/n1m-N	67 6 1hd 1hd 2½ 67½ 610¼	Thompson T J	LB118 fb	*2.50	78-19	Promise of War1151¾ Dirty Mike116no Kiss of Lion1153½	Dueled, gave way	6
27Mar03-3OP	fst	1 1/16	:233 :463 1:111 1:443	4+ Clm 30000(30-25)	95 6 1hd 1hd 1½ 1hd 1nk	Thompson T J	L118 fb	*1.20	87-24	Fan the Flame118nk It's Roo11811 Del Mar Danny1141	Dueled, all out	6
14Mar03-5OP	fst	1	:232 :471 1:113 1:372	4+ Clm 30000(35-30)	83 7 11½ 11 1½ 2hd 2¾	Thompson T J	L113 fb	3.60	95-18	Screenplay116¾ Fan the Flame113½ It's Roo1165¾	Pace, stubborn	8
Previously trained by Vance David R												
23Feb03-8OP	my	1 1/16	:24 :484 1:143 1:481	4+ Clm 25000	86 3 1½ 1½ 11½ 1½ 12¼	Thompson T J	L116 fb	*2.60	69-31	FntheFlme1162¼ TemperncTim1181½ Amrttitorumbl1162	Clear again late	8
9Feb03-7OP	sly	1 1/16	:241 :484 1:142 1:461	4+ Clm 30000(30-25)	76 5 31 31½ 3½ 33 36	Thompson T J	L118 fb	4.40	73-18	Afleet Buck118nk Eyebrow Raiser1185¾ Fan the Flame1183¼	Best of rest	7
27Dec02-9TP	fst	1	:232 :471 1:12 1:374	3+ Clm 45000(50-40)	78 3 43 42½ 44 45½ 48½	Lopez J	L114 fb	7.30	76-25	FightforAlly1194¼ LkeSilver114no WinningConnection1224¼	4-5w trip,empty	8
23Nov02-1CD	fst	1 1/16	:242 :481 1:124 1:442	3+ Clm 50000(50-45)	73 2 54 54 53¼ 54¾ 511	Sellers S J	L117 fb	5.30	75-19	Valid Prime117nk Liberty Run1152¼ Wave1174	Off slow in tangle	6
8Nov02-4CD	fst	1	:223 :451 1:093 1:351	3+ Alw 48240n1x	78 7 42¾ 43½ 46 512 515¼	Sellers S J	L117 fb	15.00	76-21	Horrible Evening123nk E Z Glory1197¾ Dayton Flyer119¾	Sw,empty in lane	7
29Aug02-8AP	fst	6½f	:224 :454 1:094 1:16	3+ OC 100k/n$y-N	77 5 4 1hd 2hd 77¼ 79½	Meier R	L117 fb	16.10	86-09	Chindi119no Big Bad George1191 Bet On Sunshine121½	Tired	7
Previously trained by Morse Randy L												
24Nov01-10CD	sly	1 1/16	:234 :472 1:114 1:431	3+ OC 100k/c-N	86 1 12 11 2½ 35 510½	Albarado R J	L118 fb	7.20	83-10	BetOnSunshine1137¼ PrdeLeder1181 NoblRulr1161¾	Pace,inside,weakened	9
28Oct01-9CD	fst	7½f	:223 :451 1:101 1:283	3+ AckAckH-G3	63 10 5 4nk 62¾ 1115 1121	St Julien M	L113 fb	48.00	80-13	Illusioned1183¾ Strawberry Affair112nk Fappie's Notebook116½	5w, fad[illegible]	[illegible]
17Oct01-9Kee	gd	1	(T) :231 :462 1:103 1:374	3+ Alw 65000c	72 5 1hd 1½ 1hd 62¼ 65¼	Court J K	L119 fb	6.50	74-17	Danzatore Flag119hd Mr. Kody1191¼ Buckhari1192	Pace,inside,weakened	9
22Jly01-4Hpo	fst	1	:233 :463 1:104 1:354	3+ OmahaH100k	81 1 12 11 21 34½ 39¼	Compton P	LB119 fb	2.00	98 -	SurShotBiscuit1203½ BttlMountin1155¾ FnthFlm1191¼	Spd insd,little left	5
7Jly01-8AP	my	1	:222 :443 1:094 1:361	3+ HanshinH-G3	63 7 1hd 2½ 2½ 714 723¼	Martin E M Jr	L119 fb	4.90	73-15	BrightValour119¾ ApttoBe1191¾ Castlewood1175	Unprepared strt-stmbld	8
28May01-8LS	fst	1 1/16	:231 :461 1:091 1:402	3+ LSParkH-G3	98 8 12½ 11½ 2½ 23 27¼	Martin E M Jr	L113 fb	7.80	95-07	DixieDotCom1187¼ FnthFlm1131½ BigNumbrs1141¼	No match, clearly 2nd	8
5May01-10CD	fst	1 1/16	:24 :472 1:11 1:421	3+ Alw 50140c	95 5 11 11 1½ 1hd 1¾	Martin E M Jr	L123 fb	7.40	99 -	Fan the Flame123¾ Bet On Red1201¼ Frazee's Folly120nk	Inside, driving	11
7Apr01-11OP	fst	1⅛	:452 1:092 1:352 1:48	4+ OaklawnH-G1	97 6 2hd 1hd 2hd 64¾ 611½	Martin E M Jr	L113 fb	53.10	86-17	Traditionally1125¾ Mr Ross117nk Wooden Phone1182½	Blistering duel	7
17Mar01-7FG	fst	1 70	:241 :471 1:112 1:384	4+ OC 100k/n4x-N	85 3 32 2½ 2hd 21 35	Martin E M Jr	L122 fb	*.80	95-11	Smilin'Slew1172 PhiltheGrip1173 FantheFlame1223	Faltered final furlong	5
2Mar01-9FG	fst	1	:233 :471 1:113 1:374	4+ Alw 39000n4x	101 4 11 11 12½ 12½ 1½	Martin E M Jr	L117 fb	4.20	90-21	FntheFlme117½ CoolNCollectiv1172½ MinrsPriz1171	Well handled, held on	6
10Jun00-8AP	fst	1⅛	:471 1:112 1:362 1:50	RndTable-G3	99 1 11 15 14 15 13¼	Martin E M Jr	L114 b	4.60	95-14	Fan the Flame1143¼ Del Mar Danny1181½ Deputy Warlock116hd	Driving	6
12May00-8CD	fst	1 1/16	:241 :48 1:122 1:43	Alw 37150n1x	105 3 1hd 11 12 12½ 11½	Sellers S J	L115 b	*.70	95-12	FntheFlme1151½ FirstLiutnnt1219¾ PrsidntilFling1121½	Bobble start,driving	7
15Apr00-9OP	fst	1⅛	:464 1:113 1:363 1:49	ArkDerby-G2	72 4 52 54 73½ 1217 1219½	Court J K	L118 b	38.90	74-16	Graeme Hall1183¾ Snuck In122hd Impeachment1181¼	Faded inside	14
25Mar00-10OP	gd	1 1/16	:232 :47 1:112 1:424	Rebel-G3	93 9 11½ 1½ 1hd 3½ 34½	Borel C H	L113 b	14.80	85-16	SnuckIn113nk BigNumbers1144¼ FntheFlme1133½	Responded,falterd late	12
4Mar00-9OP	fst	1	:23 :461 1:111 1:37	Southwest75k	91 2 1hd 1hd 11½ 2hd 2nk	Lejeune S P Jr	L112 b	10.10	94-16	AfternoonAffir115nk FntheFlme112½ BigNumbers1152½	Pace, stubbornly	8
Previously trained by Hine Hubert												
5Feb00-5GP	fm	1	(T) :231 :47 1:111 1:352	+ Alw 32000n2L	83 9 61¾ 41¾ 32 21½ 3½	Bailey J D	L119 b	5.30	90-10	Clayton's Find119½ Ekundu119hd Fan the Flame1194¼	Not good enough	12
17Jan00-6GP	fst	1 1/16	:233 :481 1:134 1:454	Md 50000(50-45)	87 2 11½ 11½ 12 17 112½	Bailey J D	L122 b	*1.50	79-21	FantheFlame12212½ PersonlJourney122½ ProspectorGo1221¾	Kept to task	10
18Dec99-12Crc	gd	7½f	(T) :233 :473 1:124 1:304	Md Sp Wt 22k	54 5 3 42½ 33 55 58¼	Coa E M	120 b	3.70	74-18	Golden Concorde1202½ El Nativo120¾ My Marcie120¾	4 wide bid, tired	11
7Nov99-2GP	fst	1 1/16	:233 :473 1:123 1:441	Md Sp Wt 50k	66 6 11½ 1½ 1hd 31½ 45½	Velez R I	118 b	50.50	81-10	HomeRunChamp118hd Malgot1185¼ JcbirSezWho118hd	Inside, weakened	12
18Sep99-6Crc	fst	7f	:221 :451 1:12 1:253	Md Sp Wt 26k	40 4 8 97½ 96¾ 86½ 611¾	Velez R I	117 b	8.60	69-15	Fappie's Notebook1171¾ Equal Time1176¼ Max O Max117¾	Jostled early	11
28Aug99-9Crc	fst	5½f	:223 :47 :593 1:061	Md Sp Wt 26k	32 4 1 73½ 63½ 79½ 414¾	Velez R I	118	1.80	78-15	Jebson1185½ Prospector's Wish118hd Mr. Pentel1189¼	No threat	7

WORKS: ●Jan10 OP 6f fst 1:164 H 1/6 Jan3 OP 4f my :511 B 8/22 Nov6 CD 4f fst :513 B 49/57

ALMd40000s

This is a fairly recent addition to the Southern California racing condition book, and worth looking at for betting opportunities.

The overall condition is Starter Allowance races for horses who won a maiden claiming race and have never won any other race in their career.

These races were intended for local cheap horses that beat a maiden claiming field and are unlikely to ever win another race. They can't run fast enough to win an ALWNX1 or even a bottom level $10,000 claiming race. California doesn't run ClmNX ___ races, so this is their new alternative. It keeps owners from running in Cal-bred ALWNX races.

The condition has been dominated by horses that could easily win a 3-and-up MSWT, but instead the trainers gamble and debut the horse in a MdnClm32g and win easily for a $18,000 purse. The horses then enter these AlMd40000s races in their second career race and are able to pick up another $18,000 against the weakest competition on the grounds. (After this, they are still eligible for ALWNX1 in their third start.)

A strong debut winner usually towers over these fields of chronic losers that somehow managed to win a maiden claiming race in their lackluster history. These horses stand out so much it is silly.

Marathons

What is considered a marathon? By this book's definition, a marathon is a race consisting of three turns or more, any distance beyond 1 1/4 miles in major league racing and beyond 1 1/8 miles in minor league or low level racing. In human terms, a marathon takes 2+ hours to run. In thoroughbred terms, a marathon lasts 2+ minutes!

These races are run more often on turf but are run on dirt as well. In 2003 (excluding 2-year-old races), almost half of the races in North America were run at a distance of 6 furlongs or less:

6 furlongs or less: 49%
Over 6f, under 1 mile: 15%
1 mile to 1 1/4 miles: 35%
Over 1 1/4 miles: Only 1%!

Speed is king in North America. Already in the minority, long distance races become fewer and fewer in number with each passing year in the U.S. Distance races remain much more common abroad, leading to many American distance races attracting overseas runners that have an experience edge.

Things To Consider:

Overall, the keys for this kind of race are:

1. Pace,
2. Jockeys that can judge pace, and
3. Pace.

Why isn't "Breeding" the key to judging marathons? Although breeding limitations can hinder horses beyond certain distances, breeding is not as important a factor as pace. If a horse has tried marathon distances without diminished performances, bloodline analysis can be set aside. Defer to the trainer's judgment that the horse belongs in the race.

Pace is the most critical aspect to picking consistent marathon winners. If the field runs in a slow-paced European style canter early, and then accelerates in the final 1/2 mile, every runner in the pack is on nearly equal footing turning for home. It is then a question of who can close the strongest.

Frontrunners do not gain as much from the slow pace as you would think, because they still have to close very strongly to win. The ideal frontrunner sets a pace that drains the pursuers of their energy, negating their closing kicks.

Closers at the back of *tight packs* rarely do well. Instead, closers need to save much more energy than the other runners by staying far back. At least a "distant trailer" is clearly spending much less energy than its competition.

Bunched-up tight packs lead to free-for-alls. This means a lot of troubled trips, split second jockey decisions, and horses spread out all over the track down the stretch.

Look For:

— Distance specialists, especially if they ran "evenly" at a shorter distance 2 to 3 weeks prior to today's event.

— Frontrunners that can set a fast pace and coast alone on the lead. The longer the race and the smaller the field, the more dangerous the frontrunner. Front running speed is almost universally an advantage to a racehorse. Races over a marathon distance are no exception.

The great misconception is that the longer the race, the less likely a frontrunner will win (or the more likely a closer will catch the early leaders). This is not true. The farther the race, the longer the horses must run before making their final thrust to the finish. The more they run, the more energy they expend so the less "kick" all of the competitors have. As a result, the frontrunners only get caught if they run out of gas or if another runner has some punch to "close the gap."

Think of a race car. The throttle determines how much horsepower is being released, but the gas tank limits how far you can go and still continue to compete. Wait too long, run out of gas, and you can hold the pedal to the floor and you still aren't going anywhere!

The more entrants there are, the more likely one of the riders will vie for the lead or get into a pace duel. Big fields increase the chance that someone will contest the early pace. Small fields tend to bunch up, pelleton-style, often settling into a slow, or at least comfortable, pace. The leader need only dole out enough effort to maintain a lead. With fewer runners applying pressure, the frontrunner has an advantage.

The public consistently favors closers in marathons, even though closers do not gain any advantage by waiting that long to go after the leaders. Try to take advantage of this common misconception and favor the horse that tries to take the field wire to wire. Lone frontrunners stretching out—they'll get an easy lead and a slower pace, as they can run comfortably at a quicker pace than the traditional marathoners are used to.

Steeplechases

Racing over hurdles remains a key part of racing at Saratoga, Colonial, and a number of eastern United States meets. The vast majority of steeplechases are run at venues that do not allow wagering. This is unfortunate, because when it is possible to bet on them, they should not be passed over without an effort to find a wager based on top steeplechase connections.

Although very unusual to those players accustomed to flat races, steeplechases are actually among the simplest races to handicap. Steeplechase races cannot be judged using speed or pace figures. This fact alone probably drives many handicappers away. The horses tend to run in a slow-paced herd until the final 1/2 mile, then accelerate and "race" to the wire in earnest. At the finish, the field is often spread out over dozens of lengths and multiple runners are likely to "leave the course," a term for failing to complete all required jumps. So what about this makes steeplechases easy to handicap? The answer is the statistics about which connections win the majority of races.

Compare this information for 2004: In 2004, approximately 53,000 thoroughbred "flat" races were run in North America. The top 5 trainers based on number of wins were Steven Asmussen, Scott Lake, Jerry Hollendorfer, Cole Norman, and Todd Pletcher. Together, these five trainers accounted for wins in only 3% of the races. Extend this analysis to the top 10 trainers of 2004, and those 10 trainers accounted for 5% of all wins.

The same analysis produces startling results when applied to steeplechases. The top 5 trainers won 40% of the 228 steeplechase events during 2004, and the top 10 trainers won 59%! Particularly when contrasted with flat races, these statistics show that steeplechases are dominated by only a handful of connections.

A handicapper can easily follow the few "major players" in steeplechasing. Now for the bad news for handicappers. In nearly every betting event for steeplechases, the races are likely to contain multiple runners from the top 10 trainers in the game. Furthermore, several of the top 10 riders are likely to be riding.

Betting on half the field is no way to profit in any horse race, so more information is required to ensure a profit betting steeplechases.

The key steeplechases where betting is allowed are the National Steeplechase Association (NSA) events at the Saratoga meet. Since there are no maiden hurdle events at the meet, in order to enter a Saratoga steeplechase event, a horse must already be a winner over the hurdles. Saratoga hosts a non-betting Open House each year on the Sunday before opening day, offering maiden steeplechase races in addition to training races on the flats. These steeplechase winners qualify for the races to be run at the Saratoga meet. These races also allow the owners to cheer wildly, hoping for a cut of the $15,000 purse. And only the connections are cheering insanely, because Open House races are non-betting events unlike the steeplechases offered once the official Spa meet begins.

Most racegoers consider any hurdle race to simply be a steeplechase event. But the conditions vary, just like flat races, from graded stakes to claiming to allowances that can compete with the complexity of a flat allowance condition, like Optional Allowance / Starter Hurdle, NW2 or Started for $35,000 or less in the last two years.

At Saratoga, several steeplechases will be run each meet. Eight were run in 2002, and nine were run in each of the 2003 and 2004 meets. Usually the first race of a midweek racing day, a first-race steeplechase often attracts less betting than a flat race starting the day's card. At Saratoga, though, that's a pretty lofty comparison—around $180,000 versus $300,000. Don't be one of the bettors avoiding these races. Show up in time to bet, watch and win.

There are some important overall facts to know about steeplechase events:

— Opportunities to bet steeplechases are rare—most steeplechases run in America are non-wagering events.

— Except for Saratoga and Colonial, other tracks hold one or two steeplechases per meet as a featured event that draws little betting handle. At Saratoga, the purses for steeplechases are comparable to or better than many flat races, ranging from $35,000 to over $100,000 for the Grade 1 feature each meet.

— Riders weigh around 140 lbs. and follow the NSA circuit. It is uncommon to see a steeplechase rider competing in a normal flat race, and virtually unheard of for a "flat" jockey to ride in a steeplechase.

— There are two distinct levels, especially at Saratoga: Maiden, claiming or allowance races at around 2 1/16 miles (weight around 140 to 154 lbs.), and higher level allowances or stakes, at a longer distance and more weight—usually closer to 2 5/8 miles and up to 160 lbs. Between the levels, a huge chasm of ability separates the competitors. Success at the shorter races against easier competition does not mean a horse will be a factor in stakes.

— As previously discussed, one big plus for the handicapper is the small number of "major" connections. A relatively small number of trainers dominate, and the group shows low volatility from year to year. This makes steeplechasing easy to catch up on each summer before Saratoga opens. (Standings are maintained and available at the NSA website, *www.nationalsteeplechase.com.*)

— Finally, of key interest to the handicapper, favorites in steeplechases win about 40% of the time at events where parimutuel wagering is permitted.

Betting Steeplechase Races

There are three main areas of overlap with flat racing to be aware of.

First, many of the competitors will be former flat racers, who retired and transitioned to hurdles. Jack Flash, for example, appeared as a steeplechase competitor at Saratoga in 2000. His previous 23-race career included a decent 7th in the 1997 Kentucky Derby. A horse's most recent races over both jumps and flat racing will show in its past performances, so be sure to distinguish performance over hurdles from attempts on the flats.

Secondly, steeplechase trainers occasionally enter their horses in flat events for training and conditioning purposes. If this involves competing at another track, this sometimes looks like a trainer change. In general, a steeplechaser is not competitive in a flat race (unless all entrants are steeplechasers as a special race condition, a "training race" that is always designated as a non-wagering event).

Finally, the third area of overlap involves reporting of racing statistics. Past performances generally reflect starts at thoroughbred tracks, including steeplechase events as well as normal races. From the perspective of handicapping steeplechases, however, it is critical to know the trainer's success within that specialized arena. Take the time to access steeplechase-specific standings through the NSA website, *www.nationalsteeplechase.com*. Although there is virtually no overlap between steeplechase and flat race jockey colonies, the top steeplechase trainers often start a decent number of horses in non-hurdle events. Thomas Voss and Jonathan Sheppard are both known as strong conditioners with turf runners.

Saratoga draws in top connections, and in many events, virtually all of the entrants will have a recognizable trainer. Individual trainers and riders remain in that "top" group year after year, again making it relatively easy to stay familiar with connections.

As an extreme example, Jonathan Sheppard has been a top steeplechasing trainer for decades. In 1969, Sheppard won 27 races and was the #2 steeplechase trainer in North America by number of wins (#5 by money won). Most of his wins were for owner Augustin Stable, and some were even ridden by George Strawbridge, Jr. As one becomes familiar with the steeplechase circuit, it is no surprise that the trainer-owner combination continues to perform strongly year after year. Sheppard is not alone in his consistency both in training success and focus on hurdles rather than flat.

The below table looks back at the Top 10 trainers from 2004, showing that 9 of the 10 trainers have been a "Top 10" steeplechase conditioner for three years in a row:

Trainer Name	2004 Top 10	# wins (win %)	2003 Top 10? (win %)	2002 Top 10? (win %)
Jack Fisher	#1	27 (18%)	#1 (20%)	#4 (14%)
Sanna Hendriks	#2	19 (25%)	#5 (19%)	#3 (30%)
Jonathan Sheppard	#3	18 (20%)	#9 (9%)	#5 (22%)
Doug Fout	#4	16 (18%)	#7 (11%)	#10 (17%)
Neil R. Morris	#5	12 (17%)	#6 (25%)	#9 (22%)
Katherine Neilson	#6	10 (10%)	#2 (20%)	#6 (16%)
Ricky Hendriks	#7	10 (14%)	#4 (13%)	#2 (15%)
F. Bruce Miller	#8	9 (11%)	#10 (7%)	#7 (16%)
Thomas H. Voss	#9	8 (12%)	#3 (20%)	#1 (35%)
Chip Miller	#10	6 (26%)	N/A	N/A

Source: National Steeplechase Association, Inc. (*www.nationalsteeple chase.com*), Annual Standings

The trend with riders is similar:

Rider Name	2004 Top 10	# wins (win %)	2003 Top 10? (win %)	2002 Top 10? (win %)
Matthew McCarron	#1	24 (22%)	#2 (16%)	#6 (20%)
Tom Foley	#2	16 (21%)	#3 (13%)	#9 (9%)
David Bentley	#3	13 (15%)	#1 (13%)	#1 (17%)
Danielle Hodsdon	#4	13 (18%)	#8 (14)%	N/A
Gus Brown	#5	11 (17%)	#6 (15%)	#2 (20%)
Robert Massey	#6	11 (13%)	#4 (14)%	#3 (15%)
Chip Miller	#7	11 (18%)	N/A	N/A
Robert Walsh	#8	9 (11%)	N/A	N/A
Jody Petty	#9	9 (16%)	#7 (12%)	#5 (20%)
Xavier Aizpuru	#10	8 (12%)	N/A	N/A

Source: National Steeplechase Association, Inc. (*www.nationalsteeple chase.com*), Annual Standings

Clearly, being able to identify the top trainers and riders in an event is key to finding winners. Betting these top outfits can lead to longshots as well as favorites. Don't hesitate to back a horse ridden by a top rider just because the odds are huge. Favorites win more than their fair share, but winning these events takes unique riding skills, and the top hurdle riders win on horses at a wide range of prices. If a horse fits the race conditions and distance and is in the hands of a top outfit, ignore the odds board and even the past performances, and bet that the connections know what they are doing.

The bottom line for betting: Steeplechases add a spice of variety to racing cards. With little work, a handicapper can become familiar with the top trainers and jockeys, and add that knowledge to the past performances. Don't rely exclusively on past performances for a steeplechase race. The exercise is unnecessary, and rules of pace, distance and layoffs rarely apply. Key on jocks, trainers, and favorites. Top jocks and trainers often produce results at long odds, so combining favorites with top connections in exotics can pay off in spades.

Handicapping Stakes Races

The feature race draws as many as half the weekend bettors to the track or OTB. Superstars dominate American sports, and that's what fans want to see. A race is just a race, but a stakes is an *EVENT*. Convince the fans that an *EVENT* will be happening, and you can double or triple attendance. Just ask Belmont Park about the Triple Crown bids in the last few years.

This means more money gets bet on stakes, name recognition plays a big part in that betting, and opportunities are always available to the astute handicapper.

Who Wins Stakes? (2-year-olds)

This section will be brief. The concept is simple and there's no reason to belabor it. Two-year-old stakes are won by the juvenile with the fastest raw speed. The horse that has run the fastest opening 1/2 mile will usually dominate the field.

The single dominant factor in 2-year-old stakes is speed. 2-year-olds leave the gate with the throttle wide open and run as fast as they can for as long as they can. They do not yet have the seasoning to show patience and be able to rate. For some, this means a brilliant opening quarter followed by a rapid deceleration. Others expend energy more steadily, and these "closers" are still able to run excellent final times even though they too decelerate in the stretch.

Juveniles with Quarter horse-like gate speed will dominate early stages at 5, 5 1/2, 6 and 6 1/2 furlongs. As the distance increases, sustaining the hard charge becomes ever more important. The ability to rate is still not expected. It is the training and genes that enable the youngsters to avoid burning out in the opening 1/2 mile. But make no mistake, 2-year-olds tend to give their all for as long as it lasts, and can fade like an Indy car out of gas. Only when races extend to route distances does the situation change.

As a result, speed figures and final times are great indicators of ability. The fastest 2-year-old usually prevails. This is why 2-year-old stakes favorites are among the most reliable bets in racing.

Who Wins Stakes? (2-year-olds Excluded)

The good news in major stakes races is that the contenders usually have established credentials and are fit, healthy athletes—fine examples of the equine form. Although this clears up some confusion, stakes also tend to attract runners from top connections that don't really have the ability to win. This last group may be divided into three categories:

— Running to compete and win,
— Entered because the connections think their horse has a chance to improve enough to upset the field (either due to improved condition or ability, or due to ideal circumstances and questionable competition), and
— Running to be in the post parade and maybe get lucky.

At every level of stakes competition, these three categories are discernible. As a general rule, the more important the stakes, the more obvious the categories should be.

Stakes Levels, In Order Of Prestige

In order to assess a stakes race, it is important to have a feel for how a particular race stacks up. This is not always evident simply through purse size. Here is a look at relative stakes levels and examples of races found at each level.

— *Classic*: Kentucky Derby (Churchill Downs), Preakness (Pimlico), Belmont Stakes (Belmont), Travers (Saratoga), Breeders' Cup World Thoroughbred Championships
— *Grade I open*: Whitney (Saratoga), Stephen Foster (Churchill Downs)

— *3-year-old Grade I/II*: Florida Derby (Gulfstream Park), Santa Anita Derby (Santa Anita), Haskell Invitational (Monmouth)
— ***Track Marquee Events***: Pimlico Special (Pimlico), Arlington Million (Arlington Park)
— ***Grade II/III routes***: Often dominated by top stakes earners with best record at the distance
— ***Grade II/III sprints***
— ***Grade II/III turf***
— ***Ungraded stakes that are important to minor tracks***: Marquee events for the best horses on the grounds, even attracting shippers for the relatively rich purse
— ***Ungraded stakes***
— ***Restricted stakes*** (state bred, sales restricted, etc.): Often lead to lopsided victories due to a limited number of stakes-quality runners in a given class
— ***Overnight handicaps***: Glorified allowance events often lead to big upsets; the top contenders' focus is often looking ahead to a bigger race

The Modern Traveling Handicap Star

Shipping horses around the country (and around the world, for that matter) is not new. But a new standard of handicap star has evolved over the last 15 years to suit the handicap circuit in place today.

Prior to the Breeders' Cup, it was normal for a divisional leader to ship to New York for the Jockey Club Gold Cup, or to Gulfstream for the Donn Handicap, or to Santa Anita for the Big 'Cap. A road trip or two during the year was pretty much the extent of it for most stars. If you wanted big purses, you had to stay in New York or California. The Breeders' Cup started to change all that. It became clear that the biggest prize of all would be in a different location every year. Trainers adapted accordingly.

The conglomerates like Team Lukas had outposts around the country, so his stars could stay in a Lukas barn pretty much anywhere they traveled.

But the first big horse to set the standard for the Modern Tour d'Handicap was Alysheba. After the Triple Crown, Alysheba began a Grade I campaign that took him to:

2nd: Haskell Invitational Handicap *(Monmouth Park)*
6th: Travers *(Saratoga)*
1st: Super Derby *(Louisiana Downs)*
2nd: Breeders' Cup Classic *(Hollywood Park)*
1st: Strub Stakes *(Santa Anita)*
1st: Santa Anita Handicap *(Santa Anita)*
1st: San Bernardino *(Santa Anita)* (Grade 2)
4th: Pimlico Special *(Pimlico)*
2nd: Hollywood Gold Cup *(Hollywood Park)*
1st: Iselin Handicap *(Monmouth Park)*
1st: Woodward Handicap *(Belmont Park)*
1st: Meadowlands Cup Handicap *(Meadowlands)*
1st: Breeders' Cup Classic *(Churchill Downs)*

Twelve Grade 1 races and one Grade 2. Seven Grade 1 wins and one Grade 2 win, three track records, three Eclipse Awards, and Beyer Speed Figures reaching the 120s.

All of this following an early career that included a third in the Breeders' Cup Juvenile, a win but DQ in the Blue Grass, wins in the Kentucky Derby and Preakness followed by a dramatic, troubled defeat in the Belmont Stakes in an effort to be the first Triple Crown winner since the 1970s.

The success of Alysheba, followed shortly by stars like Easy Goer and Sunday Silence, gave rise to the American Championship Racing Series. The rejuvenated Pimlico Special and the new Pacific Classic added two big purses to the 1 1/4 Grade I roster.

Unfortunately, 1990 through 1994 passed by without a star campaigner. Lots of solid talented horses without the big standout star that could take the show on the road. The series fell apart for reasons beyond the talent in the fields. In November 1994, Bill Mott took an AlwNX2 eligible turf running 4-year-old, and put him in a dirt allowance at Aqueduct. The horse won so easily he was entered in the Grade I NYRA Mile 3 weeks later. With devastating ease, Cigar won the race by a widening 7 lengths.

No one could have guessed that cold Thanksgiving weekend was just the beginning of things to come, with 16 consecutive victories waiting for the great Cigar. Over 20 races, 17 of which were Grade Is, Cigar racked up 17 wins, 2 seconds, and 1 third. Cigar switched tracks 14 times, with 11 different tracks in all.

Cigar
Own: Paulson Allen E

B. h. 14 (Apr)
Sire: Palace Music (The Minstrel) $3,754
Dam: Solar Slew (Seattle Slew)
Br: Allen E. Paulson (Md)
Tr: Mott William I

Life	33	19	4	5	$9,999,815	121	D.Fst	20	17	2	1	$8,357,800 121
1996	8	5	2	1	$4,910,000	117	Wet(310)	2	1	0	0	$1,560,000 117
1995	10	10	0	0	$4,819,800	121	Turf(286)	11	1	2	4	$82,015 99

26Oct96-10WO	fst	1¼	:462 1:104 1:352 2:01	3↑BCClasic-G1	115	7	85½	63½	4nk	4¾	3hd	Bailey J D	L126	*.65	- -	Alphabet Soup126no Louis Quatorze121hd Cigar126½	Bid,hung	13
5Oct96-10Bel	fst	1¼	:473 1:112 1:354 2:003	3↑JkyClbGC-G1	115	6	34½	34½	31	3½	2hd	Bailey J D	L126	*.20	- -	Skip Away121hd Cigar1262 Louis Quatorze1211	Drifted late,game	6
14Sep96-8Bel	fst	1⅛	:461 1:102 1:343 1:47	3↑Woodward-G1	116	4	42½	42½	3½	11	14	Bailey J D	L126	*.35	- -	Cigar1264 L'Carriere126½ Golden Larch126¾	Swept wide,ridden out	5
10Aug96-6Dmr	fst	1¼	:454 1:091 1:333 1:594	3↑PacClasc-G1	111	4	21	2½	11	2½	23½	Bailey J D	LB124	*.10	- -	Dare and Go1243½ Cigar1247 Siphon1248	Stalkd fst pce,2ndbest	6
13Jly96-10AP	fst	1⅛	:464 1:101 1:353 1:481	3↑CitatnChlg1075k	117	10	63½	62¾	31	1½	13½	Bailey J D	L130	*.30	- -	Cigar1303½ Dramatic Gold118nk Eltish1182	Lost ground drew clear	10
1Jun96-10Suf	fst	1⅛	:454 1:101 1:361 1:493	3↑MassH500k	112	3	46	33	13	14½	12¼	Bailey J D	LB130	*.10	- -	Cigar1302¼ Personal Merit11110¼ Prolanzier112nk	Handily	6
Previously trained by Mott William I																		
27Mar96♦Nad Al Sheba (UAE)	ft	*1¼	LH 2:034	4↑Dubai World Cup Stk 4000000							1½	Bailey J	125	-		Cigar125½ Soul of the Matter1258 L'Carriere125¾	5th after 1f,bid 4f out,led 2f out,dueled 1-1/2f out,prevailed	11
Previously trained by Mott William I																		
10Feb96-10GP	fst	1⅛	:464 1:104 1:353 1:49	3↑DonnH-G1	117	1	31½	32	2hd	12½	12	Bailey J D	L128	*.20	- -	Cigar1282 Wekiva Springs1174 Heavenly Prize1153	Rated, easily	8
28Oct95-8Bel	my	1¼	:481 1:121 1:353 1:592	3↑BCClasic-G1	117	10	31	4¾	11½	12	12½	Bailey J D	L126	*.70	- -	Cigar1262½ L'Carriere1261 Unaccounted For126¾	Took over 4w trn,drvng	11
7Oct95-10Bel	fst	1¼	:48 1:112 1:36 2:011	3↑JkyClbGC-G1	111	6	31	21	21	11½	11	Bailey J D	L126	*.35	- -	Cigar1261 Unaccounted For1263¾ Star Standard1212	Stalked outs,clear	7
16Sep95-9Bel	fst	1⅛	:454 1:093 1:334 1:47	3↑Woodward-G1	111	5	32½	34	2hd	14	12¾	Bailey J D	L126	*.10	- -	Cigar1262¾ Star Standard1213 Golden Larch126¾	Cruised in hand	6
2Jly95-6Hol	fst	1¼	:453 1:092 1:34 1:592	3↑HolGldCp-G1	118	1	42	41½	11	13	13½	Bailey J D	LB126	*.90	- -	Cigar1263½ Tinners Way118hd Tossofthecoin118½	Much best, driving	8
3Jun95-10Suf	fst	1⅛	:471 1:102 1:351 1:483	3↑MassH750k	117	6	33½	31½	2½	13	14	Bailey J D	LB124	*.20	- -	Cigar1244 Poor But Honest1075½ Double Calvados113nk	4 wide, ridden out	6
13May95-10Pim	fst	1 3/16	:48 1:112 1:351 1:533	4↑PimSpclH-G1	114	1	11½	11	11½	14½	12¼	Bailey J D	L122	*.40	- -	Cigar1222¼ Devil His Due1212¼ Concern1214½	Steady hand drive	6
15Apr95-9OP	fst	1⅛	:462 1:104 1:352 1:471	4↑OaklawnH-G1	121	4	42½	43½	42	1hd	12½	Bailey J D	L120	*1.70	- -	Cigar1202½ Silver Goblin1194 Concern1221	Rallied, drew clear	7
5Mar95-9GP	fst	1¼	:472 1:114 1:364 2:024	3↑GPH-G1	116	9	43½	43½	3nk	14	17½	Bailey J D	L118	*.50	- -	Cigar1187½ Pride of Burkaan1141 Mahogany Hall1132	As rider pleased	11
11Feb95-9GP	fst	1⅛	:462 1:103 1:363 1:493	3↑DonnH-G1	114	4	11	12	1hd	1½	15½	Bailey J D	L115	4.00	- -	Cigar1155½ Primitive Hall1122 Bonus Money1123½	Dueled, drew off	9
22Jan95-10GP	fst	1 1/16	:231 :464 1:112 1:431	4↑Alw 33000n4x	108	5	1hd	1½	11	11	12	Bailey J D	L122	*.50	- -	Cigar1222 Upping the Ante1198¾ Chasin Gold1221	Led throughout	8
26Nov94-8Aqu	fst	1	:223 :454 1:111 1:36	3↑NYRAMiH-G1	115	6	41¼	41	12	15	17	Bailey J D	111	8.90	- -	Cigar1117 Devil His Due1242½ Punch Line1121	Drew off, rddn out	12
28Oct94-6Aqu	fst	1	:222 :443 1:094 1:353	3↑Alw 34000n2x	104	6	2hd	11½	13	14	18	Smith M E	117	3.50	- -	Cigar1178 Golden Plover1193½ Gulliviegold1092	Ridden out	6
7Oct94-8Bel	fm	1 1/16 [T]	:232 :463 1:104 1:412	3↑Alw 36000n3x	79	2	42½	33½	2hd	33	38½	Krone J A	117	3.40	- -	UnaccountedFor1142½ SameOldWish1196 Cigr117½	Mid move, 4 wide turn	6
16Sep94-7Bel	fm	1 (T)	:23 :452 1:083 1:33	3↑Alw 34000n2x	76	10	84¾	74	46	65½	78¼	Bailey J D	117	*1.90	- -	Jido1082½ Bermuda Cedar1142 Limited War1132	Wide all, no threat	11
8Aug94-1Sar	fm	1⅛ [T]	:472 1:12 1:363 1:483	3↑Alw 34000n3x	86	1	42½	43	41½	41¼	33	Smith M E	117	3.20	- -	My Mogul1191½ Next Endeavor1191½ Cigar117nk	In tight, steadied	8
8Jly94-7Bel	fm	1 1/16 [T]	:243 :482 1:123 1:43	3↑Alw 34000n3x	77	5	2hd	1hd	2hd	41¼	49	Smith M E	117	*1.70	- -	Dancing Hunter117½ Compadre1173 I'm Very Irish1125½	Dueled, tired turn	5
Previously trained by Hassinger Alex L Jr																		
20Nov93-6Hol	fm	1⅛ (T)	:461 1:102 1:341 1:464	HolDerby-G1	71	9	52½	54½	41½	75½	1114¼	Valenzuela P A	LB122	24.80	- -	ExplosiveRed1221¼ JeuneHomme122nk ErlofBrking122½	Bid turn, gave way	14
5Nov93-8SA	fm	1⅛ (T)	:48 1:121 1:36 1:48	VolanteH-G3	98	4	44	42½	32	21½	22	Valenzuela P A	LB117	7.70	- -	Eastern Memories1132 Cigar117nk Snake Eyes120½	Finished well	9
25Sep93-5BM	fm	1 1/16 (T)	:23 :453 1:10 1:413	AscotH-G3	99	1	53¾	54¾	41½	13½	3nk	Valenzuela P A	LB117	4.10	- -	Siebe115nk Nonproductiveasset114hd Cigar1172¼	Room rail, led, wknd	11
3Sep93-8Dmr	fm	1 (T)	:224 :47 1:11 1:35	3↑Alw 40000n3l	96	4	22	22	21	2hd	2½	McCarron C J	LB115	3.30	- -	Kingdom of Spain115½ Cigar115½ Saturnino1173	Bid 1/8,outfinished	6
18Aug93-5Dmr	fm	1 1/16 (T)	:231 :472 1:111 1:414	3↑Alw 36000n$y	94	5	43½	43½	53½	1hd	12¾	McCarron C J	LB115	*1.90	- -	Cigr1152¾ OurMotionGrnted122hd TheBerklyMn1142¼	Quick gain early str	10
12Jun93-10Hol	fm	1 1/16 (T)	:231 :48 1:113 1:412	Alw 39000n2l	84	10	75	72½	4¾	31½	31¾	Valenzuela P A	L117	2.90	- -	Nonproductiveasset115½ Tossofthecoin1191¼ Cigar1172¾	In tight 1/4,rallied	10
23May93-9Hol	fm	1 1/16 (T)	:232 :471 1:103 1:411	Alw 39000n$y	85	11	32	31	2hd	11½	41¾	Valenzuela P A	LB117	3.80	- -	Pleasedontexplain117½ SttelyWrrior115½ FleetWizrd115¾	Lead 1/8, faltered	12
9May93-3Hol	fst	6f	:22 :443 :564 1:092	3↑Md Sp Wt 32k	93	3	4	21	1hd	12	12¼	Valenzuela P A	117	5.20	- -	Cigar1172¼ Golden Slewpy1165½ Famous Fan115hd	Off slowly, rushed	6
21Feb93-6SA	gd	6f	:214 :452 :58 1:104	Md Sp Wt 28k	53	9	7	64	75¾	67	713	Valenzuela P A	B118	5.10	- -	Demigod118nk Cardiac1182 [D]Sir Hutch1182½	No factor	9

It is this 24-month terror that remains the modern standard for a champion handicap horse. In the seasons since Cigar retired, Eclipse winners like Silver Charm, Victory Gallop, Medaglia d'Oro, and Pleasantly Perfect have tried to emulate Cigar, but have never stayed the course. Three, four, five wins in a row, but longer has yet to be accomplished. Mineshaft's 2003 Horse of the Year title was accomplished without running in the WTC Breeders' Cup Classic and, in 2004, Ghostzapper won the 4 races he contested. Does Ghostzapper's 4 for 4 season compare to Cigar winning 10 of 10 in 1995, including 8 Grade 1s? Hardly.

Compare Cigar's campaign with Skip Away's handicap performances, below. Skip Away strung together 9 graded stakes wins, the closest recent comparison to Cigar's streak. However, Skip Away only won 4 of 11 races as a 4-year-old while earning Horse of the Year honors. His repeat as Horse of the Year in 1998 included 7 straight wins as the odds-on favorite. Skip Away failed to win past the month of September as his career wound down, in a very similar fashion to Cigar's final races. Time catches up with even the best handicap horses.

Skip Away
Own: Hine Carolyn H

Gr/ro. h. 12 (Apr)
Sire: Skip Trial (Balljumper) $5,000
Dam: Ingot Way (Diplomat Way)
Br: Anna Marie Barnhart (Fla)
Tr: Hine Hubert

Life	38	18	10	6	$9,616,360	125
1998	9	7	0	1	$2,740,000	121
1997	11	4	5	2	$4,089,000	125
D.Fst	34	16	9	5	$8,615,740	125
Wet(335)	3	2	0	1	$994,000	118
Turf(259)	1	0	1	0	$6,620	72

7Nov98-10CD	fst	1¼	:473 1:12 1:371 2:02	3↑ BCClasic-G1	110	6	21	2½	4¾	63½	64	Bailey J D	L126 b	*1.90	91-07	Awesome Again126¾ Silver Charm126nk Swain126no	Pressed, empty	10
10Oct98-10Bel	sly	1¼	:462 1:093 1:341 2:003	3↑ JkyClbGC-G1	100	4	2hd	2½	22	34	310½	Bailey J D	L126 b	*.35	81-14	Wagon Limit1265½ Gentlemen1264¾ Skip Away1264	Dueled outside, faded	6
19Sep98-9Bel	fst	1⅛	:452 1:09 1:341 1:474	3↑ Woodward-G1	119	2	2hd	1½	11	12	11¾	Bailey J D	L126 b	*1.10	91-18	Skip Away1251¾ Gentlemen1268 Running Stag1259	About his business	5
30Aug98-11Mth	fst	1⅛	:463 1:10 1:344 1:471	3↑ PlselinH-G2	114	4	31	2hd	11	1hd	1no	Bailey J D	L131 b	*.05	102-09	Skip Away131no Stormin Fever1139 Ⓓ Testafly1142¾	Driving	7
28Jun98-7Hol	fst	1¼	:462 1:093 1:34 2:00	3↑ HolGldCp-G1	117	2	11	1hd	1hd	11	11¾	Bailey J D	LB124 b	*.40	95-05	Skip Away1241¾ Puerto Madero1241 Gentlemen1243	Gamely, kicked clear	8
30May98-9Suf	fst	1⅛	:462 1:101 1:344 1:471	3↑ MassH-G3	121	1	1hd	12½	11½	12	14¼	Bailey J D	L130 b	*.30	103-07	SkipAway1304¼ PuertoMdero1164¾ KJsAppel1134	Set pace much the best	5
9May98-7Pim	gd	1 3/16	:47 1:112 1:354 1:541	3↑ PimSpclH-G1	118	4	12	12½	12½	14	13¼	Bailey J D	L128 b	*.20	94-16	Skip Away1283¼ Precocity115nk Hot Brush113¾	Contrlld pce 2w, drivng	5
28Feb98-10GP	fst	1¼	:463 1:101 1:351 2:031	3↑ GPH-G1	114	2	21	2hd	11½	12	12¼	Bailey J D	L127 b	*.10	95-16	Skip Away1272¼ Unruled1121¾ Behrens1141¼	Fast pace, drew off	6
7Feb98-10GP	fst	1⅛	:463 1:104 1:362 1:50	3↑ DonnH-G1	109	3	2hd	31	2hd	12½	12¾	Bailey J D	L126 b	*.40	87-24	Skip Away1262¾ Unruled112½ Sir Bear113nk	Angled out, ridden out	10
8Nov97-8Hol	fst	1¼	:461 1:093 1:334 1:59	3↑ BCClassc-G1	120	1	31	12½	15	15	16	Smith M E	L126 b	*1.80	102-06	SkipAwy1266 DputyCommndr122¾ Ⓓ WhiskyWsdom1263	Drew off, handily	9
18Oct97-9Bel	fst	1¼	:47 1:10 1:334 1:584	3↑ JkyClbGC-G1	116	1	2½	1hd	1hd	16	16½	Bailey J D	L126 b	1.45	103-04	SkipAwy1266½ InstntFrindship12610 WgonLimit121¾	Spd on rail, ridden out	7
20Sep97-9Bel	fst	1⅛	:471 1:111 1:35 1:472	3↑ Woodward-G1	116	2	1hd	2hd	33	34½	25½	Sellers S J	L126 b	1.35	87-15	Formal Gold1265½ Skip Away126nk Will's Way12640	Gamely for 2nd	5
23Aug97-9Mth	fst	1 1/16	:224 :452 1:09 1:401	3↑ PlselinH-G2	115	1	44	45	32½	25	25¼	Sellers S J	L124 b	*.90	101-07	FormlGold1215¼ SkipAwy1242½ DstortdHumor1156	No match 2nd best late	4
2Aug97-8Sar	fst	1⅛	:47 1:104 1:352 1:481	3↑ WhitneyH-G1	115	2	33	33	31½	35	36½	Sellers S J	L125 b	*1.10	88-25	Will's Way117no Formal Gold1206½ Skip Away1259½	3w 2nd turn, no bid	6
4Jly97-9Bel	fst	1¼	:472 1:12 1:371 2:021	3↑ SuburbnH-G2	118	1	3½	41	31	3nk	11½	Sellers S J	L122 b	*1.00	86-23	Skip Away1221½ Will's Way116¾ Formal Gold12015	3w move 1/4 pole	6
31May97-11Suf	fst	1⅛	:471 1:104 1:351 1:474	3↑ MassH-G3	122	3	2hd	2½	1hd	1½	1hd	Sellers S J	L119 b	*.70	104-01	Skip Away119hd Formal Gold1143½ Will's Way1142¼	Dueled, prevailed	6
10May97-9Pim	fst	1 3/16	:463 1:10 1:343 1:53	4↑ PimSpclH-G1	125	8	41½	42	32	22	2½	Sellers S J	L119 b	3.30	101-17	Gentlemen122½ Skip Away1196½ Tejano Run1148	3wd trip, closed gamely	8
20Apr97-7LS	fst	1	:232 :461 1:093 1:342	3↑ TexasMile250k	92	5	67	52½	43½	34½	37½	Sellers S J	L116 b	*.60	- -	Isitingood1233 Spiritbound1164½ Skip Away1162½	4wide 1st turn, dull	7
1Mar97-10GP	fst	1¼	:46 1:104 1:354 2:021	3↑ GPH-G1	115	2	2½	1hd	1hd	2½	22¼	Sellers S J	L122 b	*.40	89-19	Mt. Sassafras1132¼ Skip Away122nk Tejano Run1142	Fast pace, held place	6
8Feb97-10GP	fst	1⅛	:47 1:104 1:35 1:472	3↑ DonnH-G1	112	7	21½	2½	21½	21½	21¼	Sellers S J	L123 b	*.70	100-04	Formal Gold1131¼ Skip Away1236 Mecke120hd	Stalk fast pace, hung	10
5Oct96-10Bel	fst	1¼	:473 1:112 1:354 2:003	3↑ JkyClbGC-G1	115	4	2½	2½	2hd	1½	1hd	Sellers S J	L121 b	5.80	94-10	Skip Away121hd Cigar1262 Louis Quatorze1211	Dug in, prevailed	6
15Sep96-9WO	fst	1⅛	:464 1:103 1:36 1:49	WoMilion-G1	108	1	55½	55	53¾	1½	14	Sellers S J	L126 b	*1.15	101-09	Skip Away1264 Victor Cooley119no Stephanotis1193½	Driving, drew clear	7
24Aug96-7Sar	fst	1¼	:461 1:103 1:361 2:022	Travers-G1	111	3	31½	41	3½	31½	31¾	Santos J A	L126 b	*1.45	95-03	Will's Way126¾ Louis Quatorze1261 Skip Away1263½	Stdied on rail backstr	7
4Aug96-10Mth	fst	1⅛	:461 1:094 1:342 1:473	BckHskIH-G1	113	2	43	44	31½	3½	11	Santos J A	L124 b	*.60	103-01	Skip Away1241 Dr. Caton1151 Victory Speech1214½	Driving	7
23Jun96-14Tdn	fst	1⅛	:461 1:104 1:353 1:474	OhioDrby-G2	110	10	52¾	52	1½	13	13½	Santos J A	LB122 b	*.70	103-08	SkipAwy1223½ VictorySpeech1189¼ ClshbyNight118nk	Rallied, 5w. riddn out	10
8Jun96-9Bel	fst	1½	:464 1:104 2:02 2:284	Belmont-G1	105	13	63¾	2hd	11½	1hd	21	Santos J A	L126 b	8.00	89-13	Editor's Note1261 Skip Away1264 My Flag1216	4w move 2nd trn, dug in	14
18May96-10Pim	fst	1 3/16	:461 1:094 1:342 1:532	Preaknes-G1	107	11	31	23	22	21	23¼	Sellers S J	L126 b	3.30	98-10	LouisQuatorze1263¼ SkipAwy1263 EditorsNote1262½	Stalked, bid 1/8, 2d best	12
4May96-8CD	fst	1¼	:46 1:10 1:35 2:01	KyDerby-G1	87	16	64½	84½	79½	1216	1216¾	Sellers S J	L126 b	7.70	- -	Grindstone126no Cavonnier1263½ Prince of Thieves126nk	Close up no rally	19
13Apr96-9Kee	wf	1⅛	:462 1:101 1:344 1:471	BlueGras-G2	113	5	2½	1hd	1½	14	16	Sellers S J	L121 b	4.60	- -	SkipAwy1216 LouisQutorze1211½ EditorsNote1213	Drew clear, ridden out	7
16Mar96-10GP	fst	1⅛	:462 1:094 1:343 1:474	FlaDerby-G1	104	3	53	44½	45½	23	36¼	Sellers S J	L122 b	7.90	- -	Unbridled's Song1225¾ Editor's Note122½ Skip Away1222¼	Fast pace, evenly	8
10Feb96-8GP	fst	1 1/16	:233 :474 1:114 1:441	Alw 26000n1x	100	4	53½	31	1½	16	112	Sellers S J	L117 b	*1.10	- -	SkipAway11712 Hedye120no NaturlSelection1201½	Much the best, handily	12
10Jan96-1GP	fst	1 1/16	:23 :463 1:114 1:454	Alw 26000n1x	-	1	43½	53	58¾	-	-	Bailey J D	117	*.40	- -	Blushing Jim1171½ Head Minister1171¼ NightRunner1177¾	Distanced, bled	5
25Nov95-7Aqu	fst	1⅛	:471 1:114 1:373 1:501	Remsen-G2	94	1	63½	43	32	1½	2nk	Bailey J D	112	2.30	- -	Tropicool112nk Skip Away1122 Crafty Friend1133	Led 1/8, 2nd best	11
29Oct95-7Bel	fst	1	:223 :461 1:113 1:37	Cowdin-G2	79	7	31½	31½	2hd	2hd	2no	Wilson R	122	5.30	- -	Gator Dancer122no Skip Away1223 In Contention1224¾	Dueled, led, missed	8
6Oct95-9Med	fst	1 Ⓢ	:23 :463 1:104 1:371	WrldAppeal40k	79	10	67¼	64	35½	36	33¼	Wilson R	115	1.80	- -	Spicy Fact1153¼ Play ItAgainStan117no SkipAway1159	Quick move, gamely	10
16Aug95-5Mth	fst	1	:24 :474 1:13 1:39	Md Sp Wt 22k	78	2	33	23½	21½	110	112¼	Wilson R	118	*.80	- -	Skip Away11812¼ Clash by Night1187½ DarnThatErica1134¼	Drew off, easily	8
9Jly95-9Mth	fm	5f Ⓣ	:22 :451 :572	GildedTime33k	72	4	7	79	67	36	21½	Marquez C H Jr	112	5.00	- -	Cold Snap1181½ Skip Away1121 Cobb's Creek1211¾	Slow early, rallied	7
16Jun95-5Mth	fst	5f	:22 :462 :584	Md Sp Wt 17k	47	2	10	89¾	711	514	48¾	Marquez C H Jr	118	*.80e	- -	Cold Snap1134¼ Foolspruce1182 Beau Coup1182½	Off slowly, rallied	10

Today, the following races could be considered the Handicap Circuit:

Donn Handicap *(~$500k, Gulfstream Park, 1 1/8 miles)*
Santa Anita Handicap *(~$1 million, Santa Anita, 1 1/4 miles)*
Dubai World Cup *(~$6 million, Dubai, 1 1/4 miles)*
Oaklawn Handicap *(~$500k, Oaklawn Park, 1 1/8 miles)*
Stephen Foster Handicap *(~$750k, Churchill Downs, 1 1/8 miles)*
Hollywood Gold Cup *(~$1 million, Hollywood Park, 1 1/4 miles)*

Whitney Handicap *(~$750k, Saratoga, 1 1/8 miles)*
Pacific Classic *(~$1 million, Del Mar, 1 1/4 miles)*
Woodward Stakes *(~$500k, Belmont, 1 1/8 miles)*
Jockey Club Gold Cup *(~$1 million, Belmont, 1 1/4 miles)*
Breeders' Cup WTC Classic *(~$4 million, location varies, 1 1/4 miles)*
Clark Handicap *(~$500k, Churchill Downs, 1 1/8 miles)*

Adding in the Pimlico Special and Massachusetts Handicap as equivalent races during his campaign, Cigar won nine of these premier races over a 2-year period, some of them twice. Skip Away won a fair share as well, however his success was generally limited to the New York / Florida circuit. To be a top handicap horse, a runner needs to claim a number of these titles.

Instant Stakes Contenders

Because of the public interest, purse money, and higher betting pools, stakes races often get extensive press coverage. For the Kentucky Derby, even the mainstream press reports daily on Derby entrants for the entire week. All major stakes receive more than the usual amount of public attention. It can be difficult to sift through information—from useless comments to reporters to extensive past performances at the highest racing levels.

As a starting point, a horse that meets certain criteria can instantly be considered a stakes contender:

— Horses with multiple wins in stakes at today's distance. As silly or obvious as this sounds, it is often overlooked in favor of other horses. A miler may only run in three 1-mile races in a 10-race season. If a true specialist, those three races may be the best performances by far. Proven commodities are dependable!
— Horses with multiple stakes wins at today's class level or higher.

Runners that fall into either of these categories must be the measuring stick for analyzing the field. There must be strong mitigating circumstances to think that horses that don't fall into these categories will beat the ones that do!

If you want to do speed figure analysis, fine. The ones in the above categories will usually come out on top, except for the occasional huge effort by an allowance runner, etc. Will they be a favorite? Maybe. If there is more than one in a race, one will often be favored offering value on the other(s). If there is only one, then favoritism would be justified and value takes on a different meaning. If there are none in the field, then any "heavy" favorite is probably underlaid and/or vulnerable.

These are the horses that primarily win stakes races—proven campaigners. This is less frequent in juvenile races, 3-year-old races, and to some extent at minor league tracks.

In all cases listed above, when an "instant contender" is entered, pay attention. It is—more likely than not—a standout.

When a legitimate "instant contender" in stakes races does not present itself, how does one separate the other entrants?

I evaluate stakes races in the following order:

- *Instant contenders*: As discussed above, instant contenders are horses with multiple stakes wins at today's distance, or at today's class level or higher.
- *Distance*: Horses that have failed miserably at today's distance can be eliminated. Horses that have yet to try it must be scrutinized for signs that they can handle it. Those that have run well at the distance before, even if against lesser company, survive this first inspection.
- *Pace*: The faster the pace a horse can endure and still contend in the stretch, the better. Pace figures aside, the best sign that the horse can handle today's field is when the horse has run at today's class/distance in the past, and not lost ground significantly in the stretch. It's proof of survival. For plodding closers, it isn't enough of a positive. They don't really survive the pace—they are at the mercy of it.
- *Speed*: The speed figures *most closely resembling* today's distance/class level remain an excellent indication of

capability. The last speed figure earned is nowhere near as important as an overall assessment of figures earned under similar conditions. Recommended groupings of distances to compare appropriate figures:

5 1/2f to 6 1/2f
7f to 1 1 1/6 miles (one turn)
7f to 1 1 1/6 miles (two turns)
1 1/16 to 1 1/8 miles more than 1 1/8 miles

Dirt to dirt, turf to turf, mud to mud counts. One-turn to one-turn and two-turn to two-turn also count to a lesser extent.

— *Familiarity*: This means stakes experience and track experience over today's oval. These are important but often overlooked signs that a horse is in position to win, or, when lacking, that it may be vulnerable.

Summer Favorite-itis

Perceived or otherwise, for years now the season between the Triple Crown's conclusion and the opening of Saratoga and Del Mar seems to be a time with a lot of odds-on favorites. Field sizes getting smaller and top connections having multiple choices of race options have led to quality runners only saddling up when everything sets up just right. They either win or *real* longshots romp.

It makes the bettor feel like there are only two choices: go with the favorite, or try to beat the favorite. It shouldn't be so binary, with only two choices. Every race should be a banquet of opportunities, waiting for the bettor to select one. If a runner opens at 1/5, it can't be ignored. All handicapping aside, the pool may only be 10% of the total at post time but a vast majority of bettors will still react to it.

Heavy early play is important.

With a favorite at 1/5 early on in the betting, every other runner may be 10-1 and up. By a few minutes to post, it is not uncommon for the second and third choices to get hammered as possible upsetters with value. Such runners can drop from 12-1 down to the 5/2 range, and the amount of money required will only raise the odds on the favorite from 1/5 to 2/5 to 1/2. In such instances, any chance for real value is probably shot.

Heavy early play may be important but it can be misleading.

The heavy action can be the result of inside information, or a "mad bomber," or a sentimental owner. The size of the typical pool can indicate how reliable early money is. If the pool already has $50,000 when it opens, it would take a very large amount of money for a favorite to open at 1/5. If the pool only has $1,000 (or even $100 at small tracks or fair circuits), it takes a lot less money to show up as heavy early betting.

Arapahoe Park, Colorado: At some tracks, a bettor can influence the early money with only a small bet, if placed early enough. I quickly found that Arapahoe Park in Colorado fell into this category.

Sometimes a horse would inexplicably open at very low odds. What was often notable is that the horse should have been 20-1, doesn't have a popular trainer, doesn't have a popular jockey, isn't in good form. The odds steadily drift up as the horses come on the track. I studied the horse—what am I missing that a bunch of early bettors saw?

This happened more than a few times. The first couple of times I sat out and didn't bet. Sometimes the horse won, sometimes it lost. What was important was that the horse did not win as often as expected based on the mythical expectations for an "early money" horse.

To this day, I'm not sure which connections loved their own horse enough to put an early $100 down—thus causing the horse to open up with $98 more than any other—or which connections loved their horse and put an early $100 on someone else's to misdirect the public. In the second situation, the odds they get for their real win bet—on a horse they think should be the favorite without that "early money"—can make up for the lost $100. I doubt this happened often, but there can be other reasons for early money.

What are the suspected causes of favorite-itis? Why does this particular time of year seem to bring about this phenomenon?

There are a lot of stakes offered each weekend.

When two or more tracks offer stakes with similar conditions, trainers with ready contenders can pick their spots. Carding such stakes simultaneously dilutes the competition. The best runner in each race ends up with an easier field.

This is a mid-year race time for many top outfits.

Horses that have steadily raced from February through June need a breather before the second half of the year. The races they enter may be soft spots, several class levels below their own abilities. However, the runner may not be asked for a 100% effort. Which ties into the next reason.

This is a prep race time for many top horses.

Allowances will often contain a stakes runner and on paper (pace figures etc.) they stand out so much that they deserve to be odds-on. Whether or not this is an all-out try or a checkride is merely speculative (unless your cousin is the trainer or you have other real inside info).

Even becoming familiar with the trainer patterns may not provide enough information to instill confidence in either a pro or con opinion. The allowance money is so good that winning an allowance at a major track is usually worth more than running second in a $100,000 stakes race.

Trainers become streaky (hot-cold) based on overall campaign plans.

Some are using this as down-time training for Saratoga or Del Mar, when prestige and purses increase with a win. Others see this as "now time" and take advantage of the top operations taking a rest. One trainer's key meet is another's siesta. Following trainer patterns is a big help, but trainers change patterns from year to year and are likely to fool you. This happens year round, but in the June/July timeframe it seems more common.

A Better Way To Deal With Summer Favorite-itis

When dealing with small stakes fields often containing one standout and a supporting cast, do not feel compelled to take short prices on obvious choices. More than any other situation, these plays offer nothing that the entire betting public can't see as well.

If you find yourself passing a lot of races during the heat of the summer, do not despair. Connections of many of the top thoroughbreds are doing the exact same thing, waiting for more prestigious (and more contentious) races at late summer meets like Del Mar and Saratoga. Be patient and hold out when it's slim pickings for handicappers.

Here is an example. Situation: Grade II 6 1/2f F&M 3-and-up stakes at Belmont. In the following 5-horse field, I give all 5 a relatively equal chance (4-1 each) for this example. The challenge is to find and bet value in a short field. The odds are as follows:

#1: 5/2 *(underlay)*
#2: 8-1 *(overlay)*
#3: 9-1 *(overlay)*
#4: 3/5 *(underlay)*
#5: 5/2 *(underlay)*

I'm foregoing the handicapping—all are talented Grade III competitors. Three won their previous starts. The other two have been competitive and also appear in good form. None are ill-suited for the distance.

I re-check the past performances to see if I overlooked something during my first quick review. All five horses still appear to be relatively evenly matched. The #4 was morning line 7/2 fourth choice. It opened at 1/5 and looks like it will go off at final odds of 3/2 or so. Because the horses appear more closely matched in my review, this is an opportunity to bet against the favorite.

Based on my estimates, the #2 and #3 are overlays, and 100% overlays at that. I bet both to win, box them in an exacta in case I'm really right, and use both in daily doubles.

Epilogue

The odds-on horse broke right on top, showed speed all the way, then lugged in throughout the stretch drive under strong right-handed whipping. The #2 ran second, the #3 ran third. After an inquiry, the favorite was disqualified, the #2 paid $19.80 to win. Too bad the winner wasn't DQ'd below second—that would have left me with the two longest shots in the field in an exacta. The favorite only interfered with the second place finisher.

The key to this bet wasn't that the favorite would be disqualified. It was that the favorite was evenly matched against four strong contenders. I was betting on my assessment of the race, that the horses were actually evenly matched even though the odds were not even.

If I went $20/$20 win on the two overlays, a $4 exacta box of them, and $2 daily doubles with three logical contenders in the other half, I would have cashed for:

- — $198 on the win bet,
- — Near miss on a $100 plus exacta that I would have had twice, and
- — Three live doubles with $100 will pays.

If instead of $4 exactas I went with a $2 exacta box, and $2 exactas of both overlays over the favorite, I would have made $45 more. So? The win bet guarantees profit for the race if it hits. The exacta is to really capitalize on the situation and make a real score if I'm exactly right.

Focus On Fall

There are stakes everywhere during the fall racing meets, and three kinds of horses will show up in them.

1. *Top horses heading for the Breeders' Cup World Thoroughbred Championships.*

These horses are frequent stakes runners that need one or two solid preps for the big day. With so many stakes to choose from, they can pick the race that best suits the horse, and they expect a win. These horses are usually legitimate and may not be at bettable odds. Great to use in Rolling Pick 3s.

2. *Overachievers.*

These horses aren't thinking Breeders' Cup WTC. They are fit, healthy and used to finishing in the money more often that not, be it in high-priced claiming, allowance, or minor stakes races. They are not likely to beat a legitimate favorite, but are good additions to exotics. And, in the absence of a legitimate favorite, these horses are great—and often overlaid—contenders.

3. *Wishful thinkers.*

Horses jumping way up in stakes level following a MSWT or allowance win. Horses with numerous races between conditioned wins, usually at low odds. These aren't horses roaring through their conditions.

Trainer intentions in the fall mean as much as trainer intentions for 3-year-olds in the spring, leading up to the Triple Crown races. If the horse's connections want it in the Breeders' Cup WTC, they have to establish some kind of claim to the selection committee. This leads to two types of placement: entering a horse in a Big Race against probable Breeders' Cup WTC contenders, such as in the Jockey Club Gold Cup, hoping for a third or fourth that can make their horse look like the "third best horse in the country."

The other places the horse into a really easy race hoping to win by double digits. The logic is their horse is as good as the top horses and (intentionally) just hasn't run against them yet. Examples are a 2-year-old winning the "big race" at a minor track, and a handicap horse trying to win a minor stakes at a big track. Either way, the telltale sign would be a horse's connections talking big about the horse in terms of Breeders' Cup WTC. The connections expect a big win at low odds.

On Big Stakes Days:

— Demand 5/2 on win bets. When legitimate favorites don't offer that price, look to daily doubles and Pick 3s, not to exactas, and certainly not to trifectas.

— Be well bankrolled for Pick 3 play, and bet $50 win (minimum) on legitimate favorites with odds of at least 5/2.

— Look to exactas and trifectas in 2-year-old/3-year-old races with fields of eight or more.

— Bet to win selectively, but on the heavy side. Good looking, well spotted contenders should win. Their connections aren't playing games this close to Breeders' Cup WTC.

Winter Racing

It is 25 degrees outside, the wind is blowing at 20-30 mph. The track is a gritty sand, which stings your face when the wind picks up. After rain, the wet sand is even worse to run on. It sticks to your body giving you the chills. It's too cold to really warm up before a race, too cold to breathe the raw air for very long, and the shoreline 2 miles away adds salt to an already bitter arctic breeze. A miserable time to race—even if you are a horse with a full winter coat. How to guess who will brave the cold the best? It isn't easy, but there are signs.

Sharp moves in winter are the single best forecaster of a winning performance. The horses are generally overworked, under rested, and running a bit dull. When looking at a field, many are consistently giving mediocre efforts. It is one of the hardest times of the year to handicap, maybe because it is one of the hardest times for a horse to compete. (Perhaps comparable to running in Florida in July—Calder isn't known for handicappable events at that time of year.) But the outcomes of winter events are predictable to some extent.

Let's start with a look at the typical winter racehorse at Aqueduct. Most have started 20 or 30 times in the past 12 months. Most are racing for lesser purses than they were 6 months earlier. The words "tired" and "dull" describe a good number of their past performances. A large number have not won a race since Aqueduct was open the year before.

In the stakes events are animals that were not competitive with their summer rivals, but stand a better chance of winning now that most of the competition has taken the winter off. In the maiden events are a handful of first time starters that were late bloomers, but most are hopeless creatures that are not truly destined to be a racehorse. Also, a number of races are carded at a level that are not run at the track from May to November, such as Maiden Claiming $25,000, or Claiming $12,000-$16,000.

With each race run, a horse pays the price. Every big effort is taxing. As horses get older, it gets harder and harder to maintain winning form. Most cannot summon up one big effort to win. Of those that do, only 7% are able to repeat their performance a second time in a row, and only 1% will get a third or fourth win.

The toughest situation is a wire-to-wire win. Its toll is just too much for most horses to follow it up with another victory. In general, one can expect any big effort to knock the typical horse off form for the next two races. Some bounce back faster, and some are thrown off form for the rest of the season. The point to be made is that every major exertion has its price.

More than a few of the winter campaigners have learned that win or lose, there will be oats in the feed tub when they return to the barn. These old sports have little incentive to win and have felt the whip too many times to be particularly motivated by it either. Their past performances resemble an animal running with the herd.

What brings a horse like this victory is often a deviation from the routine. Maybe a 4-week layoff to freshen up. Shortening up in distance might leave him less tired in the stretch. Lengthening the distance might have the herd falling by the wayside, and plodding along puts him on the lead at the end. Even a slight change in race conditions can put him in a situation which he is better suited to. Anything to snap out of the doldrums of running every 10 days against 8 of the 30 or so horses fitting the same condition.

One thing to watch for is any, repeat any, uncharacteristic sign of improvement. A habitual plodder who suddenly moved up to run with the leaders down the backstretch before tiring has shown a spark of new life. Something perked him up, and it may be a sign of improvement to come. Often a horse will break sharply and run on the lead for half a mile, tire and fade, then win enthusiastically next out. These are positive signs and at a time of year when any good signs are rare, ones like this cannot go unnoticed.

Sometimes another factor comes into play that has nothing to do with the condition of the horses running. It is the horses that are ***not*** running that make the difference.

This time of year, many trainers pull their horses out of races the morning of the event. In such a situation, it is not unheard of to find a horse as the lone speed, even though the race had set up as a 4-way battle for the first 1/4 pole. In such cases, a horse that may have previously struggled for the lead time and again only to tire late, will be alone on a soft pace and face its easiest jaunt in months.

Few of these situations will go entirely unnoticed by the betting public, but often remain great betting opportunities. At most tracks the morning line is not adjusted after scratches, and a speedy longshot may offer good odds even after all other speed horses scratch.

Even the subtlest of signs can lead to finding a longshot to complete an exacta or trifecta. The maiden rat that hasn't hit the board in five tries may show a middle-race move last out to get within a length of the lead, then fade drastically from the new tactic. Next out he may just hang tough for second or third place at a huge price in the exotics.

During this time of year there are few standouts on the speed figure scale. Most have run a near-equal top number, and most usually run to about 85 to 95% of that number. That means on any given day, on paper most of the entrants appear capable of being competitive in their field. But the one that is peaking today is going to win. That may translate to a 5, 8, or 10 point improvement from their last race.

This does not mean that the winning horse has climbed from its plateau. It instead put out a bit better effort than usual. It will probably go back to normal range, if not lower, in its next time out.

Below is a general figure comparison between two winter competitors:

Real Cielo

93

88

84

79

90

83

Red Hot Red

85

86

91

94

87

93

When looking at the most recent starts of these two horses, Real Cielo seems to have an 8-point edge. But look closer. It is easy to see that each on his best day could beat the other. Their efforts are really quite the same, they just have their better moments on different days. The fact that Red Hot Red was 8 points slower last time in no way promises a repeat of that today.

Another comparison:

Onnagata
97
78
82
73
99
68

Launching
92
90
89
91
94
90

These two offer a different matchup. Onnagata at his best can beat Launching. But his best efforts are infrequent, and perhaps unpredictable. Launching is a proven commodity. Even on an "off" day he stands a good chance of beating Onnagata, especially since Onnagata seems to be thrown for a real loop every time he runs big.

Look for opportunities where equal contenders get bet unequally due to heavy public emphasis on recent form. Especially during winter racing, the odds between equals may be more uneven and offer good betting opportunities.

Handicapping Contests

Handicapping contests become more popular with each passing year. There are the traditional contests held at tracks and simulcast centers across America, as well as an emerging range of on-line no cost offerings. These are intended to attract new fans to the sport, or at least attract handicappers to horse racing websites.

Traditional Tournaments

The good news is, in almost every handicapping contest, 100% of the entry fees are returned to the contestants as prize money. Theoretically, this is a better deal than fighting the track take any day. However, the amount of skill required to win one of these contests completely depends on the rules.

Some contests encourage bettors to pick wild longshots in the hope of hitting one huge payoff. Others cap the payoff on a single play at 20-1, 25-1, etc. to keep one or two improbable longshots from completely determining the outcome of the contest. Nevertheless, when competing against 300 or more of your peers, if a longshot wins, someone if not dozens will have it. As a result, many contestants use each selection to pick the longest shots on the board in the hope that something crazy will happen, and that longest shot will be in the money.

Is this handicapping? Not exactly, and this kind of play would surely lead to ruin in a parimutuel system. However, contest after contest is often won by the blind stabbers. Still, contests can be a lot of fun. They often come with perks, such as free T-shirts or free food and/or lodging.

The following is a general description of how a typical contest plays out.

Tournament Format: Select 10 races from cards at three selected tracks each day of a 2-day tournament, 300 tournament entries.

— Of 300 people, 150 wildly pick longshots.

— Everyone must pick 10 of the available 30 races each day.
— Any given race has 100 people using it.
— 50 people in that given race (50%) will be picking wild longshots.
— 3 to 4 horses in any field will get that "wild" action.
— Therefore any big longshot, *no matter how improbable*, will get 12 to 15 people's tickets. Again, even an improbable longshot will have 12-15 people on it!
— 90% of the longshot hunters will earn a zero on the first day.
— People with a zero on the first day will pick 10 really wild longshots on the final day.
— If a big longshot hits and you don't have it, you will immediately be behind 12-15 people.
— If *no* big longshots hit, the majority of the field is lost on a wild goose chase.
— If two big longshots hit, at least 1 of the 12-15 with the first longshot will also have the second, thus building an insurmountable lead.
— The typical race day will have:

3 favorites win (1 at odds-on)
2 second choices win
2 4-1 to 6-1 range
1 6-1 to 12-1 range
1 12-1 or up

This is what will cause your train to derail every time! A non-typical race day with just one more horse hitting at 12-1 or up will drastically affect the contest results.

Keep this in mind if you play tournaments. One upset and everyone's game plan goes right out the window. The best advice? Go for it. Handicap each race with a mindset of judging any 15-1 shot as feasible, or not feasible. If you can eliminate a longshot with confidence, great. If you can make even a mediocre case for a longshot, take a shot.

On-Line Tournaments

Free on-line contests should be played by any handicapper with internet access. Many racetrack websites as well as other horse racing information service provider sites such as BRISnet.com and NYRA.com offer on-line contests with prizes in the thousands of dollars with no obligation or entry fee.

Contests come in all shapes and sizes. Some are for "serious" handicappers. Others are fun promotions or limited to on-line newsletter subscribers. Some sites offer simple contests to win marketing giveaways. West Point Thoroughbreds, for example, has held several tournaments for newsletter subscribers that pick the winners of marquee events such as the Breeders' Cup or Kentucky Derby.

Unusual contest formats can also be found on-line. Many contests award based on the number of wins you have in a day, meaning a 1/5 shot counts just as much as a 20-1 shot. For example, NYRA.com has offered Fantasy Stable and "Survivor" style contests that last the entire meet. In a Fantasy Stable contest, before a meet begins, each entrant selects a finite number of horses, trainers, and jockeys and are awarded points based on win, place, and show of their selections through a complicated points system.

Survivor-style contests require each entrant to select one horse a day that must hit the board in order to continue to the next day. If this sounds easy, try selecting one horse a day for an entire meet and see how long your show parlay will last. In the Belmont Fall 2001 contest, nearly 10,000 entrants were reduced to less than 100 after the first 3 weeks.

Any free on-line contest is worth the 5 to 10 minutes a day to play. If your selections happen to be horses you were going to bet with your own bankroll, it's one more chance to take advantage of your hard work. Keep track of which sites offer contests and take the time to enter.

SECTION 5

Putting It All Together

An Investment Strategy Guide

It's usually easier to figure out what horse you like than it is to figure out how to bet the race. How can you capitalize on the betting opportunity once you have finished handicapping? It takes a different perspective to handicap than to manage your money and your day so that you come out a winner. It is not sensible to plan on profiting by adopting a handicapping philosophy of "I will handicap the way everyone else does, but I'll do it better."

Now the tough part. You have to train your mind to formulate opinions in a controlled academic manner. When examining a race, where do you begin? Do you start by looking at the favorite? At the horses you know? With horses for the course? Or do you just begin with Post Position #1 and work your way down the past performances? You have a method in mind, but you need to form a personal strategy or methodology. Now is the time to instill some discipline into it.

This is like day trading on the stock market in many ways. You have an unlimited menu of opportunities and ways to bet each one. You have limited time to make the decision and act. A successful day trader is also a specialist, whether in particular data trends in any industry, a particular market size, or in a particular sector. Similarly, your personal strategy or method should be structured to capitalize on your specialties. Focus both your time and money on situations that you analyze most accurately. This will enable you to manage your time effectively and maximize your chance to profit.

"A Rough Sketch" Making Selections and Determining Wagers

The following is one model of how to walk through your selection process. Handicappers will benefit from either adopting the plan, adapting it to fit their own preferences, or constructing their own workflow that covers the same critical factors. Note that if at any point in this analysis the answers you seek become indeterminable, the best thing to do is pass the race. The worst thing to do is to "wing it."

One Bettor Way: A Rough Sketch

1. **Bankroll Management**

—Establish your plan for the day:

- — Daily bankroll: No more than 10% of total hobby bankroll
- — Best Bet Amounts: Best Bets deserve anywhere from 1/5 to 1/3 of daily bankroll per wager.
- — Exotic Wager Amounts: No more than 1/3 of daily bankroll for all exotic wagers.

2. **Time Management**

— Things to study before going to the track:

- — Race conditions
- — Which horses are contenders
- — Research on breeding, par times, biases, trainer/jockey combos, etc.

— Things to study once at the track:

  — Track conditions / bias
  — Scratches
  — Between races: Early heavy tote action
  — Final minutes to post: Horses acting poorly or washing out, exotic versus win pool action, and late action up or down

3. Data Management

— Bring the following to the track:

  — Past performances and handicapping notes
  — Rough plan of day's bets and note paper
  — Binoculars (if on track)

4. Evaluate races, starting with the Winner's Profile.

— What kind of race are we dealing with?
— What kind of runners usually win?
— What are the pars for this race?
— What are the most important factors in determining the outcome?
— How often do favorites win?
— How often does chaos prevail?

5. Determine the horses' capabilities—eliminate the non-contenders.

Answering these questions will determine the contender list and safely eliminate the majority (or perhaps all) of the entrants.

— Who are the pace factors? (Lone frontrunner, no frontrunner, two frontrunners, multiple frontrunners, or a dominant frontrunner?)
Pace factors may or may not be contenders. It isn't relevant.

— Who has recent form indicating fitness?
*Ignore **ability**, look for capability!*

IDEAL

— Race in last 7 days
— Race in last 14 days and 1 workout since
— Race in last 28 days and 4 workouts since

GOOD

— Race 14 days ago but no workouts since
— Race 21 days ago and 2 workouts since

MARGINAL

— Race in last 28 days and 3 workouts since
— Race in last 28 days and 2 workouts since
— Race 21 days ago and 1 workout since

BAD

— No races or workouts in the past 17 or more days

NEGATIVE SIGNS

— Bar shoes/aluminum pad
— New front bandages
— Blinkers "off" (sign of giving up)
— No activity in last 17 days (works or races)

POSITIVE SIGNS

— Adds Lasix
— Bar shoes "off"
— Front bandages "off"

— Who has won at the distance? (Or, who is bred for the distance?)
— Who has run to par?
— Who has handled the surface?

6. **Determine the likeliest scenarios.**

Answering these questions will determine which contenders are at an advantage or disadvantage.

— What does the pace project to be?
— Who is helped/hurt by post position?
— What are the track conditions (fast, hard, cuppy, sandy, muddy, heavy, tiring, sloppy)?
— Who will the track conditions help or hinder?
— Is there a track bias (inside, outside, early pace, closers)?
— Who will the track bias help or hinder?
— Which riders can handle a rail post position/outside post?

Now the wheat is separated from the chaff. The contenders are straight in my mind. In both an objective ***and*** subjective sort of way, I have a pecking order in mind, often with one contender clearly being more solid than the rest. I have the pace martyrs (cheap speed, rabbits, whatever) identified and know whether or not they have any chance of hitting the board. I also know which plodders may prey on the misfortune of those who contend the pace, and thus may suck up for third, second, or even the win.

7. **Value the contenders.**

— Determine basic forecasting percentages based on the answers uncovered so far.
— Upgrade those dropping in class or cutting back in distance.
— Downgrade those moving up in class or increasing in distance (unless bred for long distance and untested thus far at the distance).

- Two or more new things is a huge downgrade!
- Upgrade those with top jockeys and/or high percentage trainers—pay for skill!
- Downgrade those with low percentage jockeys and/or low percentage trainers.
- Slight upgrade for particularly good breeding indicators for today's distance/surface.

The next step comes when I must decide what the public has on its mind, and how I want to bet.

8. The Mind of the Public

Answer the following questions to understand what they are thinking, and if they or you have logic on your side.

- Who has the public made the favorite?
- Are any of my contenders a:

  - Legitimate favorite (never to be bet against even if an underlay)?
  - Low-priced favorite (is reasonable to be favored by the public, but is overbet in proportion to its chances of winning)?
  - Vulnerable favorite (lacks a critical element despite its strengths)?

- Is the favorite being bet based mostly on:

  - Speed figures?
  - Trainer?
  - Jockey?
  - Class edge?
  - Pre-race hype in the *Daily Racing Form* or media?
  - Pig-pile effect after a big bet moves the odds a few ticks?
  - "Mysterious" insider trading?

— How are the morning line favorites being bet?
  — Is one of them the public favorite?
  — Are any of them ***under bet*** and ***contenders*** on my list?
  — Are any of them ***over bet*** and ***not contenders*** on my list?

— Are any morning line longshots at half their morning line odds or less that I should take a second look at?

Now I know who the contenders are, and I know how the public sees the race, so I put the two together.

9. Decide on appropriate wagers.

— Is my primary contender an overlay?
— Quantify acceptable odds based on my own value line.
— Always assume that the favorite is over-used in exotics unless the favorite is odds-on in the win pool.
— Adjust based on scratches—if scratches will affect early pace, reassess the race!

Win Bets:

— Are two of my contenders overlays, racing against a vulnerable favorite? If so, both must be 4-1 or higher to ensure a healthy profit in exchange for making two bets instead of one.
— If top rated horse is a value, that's the win bet.
— If top rated horse is underlaid and the second choice is 7/2 or more, bet that second choice to win.
— If top rated horse is 3/2 or less, you don't have win pool value regardless of your line, and you can do better elsewhere.
— If both contenders are equal, bet the one with longer odds.

Exotics strategy:

— Bet exactas if your top choice over the favorite and second choice offer value.

- — Trifectas become a value when your contender list does not include two or more of the public's three favorites.
- — Doubles and Pick 3s can still offer value for underlay favorites, but should supplement other less risky bets.
- — Exotics must offer a premium for the added risk. If money spread in exotic combinations is likely to yield no more than the same money bet to win on your top selection, go with the simplest alternative—the win bet.

10. Pulling the trigger

There are still many ways to conclude this thought puzzle!

1) I like my contender(s), and the odds offer a fair value in the win category, to ensure a long-term profit if repeated consistently.

   - — One selection at 5-1+: A win/place or win/exacta reverse wheel is required.
   - — One selection at under 5-1: A straight win bet, and the exacta and trifectas can be all but forgotten.
   - — Two selections, both above 4-1, and a vulnerable favorite to beat: Two win bets and a small exacta box or quinella are in order.

2) I like my contenders, but they are not of value in the win pool, so I will indulge in them with exclusive exotic play.
3) The public is betting on a horse I did not consider a contender but they are doing so *based on a factor I already considered*—such as top figure, trainer, or jockey—and dismissed as not enough to make this horse a real contender. In this case I bet as planned.
4) The public is betting a horse I did not consider a contender, but I can only attribute the betting to *"inside stuff" because there are no good reasons to back the horse.* I either ignore it and bet half the amount I would have (without including

the "hot" horse) or pass the race altogether. Either way such horses will not get any of my money.

5) The public is betting a horse I did not consider a contender, but when analyzing WHY the public was betting it, *I was adequately persuaded that the horse has some merit.* I either incorporate the horse into my betting plan or, more often than not, pass the race altogether.

6) I liked a horse based on a long-term angle or because it is one of my All-Stars that I am betting blind to the particulars of today's other entrants. I bet that horse to win, and note the handicapping logic as academic exercise.

11. Remember:

— The public overbets information based on the most recent race!

— The horse with the highest last race speed figures will be underlaid 99 44/100 % of the time.

— The public rarely shies away from betting horses starting from impossible post positions.

— Jockeys and trainers that attract money are already adjusted for in ***your*** value line.

— Breeding information is most useful when horses are trying something new.

— Along with that, horses bred to do something they are trying for the first time should always be preferred over those that have already tried and failed.

— Horses that get creamed when in over their heads are probably not off form, and should be fine when back at the right level.

12. Frequently Asked Questions (to help you challenge and improve your handicapping decision model):

— Is this method undervaluing trainer stats?

No, trainers that win often will saddle runners that contend on their own merits. Trainers that saddle few winners start many horses that do not withstand handicapper scrutiny.

— Is upgrading a horse that fits a trainer "specialty" wise?

Yes, trainers are creatures of habit and the patterns that lead to success are predictable.

— What should you do about high percentage trainers with seemingly bad horses?

Rate them fairly on their merits, but realize the successful connections will draw money, resulting in an unlikely winner that is an underlay in the betting pools.

— What should you do about low percentage trainers with seemingly good horses?

Rate them fairly on their merits, but downgrade their chances if the trainer rarely finds the winner's circle even with contenders.

— Do you ever want to decide a particular running style **won't** win over a given surface on a given day?

Never say "Never."

— Is applying this to 40 to 50 races per day realistic?

Yes, but it is important to throw out a race as soon as it becomes clear that there is either too much ambiguity or little chance of finding value.

— Isn't this only half the battle, with Money Management being the real kicker?

Yes, all things considered. There are plenty of ways to identify winners, but converting that information to profit is the hard part.

Recommended Reading

Books

Any book by Tom Ainslie

Bernstein, Peter L. *Against the Gods: The Remarkable Story of Risk.* John Wiley & Sons, Inc.: New York, 1996.

Cramer, Mark. *Kinky Handicapping.* TBS Publishing: Maryland, 1993.

Cramer, Mark. *Value Handicapping.* City Miner Books: California, 1994.

Nafzger, Carl A. *Traits of a Winner: The Formula For Developing Thoroughbred Racehorses.* The Russell Meerdink Company: Wisconsin, 1994.

Quinn, James. *The Handicapper's Condition Book.* William Morrow and Company, Inc.: New York, 1986.

Romanelli, Charles S. *How to Make Money In One Day At the Track.* Simon & Schuster: New York, 1965, 1989.

Periodicals

Horseplayer Magazine

The Bloodhorse (for at least 1 year, to appreciate the perspective of the non-wagering side of racing)

Printed in the United States
41126LVS00002B/198

9 781413 490480